NOTARIES PUBLIC
IN ENGLAND
IN THE THIRTEENTH AND
FOURTEENTH CENTURIES

NOTARIES PUBLIC
IN ENGLAND

IN THE THIRTEENTH AND
FOURTEENTH CENTURIES

C. R. CHENEY

OXFORD
AT THE CLARENDON PRESS
1972

Oxford University Press, Ely House, London W. 1

GLASGOW NEW YORK TORONTO MELBOURNE WELLINGTON
CAPE TOWN IBADAN NAIROBI DAR ES SALAAM LUSAKA ADDIS ABABA
DELHI BOMBAY CALCUTTA MADRAS KARACHI LAHORE DACCA
KUALA LUMPUR SINGAPORE HONG KONG TOKYO

PRINTED IN GREAT BRITAIN
AT THE UNIVERSITY PRESS, OXFORD
BY VIVIAN RIDLER
PRINTER TO THE UNIVERSITY

'I think it will appear, that in This Discourse I have
done little else than laid before the Reader matters of
Fact: It being my settled Design, only to propose, not
to Dictate. If by This means the Discourse be rendred
the more Dry and Undiverting: It is withall rendred
(I conceive) the more Useful, and the more likely to
be Satisfactory to such as desire to be profited rather
than pleased.'

> Thomas Madox, A Dissertation concerning
> Ancient Charters and Instruments, *Formulare
> Anglicanum,* p. xxxiii.

Preface

THIS study aims at assembling some facts about the history and diplomatic of notaries public and their instruments in England before the end of the fourteenth century. I have not felt called upon—nor is it within my competence —to examine the legal quality inherent in the notarial instrument, according to the doctrines of the civilians, ancient or medieval, for English notarial activity before 1400 can probably throw little or no new light on the matter. My interest was first awakened in the notary by my teacher in diplomatic, V. H. Galbraith, at Oxford in 1928. When later on I succeeded him as Reader in that university, I devoted a small part of my course for graduates to notaries in medieval Europe. Recently, an international congress at Fribourg, concerned particularly with the subject, stimulated me to put into order the notes of many years and to carry my inquiries further into the records. I cannot claim to have covered the ground thoroughly; but such facts as are assembled here about the English notariate may be of use, in view of the lack of any general study.

My debts to scholars who have written on various aspects of the subject will be evident from the list of books and articles on pp. 186–194. I also gratefully acknowledge information, advice, and criticism which various friends and colleagues have given me, especially Dr. P. Chaplais, Dr. J. H. Denton, Professor V. H. Galbraith, and Professor E. L. G. Stones. Dr. Chaplais's important paper on 'Master John de Branketre and the office of notary in Chancery, 1355–75' (*Journal of the Society of Archivists*, iv, no. 3 (April 1971), 169–99) unfortunately appeared too late for this book to benefit from it. My wife has read the book in more than one draft and suggested many welcome improvements. I am grateful, too, to the authorities of the British Museum, the Public Record Office, the Archivio Segreto Vaticano, and various ecclesiastical archives in England for permission to cite and print documents in their custody. For facilities in consulting these records I wish particularly to thank Dr. William Urry and Miss A. M. Oakley (Canterbury), Mrs. N. H. K. Gurney (York), Mr. A. R. B. Fuller (St. Paul's Cathedral), Mr. J. E. Fagg (Durham), Miss P. E. Morgan (Hereford), the Very Reverend E. W. Kemp (Worcester), and Mr. N. H. MacMichael (Westminster Abbey). Leave to reproduce documents in facsimile has been kindly granted, as under, for plates 1 and 6 by the Dean and Chapter of Worcester, for plate 2 by the Dean and Chapter of Hereford, for plate 3 by the Dean and Chapter of St. Paul's, and for plates 4 and 5 by the Controller of Her Majesty's Stationery Office.

C. R. CHENEY

Contents

Contents

List of Plates

(*at end*)

1. The English Background

VERY little has been written in modern times about the notary public in medieval England. Discussion of the historical evidence by English historians has been unsystematic; and standard works on the palaeography and diplomatic of English documents, from Thomas Madox to Hubert Hall, Johnson and Jenkinson, and Hector, have nothing to say. More systematic study by lawyers has suffered from neglect of the historical evidence and from a tendency to argue backwards from the modern institution of notaries public to their very different circumstances in the Middle Ages.[1] Comparison with the institution on the continent of medieval Europe shows marked contrasts. For the modern English reader it is perhaps particularly necessary to emphasize the basic characteristic of the notary public. By definition he was a *persona publica* with some public functions, if only in the field of private law; he was authorized by a public authority to issue instruments. It is essential to bear in mind this quality of authorization and to avoid being sidetracked by reference to notaries who did not announce themselves as public.

The word *notarius* in itself presents no difficulty, and was used in classical times. The man was a scribe who wrote minutes of

[1] Valuable brief comments are in the histories of English law by Pollock and Maitland, i. 218, and W. S. Holdsworth, v. 114–15, and in Tout, *Chapters*, i. 122–3. The essay specifically devoted to 'The origin and historical development of the profession of notaries public in England' by H. C. Gutteridge (*Cambridge Legal Essays*), pp. 123–37 is quite inadequate on medieval conditions, for which the author relied heavily on [Richard] Brooke's *Treatise*, 8th edn. A brief and somewhat confused contribution by J. S. Purvis to *Archivum*, xii (1965), 121–6 ('The notary public in England') adds nothing useful to what he wrote as foreword to *Notarial Signs*. More to the point are the information and comments supplied by Mr. Denholm-Young in his notable essay on 'The cursus and by Dr. H. D. Emanuel on notaries public and their marks. Mr. H. G. Richardson had a few wise words to say about notaries in England in *Law Quarterly Review*, lvii (1941), 333–4. For notarial activity in an English diocese see Prof. Haines on the administration of the diocese of Worcester; for notaries public in civil government see Tout, op. cit., and Prof. Otway-Ruthven on the King's Secretary. Few English historians have used Baumgarten, *Von der apostolischen Kanzlei*.

proceedings, judicial or otherwise, or drafted letters. But the word was not much used in medieval England by itself as the indeterminate equivalent of scribe or secretary. It is found less in medieval English legal records than in literary works, where it had no very precise connotation.[1] It only becomes commoner when the office of notary public comes to be known in England. Occasionally, from late in the thirteenth century onwards, a man is described by a king or a bishop as *notarius noster*,[2] and by modern historians as royal or episcopal notary.[3] But when writers speak of royal or bishops' notaries their evidence needs scrutiny. These must probably be regarded, one and all, as notaries public in the permanent or temporary employment of the king or the bishop. And in every verifiable case the English notary will be found to hold his authority as a writer of public

[1] At least three *notarii* witness archiepiscopal acts of Canterbury between Theobald and Hubert (Gervas. Cant., *Hist. Works*, ii. 289; Hereford, D. & C. Archives, no. 2771; *Cal. Ch. Rolls*, ii. 361). 'Clerks and notaries of the Exchequer' are mentioned as witnesses to a fine of 1197 in a thirteenth-century note in a cartulary of Merton (*TRHS*, 4th series xv (1932), 82). The word may have later acquired a more technical meaning in a few English cathedral chapters, for chapter-clerks or assistants to the chancellor (see Edwards, *English Secular Cathedrals*, pp. 209–10, 212): the earliest cited is mentioned at Chichester in statutes of 1232. These were not all notaries public.

[2] For men known to be notaries public by apostolic or imperial authority see at Canterbury the archbishop's *notarius noster* (1281, below, Appendix II, no. 7); at York *notarius noster publicus* (1306, *Reg. Greenfield*, iii. 4); at Hereford *notarius noster* (1321, *Reg. Orleton*, p. 188); at Winchester *notarius noster* (1296, *Reg. Pontissara*, ii. 802) and *Wintoniensis episcopi notarius et iudex ordinarius* (1307, *Reg. Woodlock*, i. 170, and 1317, *Reg. Sandale*, p. 64); at Worcester *tabellio noster* (1308, *Reg. Reynolds*, p. 3). By the thirteenth century *tabellio* is synonymous with notary public; see the remarks of the Bolognese, Salatiele, and his glossator in the preface to his *Ars Notarie* (*c.* 1237–54), i. 8–9, ii. 6–7.

[3] Tout, *Chapters*, habitually refers to 'the king's notary' or 'a royal notary' or 'a notary of the chancery'. They are all notaries by apostolic or imperial authority, and are in some cases being explicitly rewarded for preparing public instruments (cf. *Chapters*, ii. 70-1). See also G. P. Cuttino, *English Diplomatic Administration* (Oxford, 1940), p. 135 : 'those in the Wardrobe were usually royal notaries'; the two he names were William de Maldon and Andrew de Tange (see below, pp. 57–8). Mr. Geoffrey de Eversley, who served both Edward I of England and Alfonso X of Castile, is described in a letter from Edward to Alfonso as *vester notarius et noster clericus* (1282, Rymer, i. ii. 606), cited by Denholm-Young, 'The cursus', p. 78. On the obscure office of protonotary in the English royal Chancery see ibid., pp. 86–7 and Wilkinson, *Chancery under Edward III*, pp. 74, 189–90. Octave Morel warned against confusion between the French *notaires royaux* (who were notaries public, cf. below, p. 54) and *notaires du roi* (who were officials of Chancery): *La Grande Chancellerie Royale . . . 1328–1400* (1900), p. 54.

instruments from either the pope or the emperor. A further warning is necessary. The person described in the records as *notarius apostolice sedis* or *notarius domini pape* or (by the pope) as *notarius noster* and by modern writers as 'papal notary' must be distinguished from notaries public—even from those who held their authority from the apostolic see. When we are told that 'the king frequently retained several papal notaries and paid them annual pensions : Master Berard of Naples, for instance',[1] the persons in question prove to have been officials of the papal Chancery, members of the ancient notarial college in the Roman Curia.[2] It is, of course, true that by the mid thirteenth century the members of the papal notarial college were commonly notaries public. But these curial officials are not our concern. The *notarius publicus* encountered in English records of the thirteenth and fourteenth centuries is not, as a rule, a curial official. He announces himself as notary public because he claims to have the quality of a public person by commission from the pope or the emperor.

Since notarial writings commonly proclaim themselves to be *instrumenta publica*, it may be well to pay some attention to this term. The *Oxford English Dictionary* defines an instrument, in its legal sense, as : 'a formal legal document whereby a right is created or confirmed, or a fact recorded; a formal writing of any kind, as an agreement, deed, charter, or record, drawn up and executed in technical form, so as to be of legal validity'. Written instruments took on different forms in different regions during the Middle Ages. Contracts and conveyances made by quite ordinary people might be validated by their seals and witnesses. Alternatively, they might be fortified through ratification by a public authority, a king, prince, bishop, or mayor of a

---

[1] *Engl. Diplomatic Administration*, p. 135. For Berard see D. Lohrmann, 'Berard von Neapel, ein päpstlicher Notar und Vertrauter Karls von Anjou', in *Adel und Kirche: Festschrift Gerd Tellenbach* (1968), pp. 477–98.

[2] For the early history of the papal Chancery see R. L. Poole; for the thirteenth century see Prof. Barraclough, *Public Notaries*, pp. 14–18, and further, Herde, *Beiträge*, pp. 8–11. Papal notaries mentioned in England in the twelfth century and after were members of the notarial college: e.g. Master Philip in 1199–1200 (cf. Cheney in *EHR*, lxiii (1948), 342–50 and *Hubert Walter*, pp. 126, 130–1) and Master Arlotus (cf. below, p. 15). I shall not concern myself with English curial officials or Englishmen practising as notaries public in the Curia (Baumgarten, p. 14; P.R.O., E. 30/67).

town. By these means such a person conferred, so to speak, the blessing of his office on acts of private individuals. From being private acts these became public acts. 'Ex qualitate personae', reads the Common Gloss to the Decretals (*Extra*, 2. 22. 9), 'approbatur vel reprobatur instrumentum.' It follows that the notary public who is said to cast legal instruments *in publicam formam* does so only because he qualifies as a *persona publica*, by delegation from a public authority. He writes, in virtue of his commission, *sub manu publica*. Bresslau observed the revival and increase of the word *instrumentum* in Italian legal proceedings of the twelfth century, and the eventual recognition, first by ecclesiastical judges, that the instrument drawn up by a notary public qualified as *instrumentum publicum*.[1] Before the end of the century the Emperor Henry VI could refer to the notaries' duty 'instrumenta publica iuxta morem eius officii condendi'.[2] In the mid thirteenth century the canonist Hostiensis will define an instrument as public 'quando confectum est per manum tabellionis qui iuravit fideliter exercere officium suum de his que videbit et audiet'.[3]

In the law and government of the Mediterranean lands the *tabellio*, *notarius publicus*, and *notarius et iudex* had a history stretching back to antiquity. The notary public authorized to act within a limited region was common.[4] But it seems to have been in the course of the twelfth century that in Italy the emperor and the pope began to grant licences to notaries to practise universally, and draw up public instruments bearing their sign manual, which would be accepted as authentic *ubique terrarum*. This development was complete when William Durand succinctly stated the position in discussing the nature of public instruments in his magisterial *Speculum* (*c.* 1271): 'Note that a notary public (*tabellio*) appointed by the emperor or the pope or

---

[1] *Handbuch*, i. 655–6, citing an act of 1169.					[2] Ibid. i. 656 n. 2.

[3] *Summa*, f. 103*ab*. Bresslau, who quoted from this passage, cited a few cases where non-notarial sealed deeds were called public instruments (ibid. i. 718 n. 1). In 1258 the chapter of Christ Church, Canterbury, described its non-notarial sealed letters patent as *instrumentum publicum* (B.M., MS. Add. 6159 f. 4ʳ). The term *instrumenta publica* occurs in a letter of English judges delegate of the pope in 1173 (Durham, D. & C. Mun., Misc. ch. 6587, imperfectly printed in *Historiae Dunelmensis Scriptores Tres* (Surtees Soc., 1839), pp. liii–liv).

[4] See Redlich, *Privaturkunden*, pp. 209–27 and de Boüard, *Manuel de Diplomatique*, ii. 161–74, etc.

by someone to whom they have granted this by special privilege, may perform their office and draw up instruments anywhere, even in France or England or Spain, not only in lands specially subject to the emperor or pope.'[1]

The Anglo-Norman world was brought closer to the Mediterranean world of ideas when Henry II, through his Aquitanian wife, joined in one 'empire' the northern parts and a dominion in France which extended to the Pyrenees. Politics, commerce, and Church affairs all created contacts. It may be that even at this time an embryonic notariate was to be found on the model of the Italian cities in the municipalities of Gascony and Provence.[2] Certainly, before the twelfth century was out, a *publicus notarius Massilie* drew up and authenticated a public instrument in Marseille.[3] One other thing is certain. During the second half of the twelfth century contacts between England and Italy were increasing to an unprecedented degree in commercial affairs and in the course of Church government. Englishmen who travelled encountered the notarial instrument in its original homeland. The evidence for the commerce actually reposes in the notarial archives of Genoa to this day.[4] The papal Curia made use of the notarial public instrument. In 1167 × 1169 Pope Alexander III addressed a decretal 'Meminimus' on a number of points of law to Bishop Roger of Worcester. It included the following passage: 'Scripta vero authentica, si testes inscripti decesserint, nisi forte per manum publicam facta fuerint, ita quod appareant publica, aut authenticum sigillum habuerint, per quod possint probari, non videntur nobis alicuius

---

[1] *Speculum*, lib. II partic. ii, § 8. 23 (pp. 304*b*–305*a*): 'Nota quod tabellio ab Imperatore, vel Papa, vel ab eo, cui hoc speciali privilegio indultum est, ordinatus, potest ubique etiam in Francia, vel Anglia, seu Hispania, non solum in terris eis specialiter subiectis, suo officio uti et instrumenta conficere.' In this Durandus was closely following what his master Hostiensis ('dominus meus') had written (*Summa*, loc. cit.); cf. Salatiele, *Ars Notarie*, i. 13–14, ii. 10. See also Baumgarten, pp. 20–1 and de Boüard, ii. 190.

[2] Cf. Giry, *Manuel de Diplomatique*, pp. 829–30.

[3] De Boüard, *Manuel*, Tome ii Album, Pl. XXIV. The document was drawn up in 1194 in the name of Ugo Fer, 'in iurisdictione castri Sancti Marcelli locum G. Biterrensis episcopi et Rocelini optinens, cognitor cause', certified by Bernardus Massiliensis publicus notarius Massilie ('et cartam scribi feci et nomen meum et signum ibi feci et sigillavi, mandato Ugonis Feri predicti').

[4] R. L. Reynolds, 'Some English settlers in Genoa in the late twelfth century [1179–90]', *Economic Hist. Rev.*, iv (1933), 317–23, cf. below, p. 50 n. 1.

firmitatis robur habere.' This gained wide currency in early English collections of decretals and eventually passed into *Extra*.[1]

Alexander III, in this decretal, did not *require* the employment of a notary public who wrote 'sub manu publica'; and in England the alternative forms of proof which the decretal allowed prevailed in the ecclesiastical courts as elsewhere. The reason why the notary public had not appeared, and did not appear, during the twelfth century is not hard to see. In short, the reason is that which explains his absence from other parts of northern Europe: customary law prevailed. The Romanizing effect of Christian missions in the early Middle Ages had indeed brought literacy to a clerical class in these regions, but the process was far from undermining completely traditional rules of private law and administration of justice. In these regions the execution of contracts and judicial sentences did not depend on written record; they might be executed and go unquestioned without written record. Writing, if it was used, simply gave additional solemnity to a transaction for which the community was guarantor. A well-known English example illustrates the fact. In the reign of Cnut a son claimed his mother's land. But his mother was angry with him and declared in the presence of three thegns that she granted her land and gold and clothing and chattels after her death to her kinswoman Leofflaed, wife of Thurkil the White. She called on the thegns to announce it to the shire-court of Hereford and to call upon the court to witness her grant. They did so. 'And Thurkil rode then with the permission and witness of all the people to St. Ethelbert's minster, and had it entered in a gospel-book.'[2]

Here we see a state of affairs often remarked upon by modern diplomatists, which has recently been put very clearly by Professor Cronne: 'The symbolic public ceremony was, for long,

---

[1] J.-L. no. 13162, found in two of the earliest collections, *Wigorniensis altera* and *Belverensis*, and many others, ultimately in *Extra*, 2. 22. 2. The passage was remarked by Bresslau (*Handbuch*, i. 656–8, cf. 718 n. 1), who was unable to assign a date. For the date see S. Kuttner, *Repertorium der Kanonistik* (Studi e Testi, 71, 1937), p. 287.

[2] P. H. Sawyer, *Guide to Anglo-Saxon Charters* (Royal Hist. Soc., 1968), no. 1462, translated by Dorothy Whitelock, *English Historical Documents*, i (1955), 556, no. 135. The gospel-book, of the late eighth century, is still in Hereford Cathedral Library (MS. P. i. 2).

all that was formally necessary for the transfer of property and rights. When written records of such transactions came to be made they were, at first, in the nature of precautionary evidences rather than, strictly, instruments of conveyance.'[1] And, as in the Herefordshire case, a precious gospel-book was often the medium of written record of a title. It fortified the title, not so much by a mode of authentication which could possibly satisfy any rational system of jurisprudence or objective test of credibility, as by its sacral, magical quality.[2]

A century after Cnut's day it was still possible to convey land without charter in England; but the advance of literacy was now touching the practice of the law, and a profession of literate lawyers was growing up.[3] To supplement livery of seisin a written deed—an act that bore on itself some mark of its own authenticity—became habitual.[4] After all, a very large proportion of eleventh- and twelfth-century land-transfers were in favour of religious corporations, and the Church cherished the traditions of the Roman law.

Written records of legal transactions developed in England along certain definite lines.[5] For contracts and conveyances there was, from early days, the chirograph, in the special sense of a bipartite document[6] (which could be made doubly secure by preparation in tripartite form), and there was the writ-charter, framed in the form of a letter and authenticated by a seal.[7]

---

[1] *Regesta Regum Anglo-Normannorum 1066–1154*, iv, ed. H. A. Cronne and R. H. C. Davis (Oxford, 1969), 1.

[2] Cf. N. R. Ker, *Catalogue of MSS. containing Anglo-Saxon* (Oxford, 1957), p. 557, s.v. Records, and P. Chaplais in *Journal of the Soc. of Archivists*, iii, no. 2 (Oct. 1965), 52–4 and idem, ibid. no. 10 (Oct. 1969), p. 541.

[3] See Galbraith, 'Monastic foundation charters', 'The literacy of the medieval English kings', and *Studies in the Public Records*, ch. ii.

[4] Even then the charter might still retain the nature of an object laid on the altar to signify the dedication of the property and the conveyance of seisin (as in earlier seisin 'per cultellum', etc.). In 1193 the abbot of Glastonbury assigned a mill at Street to his monks, by sealed charter; but the charter concludes: 'Acta est vero hec concessio anno verbi incarnati mcxciii in die Oblacionis sancte Marie et presens carta supra altare beate Marie me offerente posita, astantibus eiusdem ville clero et populo.' *Glastonbury Chartulary*, iii. 702–3, no. 1301.

[5] The best guide remains Madox's *Formulare*.

[6] Bresslau, *Handbuch*, i. 669–71; Galbraith, 'An episcopal land-grant.'

[7] See F. E. Harmer, *Anglo-Saxon Writs* (Manchester, 1952) and R. C. Van Caenegem, *Royal Writs in England from the Conquest to Glanvill* (Selden Soc., lxxvii, 1959).

For judicial decisions there was the final concord, prepared in 'chirograph' form in the court of the competent authority,[1] and there was the notificatory writ or *recordatio* with seal. Private seals, as well as the seals of corporations civil and ecclesiastical, became extremely common in twelfth-century England. Before the end of the century it was a matter for remark that every little knight now had his seal.[2] By the end of the thirteenth century even a villein could have a seal.[3]

But the proliferation of seals itself presented difficulties. Seals could be, and often were, forged. Moreover, a deed sealed by a private person was of little value once the owner of the seal and the witnesses were dead. Finally, a seal was of no value if it belonged to a person so obscure that it would not be generally recognized outside the owner's immediate circle of acquaintances.[4] The private individual who needed wider publicity for his deed was driven to ask some person of consequence or public authority to attach to it a seal which was beyond doubt: a bishop, an archdeacon, the mayor of a town, even the king himself might be solicited to put his seal to a private act.[5]

---

[1] A final concord is made in the court of William de Muntchanesi at Towcester and further 'recordata' in the shire-court of Northampton before Simon de Pateshull, sheriff (*Luffield Priory Charters*, ed. G. R. Elvey, i (Bucks. and Northants. Record Societies, 1968), 118, no. 127). Another is made *c.* 1205–9 in the court of Geoffrey de Childewic 'coram vicecomite Oxonie et coram probis hominibus eiusdem ville' as the outcome of a plea in Geoffrey's court 'per breve domini Regis Johannis de recto' (*Cart. of Hosp. of St. John the Baptist*, ed. H. E. Salter (Oxford Hist. Soc., 1914–16), ii. 69–70 and i, pl. II). C. T. Clay cites early final concords in county and baronial courts, *Yorks Archaeol. Journal*, xl (1959), 81. For much later ones (1294 and after) in the court of the archbishop of York see H. H. E. Craster in *Archaeologia Aeliana*, 3rd series xxi (1924), 192–5. For a final concord in the king's court, 1163, see *Curia Regis Rolls*, x. 334.

[2] *Chronicon monasterii de Bello* (Anglia Christiana Soc., 1846), p. 108.

[3] P.R.O., Anc. deeds A. 5781, cf. *The Norfolk portion of Chartulary of Lewes*, ed. J. H. Bullock (Norfolk Record Soc., xii, 1939), pp. 6–7, no. 21.

[4] Durandus notes: 'ignotis sigillis non creditur, nisi eis fides per aliquos, qui ea noverint, imponatur', *Speculum*, lib. II partic. ii, § 8. 6, with a reference to *Extra*, 1. 22. 1 and 2.

[5] e.g. a rector gives a receipt for £8, attaching his own seal, 'et ad maiorem ipsius securitatem sigillum venerabilis patris domini Oliveri dei gracia Lincolniensis episcopi eisdem procuravi apponi' (1299, *Reg. Sutton*, vi. 182–3, cf. 186). A private litigant appoints a proctor in a case against St. Albans Abbey, 'et quia sigillum meum pluribus est incognitum, sigillum maioritatus Londoniarum huic scripto apponi procuravi' (1386, *Gesta Abbatum S. Albani*, ed. H. T. Riley (RS 1867–9), iii. 249). But this practice was not proof against fraud; see Arch-

These conditions produced a state of affairs in which the contract or conveyance came to be cast in the form of a judicial decision in a court of law. It was a sort of double stitch which was more durable even than the charter of confirmation by a public authority. It could come about so soon as a court could count on having some literate, clerical servant and had developed the habit of making some sort of written record. The twelfth century saw the beginnings of a kind of non-contentious jurisdiction (*juridiction gracieuse* in French parlance) exercised by public authorities in northern Europe. By the mid thirteenth century it was in full swing, giving rise to records which can be compared and contrasted with the products of the Mediterranean notary public, who still sometimes bore the title of *iudex*.[1] The kings of England, in their dominions abroad, followed the example of their French overlords. Edward I, as duke of Aquitaine, provided seals for his officials in various places in Gascony to enable them to authenticate in their courts the contracts of private persons. In 1279 he sent a similar seal which was to serve the same purpose to the bailiffs of Guernsey and Jersey. This method of ratification existed in Gascony alongside notarial practice; in the Channel Islands it lasted into modern times.[2]

In their small realm of England the Angevin monarchs were establishing from the first a more strict, efficient, and far-reaching control over the community as a whole than was found in other kingdoms. As part of their control they developed a non-contentious jurisdiction unexampled in extent. Already in the twelfth century the royal Exchequer and Chancery were prepared to strengthen private contracts by allowing official enrolment of private charters.[3] And after 1195 a final

bishop John Pecham in the Council of Lambeth (1281), c. 13 (*Councils and Synods*, ii. 908–9). Cf. below, p. 12 n. 2.

[1] Cf. R. C. Van Caenegem, 'La Preuve dans le Droit du Moyen Âge Occidental', in *Recueils de la Société Jean Bodin*, xvii (Brussels, 1965), 745–9, and works there cited, especially de Boüard, *Manuel*, tome ii.

[2] For Gascony see Tout, *Chapters*, v. 302–5 and *Guide to Seals in the P.R.O.* (1954), pp. 53–4. For a clear description of the 'lettres-sous-sceau' or 'lettres-de-juridiction' of the royal courts of the Channel Islands see the introduction by J. Le Patourel to *List of Records in the Greffe of Guernsey*, vol. i (List and Index Soc.: Special series vol. 2, 1969).

[3] Pollock and Maitland, ii. 96. On this use of the Pipe Rolls, Cartae Antiquae

concord drawn up in the king's court, after genuine or feigned litigation, took the secure form of a tripartite indenture of which the 'foot' was laid up in the Treasury, in official custody, to be produced in case of dispute.[1] Maitland noted the peculiar advantages of 'litigious forms' in regard to English conveyances of land: 'In the first place we secure indisputable evidence of the transaction. In the second place, if a man is put into seisin by the judgment of a court he is protected by the court's ban.'[2] Before the end of the thirteenth century the Crown extended its oversight to private contracts of another type—mercantile debts; and it was by royal enactments that municipal authorities found laid upon them the obligation to record recognizances.[3]

The powerful example of the practice of the English lay courts must be borne in mind when we see what happens in the ecclesiastical field. In England, as in northern Europe generally, the church courts develop a non-contentious jurisdiction, notably in England in the matter of proving of wills. No attempt was made, in early days, to invoke the notary as *persona publica* to deal with business of this sort. Local authorities were sufficiently inventive, without going to Italy for models. It is a commonplace that during the twelfth century the canon law of Rome, becoming the common law of the Western Church, absorbed and diffused throughout western Europe much of the procedure and principles of Roman private law.[4] But the growth of a centralized papal government—at once universal and Italian—did not and could not establish a uniform

Rolls, etc., see also H. G. Richardson, *Memoranda Roll for I John (1199–1200)* (Pipe Roll Soc., N.S. xxi, 1943), pp. lvii–lviii. Private persons also had deeds recorded in episcopal registers: see R. M. T. Hill, 'Bishop Sutton and his archives', *JEH*, ii (1951), 51–2.

[1] The earliest is recorded as such, on its dorse, dated 15 July 1195 (*Feet of Fines, Henry II and Richard I* (Pipe Roll Soc., xvii, 1894), p. 21). For the force and value of the final concord in its developed form see C. T. Flower, *Introduction to the Curia Regis Rolls* (Selden Soc., lxii, 1944), pp. 266–75, and cf. Galbraith, *Studies*, pp. 10–13.

[2] Pollock and Maitland, ii. 95.

[3] Postan, 'Private financial instruments', pp. 38–40, and the introduction by Alice Beardwood to *The Statute Merchant Roll of Coventry, 1392–1416* (Dugdale Soc. Publications, xvii, 1939), pp. vii–xxvi.

[4] Cf. Gaines Post, *Studies in Medieval Legal Thought* (Princeton, 1964), pp. 184–9, and Barraclough, 'The English royal Chancery and the papal Chancery'.

system of administration in all parts of the Western Church. Local government still counted for a lot in ecclesiastical elections and in the proceedings of local church courts. Small wonder, then, that even in the Church Universal the customs for recording titles and legal processes varied from region to region. Differences of personnel and training led to differences of competent officers, means of authentication, form, and terminology. The law of the Decretals, although it had a good deal to say about the notary as *persona publica*, did not exclude other than notarial instruments. The canonists were content to allow various methods of proof. In the Fourth Lateran Council Innocent III allowed two fit men to replace the *persona publica* for drafting judicial *acta*, and in a decretal letter of 1207 conceded that an instrument sealed by the Scottish king could be treated as valid 'according to the custom of the country'.[1] The rubric in *Extra* to this latter ruling reads: 'Consuetudo loci facit instrumentum authenticum.' The thirteenth-century canonists enlarged upon this.[2]

[1] *Extra*, 2. 19. 11 (IV Lateran Council c. 38), 2. 22. 9 (Migne, *Patrologia Latina*, ccxv. 1128). Cf. the citations of authorities by John Athon in glossing the legate Otto's canons (Lyndwood, *Provinciale*, part ii, pp. 67–8).

[2] Cf. Durandus, *Speculum*, lib. II, partic. ii, § 7. 8 (p. 301*a*).

2. Beginnings of Notarial Activity in England

IN these circumstances we need not be surprised that the first mention of the notary public in English ecclesiastical law is the record of a non-event. Three years after the publication of *Extra* the legate Otto, cardinal deacon of St. Nicholas in Carcere Tulliano, held a council for the Church of England and Wales at London in April in 1237. In it he laid down rules for the better conduct of the church courts, and in the course of so doing said, in so many words, that 'publici notarii non existunt' in England; and again, 'tabellionum usus in regno Anglie non habetur'.[1] The legate accepted the fact and did not propose that a notary public, a *persona publica*, should be required to authenticate instruments and *acta*. He concentrated on requiring more regular use of authentic seals. Not only archbishops and bishops, but also their officials, rural deans, and cathedral and collegiate and conventual chapters were all to have seals which should be clearly inscribed with the title of the dignity, officer, or society to which they belonged.[2] Among the documents issued in England by Cardinal Otto and his delegates none has been found in notarial form, although in England, during his legation (1237–41), there were to be found numerous Italian lawyers and clerks, and persons as distinguished as Henry of Susa (later Cardinal Hostiensis) and Albert, chancellor of Cologne (probably the later legate in the Baltic lands and

[1] *Councils and Synods*, ii. 257–8, cc. 27–8.
[2] In the past rural deans did not always have seals of office. William of Drogheda, *Summa Aurea* (ed. L. Wahrmund, Innsbruck, 1914), p. 18, gives a form of letter from the dean of Oxford: 'Quia signum non habeo', and see William's comment. Examples of seals of office set by deans on a will (1325) and on a private deed (1340) are Madox, *Formulare*, nos. DCCLXXII (p. 426) and DCXI (p. 348). See also below, p. 108 n. 2. The official of the bishop of Durham in 1282 needed notarial authentication of an act sealed with his personal seal, because he had not used the seal of the officiality (Brentano, *York Met. Jurisdiction*, p. 254).

archbishop of Riga). It was still to be a long time before the notary public found a firm foothold in this country.

When he did come, the way had been prepared by various developments. To appreciate these developments it is necessary to look back a long way into the past. The vocabulary of the classical Roman law had known the *tabellio*, the publicly authorized scribe, and under that law the *tabellio* operated. The institution had survived, as has been remarked, in Latin lands, where civic notaries plied their trade and maintained the rules of testimony and instrument-making which are to be found in the *Corpus Juris Civilis*. The vocabulary and many of the collocations of words found in the late medieval notarial instrument ultimately go back to the *Code* and the *Digest*,[1] as do the basic ideas of the authentic instrument and the public person. Some ideas and words of Roman law had reached England long before the notary public. Some may have come in Anglo-Saxon times through the vulgar, barbarian, Roman law of the Goths and Franks;[2] but the range of borrowings then did not extend to the *ordo iudiciarius*, which the northern countries did not assimilate. In the twelfth century the legal renaissance encouraged rational procedure and, more specifically, procedure by written record. New emphasis was laid on this by the Italian jurists of the twelfth century, and it became the object of study by canonists both in Italy and in other parts of Europe.[3] In the north the procedures in which the notary could profitably play a part only gradually came to be cultivated. The transplants are of the thirteenth century or, at the earliest, of the second half of the twelfth. They were nourished by the increasing demands

[1] See below, p. 123.

[2] For the 'vulgar law' see Ernst Levy, *West Roman Vulgar Law: the Law of Property* (Philadelphia, Mem. American Philos. Soc., xxix, 1951), Pierre Riché, *Enseignement du Droit en Gaule du vi^e au xie siècle* (*Ius Romanum Medii Aevi*, Pars I, 5b *bb*, Milan, 1965), and Peter Stein, *Regulae Iuris* (Edinburgh, 1966), ch. vii. The influence of this law in Anglo-Saxon England was adumbrated by Paul Vinogradoff (*Roman Law in Mediæval Europe* (1909), p. 26) and is touched on at several points by Eric John in *Land Tenure in Early England* (Leicester, 1960) and *Orbis Britanniae* (Leicester, 1966). For Roman law in twelfth-century England see F. de Zulueta's edition of *The Liber pauperum of Vacarius* (Selden Soc., 44, 1927) and E. Rathbone, 'Roman law in the Anglo-Norman realm', *Studia Gratiana*, xi (1967), 255–71.

[3] See the admirable article on 'Ordines iudiciarii' by Alfons Stickler in *Dict. du Droit Canonique*, ed. R. Naz, vi (1957), 1132–43.

for full written records of legal proceedings. The thirteenth-century *artes notarie* (not only designed for notaries public by apostolic or imperial authority) played a large part in the transplanting. By the middle of the century, Bolognese teachers like Salatiele and Rolandino were producing manuals and models which became popular textbooks. Before the middle of the century, too, the official books of decretals followed the pattern of the 'systematic' unofficial decretal-collections of the late twelfth century, and had their *tituli* 'De testibus', 'De fide instrumentorum', and so on. In devoting special sections to these topics the canonists were but copying the law of Justinian. This must be borne in mind when we try to estimate the influences at work in England—particularly in the church courts—which favoured the sort of *ordo iudiciarius* in which the notary public could be serviceable and which he understood. English teachers and practitioners studied in continental law schools, at Bologna and elsewhere. Thanks to Kuttner and Rathbone and others we now know something of the background and activity of Anglo-Norman canonists of the late twelfth century. Historians of the common law in this period can talk (and dispute) about the influence of Roman civil law on Glanvill and Bracton. English lawyers in the early thirteenth century were certainly becoming familiar with concepts and phraseology of Roman origin, all the more so because this period of church history saw an unprecedented growth in the administrative and judicial activity of the Roman Curia. To the collectors and commentators and writers of manuals, and to practising lawyers too, the notary or *tabellio* was no stranger, even if he had not yet found his way in person to England.

He appears first, to my knowledge, as the draftsman of a public instrument concerning a foreign potentate twenty years after the legatine council of Cardinal Otto. On 18 December 1257, in the queen's chamber in Westminster Palace, in the presence of Henry III and his Provençal queen, Eleanor, a notary public named John drew up a contract between Richard de Clare, earl of Gloucester and Hertford, and a proctor of William, marquess of Montferrat, for the marriage of the marquess to one of the three daughters of the earl. Had the parties to the contract both been English, one would expect the document to have taken the form of a sealed chirograph. But the marquess of Montferrat's proctor (Abbot John of Locedio) presumably followed the custom of his country in bringing with him a notary public to draft and authenticate the record. It is highly probable that this notary was an Italian.[1]

This was one type of work for a notary public in England. He found more frequent employment in the normal workings of the Universal Church. Thirteenth-century England—like the rest of Europe—becomes well acquainted with the Italian tax-gatherers of the pope. As provisions become common, more and more English benefices are the subject of lawsuits in the Roman Curia. It was natural to adopt the notarial instrument for some of this business. Leaving aside the appearance of the marquess of Montferrat's notary in 1257 (who may have held his title by imperial authority) the first known notary public by apostolic authority to set foot in England came in 1258 as a servant of Pope Alexander IV's nuncio, Master Arlotus.[2] On 2 August 1258 the nuncio, surrounded by a group of Italian chaplains and clerks in the bishop of Salisbury's house in London, examined charters and witnesses to establish the right of the Austin canons of Osney to the rectory of the church of Stone (Bucks.). The outcome was that the rectory was found to be appropriated to the abbot and convent and was therefore not liable to papal provision. Master Arlotus clothed his recognition of the facts in a document drawn up by Thomas de Sancto Germano.[3] This ends with the notarial eschatocol: 'Et ego Thomas de Sancto Germano apostolice sedis auctoritate

---

[1] Locedio, O. Cist., dioc. Vercelli. Unfortunately, the record is only an abridged copy, a schedule attached to Charter Roll 42 Henry III m. 5 (cf. *Cal. Ch. Rolls*, ii. 3–5). The text preserves the formula 'in presentia . . . ac mei Johannis subscripti notarii', but the eschatocol is only indicated by the opening words: 'Et ego'. Isabel de Clare married the marquess in June 1258 at Lyon.

[2] Arlotus was a member of the curial college of notaries and a papal chaplain: see Herde, *Beiträge*, p. 13.

[3] *Oseney Cartulary*, v. 147, from Bodleian Libr., MS. ch. Oxon. a. 3, no. 188. This—the earliest surviving original notarial instrument in England known to me—is neatly written. It has a fold and tag at the foot for sealing double queue. It is badly holed in two places, and the seal is lost. Although Thomas omits the adjective *publicus* from his title in the eschatocol, he is described as notary public in the text. Two related documents written by the same hand are in the same collection, nos. 189, 191 (*Oseney Cartulary*, v. 147–8).

notarius predictis pronunciacioni et iudicio interfui et predicta omnia de mandato venerabilis viri prefati magistri Arloti domini pape notarii scripsi, et in publicam formam redegi rogatus.' It bears a notarial sign manual in a simple device, but does not refer to it with the usual formula 'et meo signo consueto signavi' (or the like). The nuncio himself corroborates the document by appending his seal. The whole document, indeed, is a hybrid, combining some features of the objective Italian public instrument with others of the subjective sealed letters patent familiar to Englishmen. It begins in the Italian notarial way with invocation and date: 'In nomine domini nostri Jesu Christi amen. Anno eiusdem mcclviii die secundo intrantis mensis Augusti indictione prima'—all decidedly un-English; but then it drops into the usual general *inscriptio* ('universis presentes litteras inspecturis'), *intitulatio* ('magister Arlotus . . .') and *salutatio* ('salutem in domino'). At the end of the text comes the corroboratory clause: 'In cuius pronunciacionis et iudicii testimonium instrumentum hoc per manum Thome de Sancto Germano publici notarii fieri mandavimus et sigilli nostri robore fecimus communiri.'[1] This is followed by: 'Actum Londoniis in hospicio reverendi patris episcopi Saresbiriensis' and a witness-list.[2] Then come the notary's eschatocol and sign.

Within a year of the making of this instrument another foreign notary is found in London. This time the transaction did not concern Englishmen at all. On 12 May 1259 Ebal of Geneva made over to his illustrious relative, Peter of Savoy, and his heirs, all his hereditary rights in the county of Geneva. The document was framed in public form by one

[1] Cf. the *transsumptum* of a sentence given by judges delegate at Cologne on 3 Nov. 1279, with the notarial eschatocol and sign manual of 'Theodericus de Colonia dictus de Porta, imperiali auctoritate publicus notarius'. It is also corroborated by the seals of the judges and of the official of the court of Cologne (Koechling, 'Untersuchungen', pp. 47–8). Italian papal tax-collectors in England found it expedient to add their seals to notarial transcripts of papal bulls. Thus William de Testa sent from London to the bishop of Salisbury (27 May 1306) transcripts 'sub manu publica nostro sigillata sigillo originalia [*sic*] penes nos propter discrimina viarum retentis' (*Reg. Gandavo*, i. 200). Cf. *Reg. Sutton*, v. 181–2 (13 Sept. 1296). For seals on other types of notarial instruments see below, p. 24 n. 4 and p. 26 n. 2 and pp. 34–5, 111–15 below.

[2] The place-date does not appear with the time-date, as was usual in notarial instruments.

Galganus de Verulis auctoritate sancte Romane ecclesie publicus notarius.[1]

The next reference to a notary in English affairs occurs in the year 1263. On 6 September 1263 Pope Urban IV authorized his chaplain, Master William, an archdeacon in the church of Paris, whom he was sending to England on urgent business of the Universal Church, to confer the *officium tabellionatus* on a suitable person, according to the customary form of the Roman Church. The notary is to set down what is needed to expedite the business in public authentic writing.[2] No details are revealed. We can be pretty sure that this mission was connected with the constitutional crisis between Henry III and the baronial party, which led in November 1263 to the ineffectual dispatch of Cardinal Gui Foulquois as papal legate and peacemaker. But at this time Simon de Montfort was in the ascendancy, and the legate was not admitted to England.[3] It seems doubtful whether the services of a notary were required or an appointment was made.

If notaries did not often come to England in the middle of the century, Englishmen engaged in litigation in the Curia found it necessary or convenient to use notarial instruments when they presented their cases to papal auditors. The Archives of the Dean and Chapter of Lincoln preserve a book of forty-five folios (incomplete at beginning and end, with a bull of Alexander IV to the dean and chapter, dated at Viterbo, 13 June 1259, serving as wrapper): it is written mostly in a single Italian hand and is an account of the proceedings between the

---

[1] The original with sign manual is at Annecy, Archives départementales de la Haute-Savoie, S A 62/18. I am grateful to Dr. Pierre Chaplais for calling my attention to the document and owe a copy of it to the kindness of M. J.-P. Chapuisat, archivist of the Archives cantonales Vaudoises at Lausanne. It was imperfectly printed by E. Mallet in *Mém. et Docs. publiés par la Soc. d'Hist. et d'Archéologie de Genève*, vii (1849), 312–13 and by L. Wurstemberger, *Peter II, Graf von Savoyen* (Bern and Zürich, 1856–8), iv. 253, no. 507. This notary appeared in 1264 at Orvieto, in the Roman Curia, concerned in a case about an English benefice (*Reg. Urbain IV*, iii. 68, no. 1073).

[2] *Cal. Papal Letters*, i. 387.

[3] *Councils and Synods*, ii. 693–4. The legate, conducting negotiations from France, made use of a notary public to exemplify the letters he received from the English barons and bishops: see J. Heidemann, *Klemens IV: das Vorleben des Papstes u. sein Legationsregister* (Kirchengesch. Studien, ed. Knöpfler, Schrörs, and Sdralek, VI. iv, Münster, 1903), pp. 210–11, 219, 221, 225, 238, 243–4.

dean and chapter and Archbishop Boniface in their dispute over *sede vacante* jurisdiction. The proctors of both parties were stating their cases in the Curia before Stephen, cardinal bishop of Palestrina, between 1255 and early in 1259. The record had been committed to writing by one Bernardus de Insula Romanus, notary by apostolic authority, and this copy was collated by him and by Peter, notary by imperial authority, who both make their signs on the copy.[1] Another example from the sixties also concerns Archbishop Boniface of Canterbury. This is a document prepared by Bonaspes Guyditii of Perugia in the court of Clement IV, which survives in the Public Record Office. In 1260 Archbishop Boniface, on his metropolitan visitation, had discovered that Bogo de Clare, the dean, and the canons of the royal free chapel of St. Mary's, Stafford, claimed exemption from the diocesan bishop and the archdeacon. He summoned the parties before him at Lambeth and on 15 February 1261 the proctor of St. Mary's appealed to Rome. The archbishop wrote a report to Pope Alexander IV on 3 March 1261; this was not drawn up by a notary, but was incorporated in an *inspeximus* in the form of letters patent of Walter de Cantilupe, bishop of Worcester, dated at Fulham, 25 May 1261. The case dragged on, its progress in the Curia doubtless impeded by political events in England. Eventually, on 8 June 1267, it reached a stage when the *inspeximus* was produced in the Curia, while Clement IV was at Viterbo, in the presence of the chaplains of Richard, cardinal deacon of S. Angelo. The Italian, Bonaspes 'apostolice sedis auctoritate notarius, habens auctoritatem instrumenta et literas exemplandi et publicandi', made a copy in *publica forma* and added his sign manual. The document must have been commissioned by Englishmen, and eventually it found its way to England.[2]

[1] Lincoln, D. & C. Archives, D ij/62/4; the signs are at the foot of f. 30ᵛ. Cf. *Lincoln Cath. Stat.*, ii, pp. cliii–clvii. The case was concluded in England by a composition, 22 May 1261 (Churchill, *CA*, ii. 46). This was drawn up 'in modum cyrograffi', the parts sealed alternately. The course of the litigation is discussed at length in the doctoral thesis (University of Wales, 1970) of Dr. Daniel T. Williams on 'Aspects of the career of Boniface of Savoy'. The same notary was employed on another case in the Curia in 1257 (*Mong. Ang.*, vi. 163).

[2] Prynne, *Records*, iii (1672), 1234–5, from P.R.O., SC 1/11/94. For the copy of another instrument in the case prepared by Bonaspes see J. H. Denton, *English Royal Free Chapels* (Manchester, 1970), pp. 164–9, and for a discussion of

Yet another example may be cited, this time from the muniments of St. Paul's Cathedral. This records the agreement
reached at Viterbo, in the Curia, before Gregory of Naples,
papal auditor, by the proctors of the bishop of London and of
the dean and chapter of St. Paul's, on 26 January 1262. The
chapter's proctor had raised objections to a letter impetrated
from Pope Urban IV by the bishop a month earlier. The
agreement took the form of letters patent of the auditor, under
his seal, which were also authenticated by the sign and signature
of Guillelmus de Alifia, a notary by apostolic authority.[1]

As Englishmen were coming to employ notaries public in the
Curia, it is not surprising that they should begin to make use of
them in England upon occasion. In the years 1266–8 there is
again some evidence of their presence in the country. The cases
which have been noticed are worth enumerating:

i] The first occasion shows an imperial notary acting for the
agents of Italian bankers. On 17 February 1266, at Lambeth in
the archbishop's chapel, Bishop John Gervais of Winchester
(soon to be suspended from office by the legate Ottobuono for
his part in the Montfortian government) bound himself and his
church to pay a debt to Spinellus and Raynucius, merchants of
Florence; and his recognizance was drawn up in public form by
'Johannes de Sancto Dimitrio imperiali auctoritate publicus
notarius'. The name of the notary has not an English sound,
and the hand is continental.[2]

ii] Late in the same year 1266 the legate Ottobuono, having
collated Opizo of Lavagna to the church of Much Cowarne
(Herefordshire) on the death of the rector, John Capel, heard
that the abbot and convent of Gloucester claimed to hold the
church appropriated. He therefore ordered the dean of christianity of Gloucester to summon the parties concerned before

the proceedings, ibid., pp. 98–101. Bonaspes also drew up Westminster Abbey,
Mun. 16751, at Orvieto, 7 May 1264.

[1] London, St. Paul's Cathedral, D. & C. Mun., A/78/2074.

[2] The original is in Winchester Cathedral Libr., Cath. Records no. II, f. 5,
no. 12. The notary's signum is inscribed on the right-hand side of the eschatocol
(cf. below, Appendix II, no. 8). The text mentions the bishop's seal, but there
is no trace of attachment: the foot of the document may have been cut off.
I am obliged to Mr. Patrick Hase for knowledge of this document. For the
involvement of Bishop John with Italian creditors see Lunt, *Financial Relations
of the Papacy with England to 1327*, pp. 470–4.

him. The dean's citations, on 16 and 18 December 1266, at Gloucester, Much Cowarne, and Hereford, are recorded in a public instrument by a notary who states that he was present at the proceedings: Andreas dictus Brito de London' sacrosancte Romane ecclesie notarius publicus. He wrote at the request of the dean of christianity. This time both name and handwriting suggest an Englishman.[1]

iii] On 22 February 1267 letters patent of Nicholas of Ely, bishop of Worcester, about the jurisdiction *sede vacante* in his diocese, dated by the bishop at Alvechurch on 6 January 1267, were inspected and transcribed at London by the hand of Radulfus de Sancto Dionisio, apostolice sedis auctoritate notarius publicus. This Ralph of St. Denis seems to be otherwise unknown, though the name of St. Denis is not rare in England: his handwriting is not distinctively English, and might be northern French. Diplomatically, the document is not an entirely orthodox or well-framed notarial instrument. It begins, to be sure, with an invocation, which uses elongated letters; and it continues with a dating clause which introduces the indiction. But then comes a general address ('Pateat universis quod ego . . .') in which the notary speaks in the first person and gives his name and title in full. He does not say at whose request or command he has inspected the bishop's letter, nor does he give a precise place-date ('Actum Londonie'). The list of four witnesses which concludes the text appears to be written by the hand which wrote the rest of the instrument, but to be written later, even after the eschatocol. These are irregular features. The eschatocol, on the other hand, is in normal notarial form.[2]

iv] On 18 January 1268, sitting in the house of the bishop of Durham at London, a notary by imperial authority named Henricus Astensis authenticated a proctorial letter of the Dean and Chapter of Hereford, who had been cited to appear in a case against the Friars Preachers in the court of the legate Otto-

---

[1] Worcester, D. & C. Mun., B. 554, the original, with the notary's elaborate sign, well written on a large sheet (see Appendix II, no. 20 and pl. 6). Twenty years later Opizo was in trouble with Gloucester Abbey over another English benefice: *Cal. Papal Letters*, i. 486–7 and *Reg. G. Giffard*, ii. 310.

[2] Worcester, D. & C. Mun., B. 1613, reproduced as Plate 1 below. On the *sede vacante* jurisdiction see Churchill, *CA*, and Haines, *Admin. of the Dioc. of Worcester*.

buono. The legate's chancellor, Master Ardicio de Comite (Ardizzone Conti), himself a canon of Hereford, witnessed the document. The notary presumably took his name from Asti, and his handwriting looks Italian.[1]

v] On 11 July 1268 one of the legate's English judges delegate, Abbot Henry of St. Radegund's near Dover, announced the appropriation of three churches to the Templars, and recited the authorization from Pope Clement IV. He caused his letters patent to be drawn up *in publicam formam* by Lucas de Wartmaun, notary public by authority of the apostolic see.[2] Among the witnesses—for the most part English—was another notary public, Master Gerard of Parma.[3] The letter concludes: 'Et ego Lucas . . . in puplicam formam redegi meique nominis signum feci' with a notarial eschatocol of unusual elaboration. Like the document of Thomas de Sancto Germano ten years earlier, this is something of a hybrid. It bore the judge's seal as well as the notary's sign. It omitted the preliminary invocation and dating clause common on notarial instruments, but retained features of the notarial style in the date after the corroboration clause: 'Datum London' in capitulo ecclesie cathedralis London' a.d. mcclxviii pontificatus domini Clementis pape IIII anno quarto indictione undecima.'

vi] On 15 October 1268 at Lambeth, Johannes Erturi de Cadomo, notary public by apostolic authority, recorded for the archbishop of York his long-standing claim to have his cross carried before him when he travelled through the province of Canterbury.[4]

vii] Finally, on 26 November 1268, at Sugwas near Hereford, Bishop Peter d'Aigueblanche lay on his deathbed and prepared his last will. The testament was drawn up in notarial

---

[1] Below, Appendix II, no. 11. For Mr. Ardicio cf. *Diplomatic Documents, 1101–1272*, ed. Chaplais, p. 279, no. 412.

[2] *Reg. Sutton*, i (1948), 78–80.

[3] The description of this man and his place in the witness-list make it hard to believe that this is *the* Gerardus Blancus de Parma, papal chaplain and scriptor, already high in papal favour who, after a distinguished career as cardinal and legate, was buried in St. John Lateran in 1302: see Herde, *Beiträge*, pp. 33–5 and, for his formulary, Herde in *Archiv für Diplomatik*, xiii (1967), 225–312.

[4] *Reg. W. Giffard*, pp. 140–2. This man's name shows that he derived eventually from Caen. But it seems likely that he belonged to a family of that name already domiciled in England. See further below, Appendix I.

form by a clerk named John of Aosta, notary public, and a codicil was written by another notary, Lambert. Both survive only in badly damaged copies in the Dean and Chapter Archives at Canterbury.[1]

Of all these documents three, at most, may have been drafted by notaries public of English origin (nos. ii, iii, and vi), and all the notaries were engaged directly or indirectly in serving the needs of foreigners. They appear about the time that the legate Ottobuono presided over the English Church (1265–8) and three of the documents concern proceedings in his court. There is nothing surprising about that. It would indeed be perverse not to associate this activity with the legate's presence in England. A legate *a latere* provided a natural channel for Italian influence throughout the Latin Church. Significantly, when Ottobuono legislated for the English Church at London in 1268, on the matter of documentary evidence he was not content, as the legate Otto had been, to say baldly that in England 'publici notarii non existunt'. To prove the vacancy of a benefice he demanded the production of *either* a document sealed with one or more authentic seals, *or* a public instrument, *or* sworn and trustworthy witnesses.[2] At the same time, other influences were at work on England from Savoy, Provence, and possibly Spain, through the marriages of King Henry III and his son Edward. Queen Eleanor's uncle, Archbishop Boniface, employed Savoyard and Provençal clerks in his household in England, although no notary has been identified among them.[3] As we have seen, Ebal of Geneva and Peter d'Aigueblanche, associates of Peter of Savoy, had notaries with them in England; Florentine bankers might bring notaries to record recognizances of debtors. But the year 1268 saw a temporary halt in

---

[1] C. E. Woodruff, 'The will of Peter de Aqua Blanca', pp. 1, 7.

[2] *Councils and Synods*, ii. 759 (c. 10, De intrusis).

[3] As lord of Tournon, in Savoy, the archbishop employed local notaries public in his home country to draw up deeds of enfeoffment: 'Willelmus de Bonvilaret notarius sacri palatii et domini comitis Sabaudie' and 'Johannes de Ugina imperiali auctoritate publicus notarius' (F. Mugnier, *Les Savoyards en Angleterre au xiiie siècle* (Chambéry, 1890), pp. 286–91, 296–8, a.d. 1255, 1263, 1265). H. Emanuel (p. 3, cf. Fig. 3) notes that a Savoyard intruded into the chapter of Hereford, Poncius de Cors, employed Petrus Nicolai de Guarcino, notary public by imperial authority, at Sugwas near Hereford in 1291: Hereford, D. & C. Archives, no. 769, whence (incomplete) *Hereford Charters*, pp. 158–9.

notarial activity in England. The foreign element in the government of Church and State was diminished. Peter of Savoy had died abroad early in the year. The legate returned to Rome. Peter d'Aigueblanche died; and the archbishop of Canterbury left for his native Savoy, soon to find there a burial place beside his brother at Hautecombe. Nearly a decade passes before notaries public are recorded again in England in equal numbers. Andrew dictus Brito of London and Ralph of St. Denis (who may have been Englishmen) seem to leave no further trace, and John Erturi de Cadomo does not appear again as notary until 1280. John of St. Dimitrio reappears once.[1]

Although at this period the English royal Chancery and law courts made no use of notaries public, the king as duke of Aquitaine employed them when he was in his Southern provinces. On his way home from the crusade, Edward I had to deal with the opposition of Gaston, vicomte of Béarn. At Limoges on the Friday after Ascension Day 1274, he heard the vicomte's complaints against his seneschal of Gascony delivered orally by two Friars Minor. The hearing of the complaints (stated in direct speech) and the king's rulings on the matter were drawn up *in publicam formam* and signed by 'Petrus Lafauria clericus Lemovicensis auctoritate apostolica notarius publicus ac iudex ordinarius'. Among the witnesses were a notary by imperial authority and the king's civilian adviser, Franciscus Accursius, the famous professor of laws of Bologna.[2]

Foreign influence had brought foreign notaries to England in the middle of the century. Business connected with benefices and papal taxes brought them here again in the late seventies.[3]

---

[1] On 10 Jan. 1273: see below, Appendix II, no. 8.

[2] Rymer, I. ii. 511 (cf. 512) from P.R.O., E 36/275 (Liber B of the Treasury of Receipt). Although the instrument has all the notarial formalities it was also corroborated by the seals of three abbots. The use of the words *ac iudex ordinarius*, common among notaries of the Lombard towns, is worth remark. For use of the title in England see below, p. 25.

[3] At the other end of Europe, in Silesia and in Hungary, the first notaries public arrived in the train of papal legates and collectors, and were foreigners. See Luschek, *Notariatsurkunde*, pp. 1, 239 (1282), Bónis, in *Archivum*, xii (1965), 90, and cf. Bresslau, ii. 633 n. 1. See also below, p. 32. For Bohemia see J. Sebánek, 'Die Anfänge des öffentlichen Notariats und der Notariatsurkunde in den böhmischen Ländern', to appear in the acts of an International Congress for Diplomatic, Fribourg, Oct. 1969 (I am obliged to Prof. Sebánek for a copy of this paper). This shows the infiltration of notarial style during the thirteenth

On 18 November 1276 Petrus dictus de Sancto Marco de Ferentino, in St. Paul's Cathedral, London, prepared an instrument of appeal for the Cistercian nuns of Sinningthwaite against the archbishop of York's visitation. He is recorded in London again, on 30 July 1278, this time in the service of Master Salvagius de Florentia, a papal chaplain and royal protégé.[1] In May and June 1277, in the church of the New Temple, London, Petrus Raynaldi de Vallecimaria of the diocese of Camerino, notary public by apostolic authority, prepared and signed half a dozen documents for papal tax-gatherers.[2] He was engaged on similar business at Blackfriars, London, in January 1279, together with another notary public, Jacobus de Briga.[3] James reappeared at the New Temple in March, to write and sign a certificate in public form that large sums—proceeds of the pope's tax—had been received by merchants of the Luccan firm of Riccardi. The instrument incorporates the merchants' autograph receipts, written in the Italian vernacular, and had their seals (now lost) appended.[4] Next year one Ildebrandinus Bonadote de Senis, notary by

century, although the earliest known native notarial instrument is of 1313. M. Boháček's inference that a private deed drawn up at Prague in 1263, described as *instrumentum publicum*, was necessarily the work of a notary public seems unjustified (*Studia Gratiana*, xi (1967), 286, and cf. above, p. 4 n. 3). The only unsealed instruments in the register of Bishop Tobias of Prague (*Formulář biskupa Tobiáše z Bechyně 1279–96*, ed. J. B. Novák (*Historický Archiv*, xxii, Česká Akademie, Prague, 1903), pp. 189–92, nos. 250–1) were drafted by the *notarius* magister Henricus Italicus (1279–80). Dr. Sáša Dušková shows that 'Italicus' may signify no more than his Italian education and that the notarial title does not prove him to be a notary public ('Kdo byl notář Jindřich (Wer war Notar Heinrich)', *Sborník prací filosofické Fakulty Brněnské University* (1960), C. 9, pp. 59–74, with German summary; and further in *Sborník* (1970), C. 17, pp. 165–6). Nevertheless, in formula 250, a private act, Henry uses the words 'rogatus . . . propria manu scripsi et meo signo signavi . . .', in the Italian notarial fashion.

[1] *Mon. Ang.*, v. 464–5; B.M., MS. Cotton Claud, D. xi ff. 231ʳ–232ʳ.

[2] Printed by W. E. Lunt, in *EHR*, xxxii (1917), 71–80. Most of them were published by Emilio Re, 'La compagnia dei Riccardi in Inghilterra', pp. 125–32. Two were translated into English by Lunt, *Papal Revenues*, i. 211–12, 307–8.

[3] *EHR*, xxiii. 82–3. Cf. Lunt, *Papal Revenues*, ii. 179–82, and, for James de Briga, ibid. i. 259–61 (Dec. 1278).

[4] Vatican Archives, Instr. Misc. 164; in facsimile, *Epistolae et Instrumenta saeculi XIII*, no. 33, and printed by Re, loc. cit., pp. 132–5. The recipients' seals were a useful safeguard in case of action in the English courts. Similarly, the seal of an English debtor was attached to a notarial record of his loan from Italian merchants at Orvieto in 1283 (Brentano, *York Met. Jursidiction*, pp. 220–5). For seals on other sorts of notarial instruments see above, p. 16 n. 1.

apostolic authority, drew up *in publicam formam* an exemplification of a proxy whereby James of Ferentino and Bartholomew, a merchant of the company of Bonaventura of Siena, were empowered to receive possession of benefices and pensions granted in England to Angelus de Urbe, canon of Châlons and Cambrai, rector of the church of Haversham and clerk of the king of England.[1] Ildebrandinus practised in England for several years, exemplifying documents arising from ecclesiastical lawsuits. In instruments of 1282 he described himself as 'sancte Romane ecclesie auctoritate notarius publicus et imperiali auctoritate iudex ordinarius ac notarius'.[2]

In 1282 a case arose in the King's Bench which shows a certain suspicion (not wholly unjustified) of these newfangled ways. One Hugh le Pope had won his suit against Florentine merchants in the king's court, but on appeal the judgement was reversed. He then persuaded a *tabellio* named Monterus, dwelling in the city of London, to compose a record of the first, erroneous judgement and send it under his witness to Florence, to the damage of the merchants. The appeal he doubtless suppressed. The King's Bench declared it to be unheard of that judgements of the king's court should be impeded by a notary—'quorum nomina non a longo tempore in regno Anglie sunt audita'. The arrest of Hugh le Pope and of Monterus (whose name hardly suggests an Englishman) was ordered.[3] This Monterus was probably the notary public by imperial authority, Monterus Benvenuti of Florence, who exemplified some papal indults for the Hospitallers at London in 1287.[4] Unpopular or not, the notary public had come to stay.

[1] The instrument, with sign manual, is dated at London 'Idus Julii indictione octava anno domini m cc octogesimo' (below, Appendix II, no. 12). Mr. Angel was described as canon of Châlons in 1263 (*Cal. Papal Letters*, i. 391) and as of Cambrai, and 'advocatus domini regis in curia', when presented by the king to Haversham in 1274 (*Rot. Gravesend*, p. 251). Cf. Chaplais, *Diplomatic Documents*.

[2] Brentano, op. cit., pp. 190–4. Prof. Brentano speaks of 'the Canterbury notary Ildebrandinus' (p. 188), but the documents scarcely suggest that he was employed by the archbishop.

[3] *Sel. Cases King's Bench*, i. 99.   [4] Westminster Abbey, Mun. 9177.

3. Early English Notaries Public

EVEN as the Italians wrote in London, the next stage of the history of notaries in England was being prepared in Rome. On 25 January 1279 Pope Nicholas III provided to the archbishopric of Canterbury an Englishman resident in the Curia, and consecrated him on 19 February. John Pecham, O.F.M., was archbishop from 1279 to 1292. During his pontificate notaries public become naturalized in England, and the archbishop himself plays an important part in establishing them. It is unlikely that any of the notaries public hitherto encountered in this country were English, except for Andrew Brito and Johannes Erturi de Cadomo.

The archbishop's first and most striking action is well known, and has found its way into the manuals of diplomatic. He brought to England an Italian notary public, author of a much-read 'Summa de his quae in foro ecclesiastico coram quibuscunque iudicibus occurrunt notariis conscribenda'.[1] This was Johannes quondam Jacobi de Bononia, apostolica et imperiali auctoritate notarius publicus.[2] Master John accompanied the archbishop to England in the summer of 1279 and, perhaps ten years later,[3] dedicated his 'Summa' to his patron. He wrote (so

---

[1] Ed. by Rockinger in *Briefsteller und Formelbücher*, pp. 593–712. Other manuscripts are indicated by Bresslau, *Handbuch*, ii. 258 n. 4, and by Denholm-Young, 'The cursus', p. 97. The Cottonian manuscript contains only the first quarter of the work. Another early-fourteenth-century copy is in Worcester Cathedral Library, MS. Q. 62, ff. 1–28 (? English, of no great merit). Dr. Ian Doyle kindly called my attention to a text in Uppsala University Library, MS. C. 53, ff. 105–33, of the same period, Italian in appearance; I am grateful to the Librarian for a microfilm. References hereafter are to *Summa*.

[2] He gives his full title in a form of proxy, *Summa*, p. 607, and uses this form, omitting the word 'publicus', in a sealed proxy for the bishop of Winchester, at Orvieto in June 1282 (*Reg. Pontissara*, ii. 381–2). Cf. *Summa*, p. 608: 'Interdum scribitur procuratorium manu publica, et nichilominus sigillo . . . roboratur.'

[3] Rockinger (p. 597) dated the *Summa* 1289 on evidence which is rather shaky, as Prof. Richard Mather has pointed out to me. The dedication to the archbishop by 'servitorum suorum humillimus' suggests that he was still in the archbishop's service, but at a distance; for he sends his book by Mr. Philip (? de Exonia,

he reminded his master) as one who had sat at the feet of many doctors of law and notarial practitioners in Bologna and the Roman Curia. He wanted to instruct English clerks in the archbishop's household and elsewhere. He deplored their total lack of training in the *ars notarie* of the Curia. He would show them how to frame the documents needed in ecclesiastical business.[1] It was only right and proper that in these matters the English Church should copy the usage of the mother of churches.[2] John was, then, concerned with the whole matter of writing business letters—the notarial art in general—not only the drafting of public instruments for authentication by the notary as *persona publica*. His work has additional interest in that his formulas introduce English litigants and officials. In the 'Johannes de Sewes rector ecclesie de Sermeden Cantuariensis diocesis'[3] one can recognize John de Bononia's colleague, Johannes de Sancto Martino Lewensis rector of Smarden, himself a notary public by apostolic and imperial authority.[4] Doubtless John de Bononia contributed much to the form of English ecclesiastical documents. His influence, too, may account for the employment of more notaries public by English bishops.

It is this appearance of English notaries in episcopal service which deserves attention next. Before Archbishop John Pecham left Rome for England in 1279 he armed himself with a papal faculty, dated 25 March, to appoint within a year three suitable men to the office of notary public.[5] He acted on this. In his hall at Lambeth, in full consistory on 24 October 1279, he delivered sentence of excommunication against certain

archdeacon of Barnstaple, Pecham's proctor at the Curia in earlier years), *Summa*, pp. 711–12, cf. below, p. 32.

[1] *Summa*, pp. 603–4, 711; cf. p. 637: 'ut tollatur insufficiens modus Anglie rescribendi . . .'. John's preface is quoted by Pollock and Maitland, i. 219, and Jacob, *Essays*, pp. 198–9.

[2] 'Quoniam sacrosancta romana ecclesia mater est omnium et magistra ipsam unusquisque debet et merito quantum cum deo potest in omnibus suis processibus inmitari' (*Summa*, p. 603). The papal Chancery had influenced the English royal Chancery before this time; see Barraclough, 'The English royal Chancery and the papal Chancery', pp. 365–78, and cf. Cheney, *Study of the Medieval Papal Chancery* (Glasgow, 1966), pp. 29–32.

[3] *Summa*, p. 615.   [4] See below, p. 30.

[5] Below, Appendix II, no. 3. The archbishop got another faculty in March 1292 to create two notaries (*Cal. Papal Letters*, i. 557).

unnamed sons of Belial, and the list of witnesses ended with 'Johanne de Sancto Martino Lewenci, Johanne Alani de Bekles notariis puplicis'.[1] On 11 November in the following year a similar document recording a sentence was drawn up at Walden Abbey, Essex, by a notary named John, and on this occasion the last of the witnesses named was 'Willelmo de Holaym notario publico'.[2]

Later traces show clearly that these three men were all members of the archbishop's permanent staff. William de Holaym, to be sure, seldom appears again, but it is significant that the archbishop collated to him the rectory of Deal in December 1280 and in an unusually fulsome letter, recording his investiture 'per nostrum anulum', spoke highly of his services in the past ('qui in nostre familiaritatis gratiam assumptus per obsequiositatis devote promptitudinem te nobis acceptum plurimum reddidisti'). One is inclined to wonder whether the letter is itself a sample of William de Holaym's skill in the *ars notarie*. In July 1282 the archbishop described William as *clericus et familiaris noster*.[3]

John de Beccles has left more record. And here it may be convenient to remark upon his practice of describing himself in public instruments as Johannes Alani de Beccles; for the same style is used by many other English notaries public in the next hundred years, and it underlines the exotic nature of their calling. By the later part of the thirteenth century Englishmen as a rule stopped recording their father's christian name, and if they did use it they usually adopted the form Johannes filius Alani. So Johannes Alani de Beccles, Andreas quondam Guilielmi de

---

[1] *Councils and Synods*, ii. 861 (from the Worcester episcopal register). A puzzling feature of the surviving copies is the substitution, in an Exchequer text, of two other notaries (otherwise unknown) for those named above (ibid., note g).

[2] *Reg. Ep. Peckham*, i. 147–50. The preamble reads: 'in presentia mei Johannis notarii', but the registrar omitted the eschatocol. This might be John de Beckingham, a witness of the document, a household clerk later sent to Rome on the same business (*Reg. Pecham*, ii. 68–9): in P.R.O., SC 1/9/2 he is described as the archbishop's notary.

[3] *Reg. Pecham*, i. 109–10, 116. Deal (Kent) was in the archbishop's gift. In 1282 the archbishop recorded that he had ordained William acolyte, 21 Dec. 1280, on letters dimissory of the archbishop of York, and had later ordained him subdeacon (8 March 1281) on the title of Deal, and deacon and priest in the same year (ibid. i. 187).

Tange, Richardus natus Philippi Lovecock, Ricardus natus quondam Henrici de Ganyo, and others like them were aping the Italian custom which was already represented by Johannes Erturi de Cadomo and Johannes quondam Jacobi de Bononia, and which was adopted by notaries elsewhere in northern Europe.[1] But those who followed this practice only used it in the formula of subscription in their own instruments. If they had to be named in the text, the name appeared in its shorter form. So in 1281 John Alani de Beccles subscribed in this form an instrument which he had drawn up for the archbishop of Canterbury; but in the text of the document he gave his name as plain John de Beccles.[2] On 6 November 1305 the notary public Philip de Londonia exemplified papal bulls at Westminster, and stated in the eschatocol that he had collated the text with the help of Master Adam de Lyndeseye and Master Henry de Colecestria, notaries public. These same men, a few days earlier, wrote exemplifications which they certified under the names of Adam filius Ade Swayny de Boterwik dictus de Lindeseia and Henricus Ricardi de Colecestria.[3] This common practice has sometimes led to misunderstanding by modern editors and scholars, who have (for instance) made an unwarranted distinction between John Erturi de Cadomo and John de Cadomo.[4] But to return to John de Beccles.

He first appears as a trusted clerk of Thomas de Cantilupe, bishop of Hereford, commissioned to act in lawsuits at Rome in November 1276 and May 1279.[5] In October 1279 he acts as executor of the will of Master Giles de Avebury, dean of Hereford.[6] But meanwhile he presumably had encountered John Pecham in the Curia and was engaged by the archbishop. By October 1279, as has been seen, he is described as notary public and is in the archbishop's company. In May 1281, when drafting for the archbishop the instrument mentioned above he makes

---

[1] The form was often adopted by notaries elsewhere in northern Europe: thus, Andreas quondam Jacobi de Cracovia, 1312, Andreas natus quondam Hotradi de Brodetz diocesis Pragensis, 1365 (Luschek, p. 162).

[2] Below, Appendix II, no. 7. Cf. the case of John de la Burghe of Shepton Beauchamp, 1315 (*Reg. Worcester Sede Vacante*, p. 173, f. 94ʳ).

[3] P.R.O., SC 7/36/2, 7/36/3, and 7/33/27.

[4] See below, pp. 143–51.   [5] *Reg. Cantilupe*, pp. 106–7, 209–10.

[6] *Reg. Pecham*, ii. 91, 221.

the archbishop describe him as *notarius noster*.[1] In the same year
he has a register in which is recorded archiepiscopal business
and in 1283 is in charge of some part of the archiepiscopal
archives.[2] In 1284 he acts as clerk to the examiners of ordin-
ands.[3] His last recorded service for Pecham is in May 1288,
when he addresses the suffragan bishops of Canterbury on
behalf of the archbishop. The bishop of Hereford's register on
this occasion describes him as *uxoratus*.[4] If in fact he was a
married clerk, this would explain why he does not appear as
incumbent of any living in the archbishop's gift. He must have
received a salary instead. John of Beccles never figures in the
register of Pecham's successor, and there seems no reason to
suppose that he entered Winchelsey's service. Instead, in 1299
and 1300 he prepared notarial instruments concerned with an
appeal by St. Augustine's Abbey, Canterbury, from the jurisdiction of the archbishop over the abbey's churches. These
were written at the abbey's request although today they are
preserved in the muniments of Christ Church.[5]

The third English notary public to be closely associated
with Archbishop John Pecham from the first year of his pontificate is Johannes de Sancto Martino Lewensis. On 30 January
1280 the archbishop collates to him the rectory of Smarden, and
he is already a priest when in May 1281 he exchanges this for
another rectory in the archbishop's gift, Buxted. In 1287 he
receives the prebend of Ratling in Wingham.[6] He prepares and
attaches his sign manual to public instruments for the archbishop repeatedly during 1282,[7] and ten years later is described
by Pecham as 'familiaris noster'.[8] In the notarial documents he

---

[1] Below, p. 35 and Appendix II, no. 7. Another of his acts (3 Dec. 1282,
in the archbishop's chamber at Leominster Priory) is Appendix II, no. 10. His
copy of letters of ordination *sub manu pupplica* was in the archbishop's archives
in 1282 (*Reg. Pecham*, i. 185). The archbishop ordered him to prepare a public
instrument at Huntingdon Priory, 10 Oct. 1284 (ibid. i. 218).

[2] *Reg. Pecham*, i. 118, 196.   [3] Ibid. i. 212.   [4] *Reg. Swinfield*, p. 179.

[5] Canterbury, D. & C. Archives, Chartae antiquae A. 208, A. 212, A. 215,
M. 375. As in earlier original instruments of John of Beccles, the sign
manual is on the right of the eschatocol, and Beccles uses the characteristic initial 'I' for
the invocation which he had used many years before.

[6] *Reg. Pecham*, i. 105, 116 (cf. above, p. 27); ibid. i. 55, 67.

[7] Ibid. ii. 38, 47–8, i. 188–90, *Reg. Ep. Peckham*, ii. 419–20. In Rymer, i. ii. 605
(21 Apr. 1282) he is described as 'apostolica auctoritate notarius publicus'.

[8] *Reg. Ep. Peckham*, iii. 987 (28 July 1292).

usually describes himself as 'apostolica et imperiali auctoritate notarius publicus'.

These three may be the trio for whom Pecham used his first faculty to create notaries public. But he attracted at least one other to his service. On 22 December 1279 Pope Nicholas III had licensed seven notaries public, after examination by his chaplain Nicolinus de Camilla, canon of Évreux. They included two Englishmen: 'pro Guillelmo de Somerdeby clerico in minoribus ordinibus etc. Lincolniensis diocesis', and 'pro Eadmundo dicto de Verduno clerico Cantuariensi in minoribus ordinibus etc.'.[1] Both these men practised in the next few years in the province of York,[2] but by 1288 Edmund de Verduno was recording institutions and resignations of benefices for the archbishop of Canterbury,[3] and in 1292 drew up in public form the record of Archbishop John Pecham's death and of the election of Robert Winchelsey as his successor.[4] Meanwhile, in 1290 he had been ordained subdeacon and deacon on the title of the Kentish church of Snargate, a rectory in the archbishop's gift.[5] Like John de Sancto Martino, Edmund de Verduno styled himself *notarius publicus* by apostolic and imperial authority.

To return to the archbishop's first notarial clerk: John de Bononia drew up an instrument for Archbishop John Pecham as early as 16 August 1279 at Mortlake, and was employed by him for the same purpose at Lambeth on 24 October 1279 and at Bicester on 19 February 1280.[6] Early in 1282 he was apparently

---

[1] *Reg. Nicolas III*, pp. 255-6, no. 597, from Reg. Vat. 39 f. 208^r. Not in *Cal. Papal Letters*.

[2] For William de Somerby see his records of the professions of obedience of bishops of Whithorn and Durham to the archbishop of York, 1282 and 1284 (*Reg. Romeyn*, ii. 83 n. 3 and *Records of Antony Bek*, p. 2). He still worked at York in 1290 (*Reg. Romeyn*, i. 99). Maybe he was the priest of this name instituted to the vicarage of Burwell (co. Linc.) 24 Nov. 1298 (*Reg. Sutton*, i. 236). For Edmund de Verduno's early career in the north see Brentano, *York Met. Jurisdiction*, with illustrations of his writing and sign manual (pl. 3). But cf. below, p. 32 n. 6. He subscribes himself 'Eadmundus de Cant' dictus de Verduno apostolica et imperiali auctoritate publicus notarius'.

[3] *Reg. Pecham*, i. 74, 77-8. He acted in this year with Adam and John de Beccles for the archbishop in his dispute with his suffragans (*Reg. Swinfield*, p. 178).

[4] *Reg. Winchelsey*, ii. 1257-8.   [5] *Reg. Pecham*, ii. 23, 29.

[6] *Reg. Ep. Peckham*, i. 45; *Councils and Synods*, i i. 861; *Oseney Cart.*, iv. 453-7.

sent to the Roman Curia to act as proctor on the arch-bishop's business; and while there, at Orvieto in June 1282, he drew up an instrument of proxy for the bishop of Winchester for transmission to the archbishop.[1] He drafted judicial records concerning English cases at Rome in March 1286 and in April 1290.[2] Documents of English concern, assigned dates after 1282 in the *Summa*, do not prove that John de Bononia returned to England later in the century. Other appearances of the name make his history hard to disentangle. One of his name, a subdeacon, was instituted in 1288 to the church of Llangennith (Glam.), in the patronage of the countess of Gloucester and Hertford.[3] It seems hardly likely that Pecham's clerk was the John de Bolonia, notary public, who witnessed a Hereford deed at Bosbury as late as 3 April 1312.[4] It cannot be utterly ruled out that the author of the *Summa*, Pecham's clerk, was the John 'dictus de Bononia clericus', who had bought property in Oxford in 1264–5, and who probably came of an Oxford family.[5] Were they identical? Was the instructor of English notaries, like John Erturi de Cadomo, himself an Englishman by birth who, before 1279, had studied in Bologna and practised in the Curia for many years? It is possible, but highly improbable.[6]

Contemporaneously, notaries public appear in other epi-scopal households of England. The example of Archbishop John Pecham may partially account for this; together with those favourable conditions in the Western Church as a whole which were remarked upon in the last chapter. It was in this same period that apostolic and imperial notaries penetrated northern France and the Low Countries, Germany, Bohemia,

---

[1] *Reg. Ep. Peckham*, i. 278; *Reg. Pontissara*, ii. 381–2.

[2] *Reg. Honorius IV*, nos. 456, 605, and *Reg. Nicolas IV*, no. 2871. I owe the last reference to the kindness of Prof. Richard Mather.

[3] *Reg. Pecham*, i. 77.   [4] *Reg. Swinfield*, p. 471.

[5] *Oseney Cart.*, i. 226; *St. Frideswide's Cart.*, i. 333–5. No trace of a James of Bologna or Boulogne, who might have been the father of Pecham's clerk, appears in Oxford records. See the next note.

[6] 'Percivallo filio domini Jacobi de Bononia iuris civilis professor'' appears with other Italians and with Philip, the archbishop of Canterbury's squire, as witnesses to an instrument drawn up by Edmund de Verduno, 19 May 1281 (B.M., MS. Cotton Vesp. F. xv, f. 177ᵛ). This suggests that Percival was John's brother and that they were of Italian origin.

and Poland, regions where—not long before—the *usus tabellionum* was rare even when local notariates existed.[1] For England the evidence consists, first, of faculties granted by the pope to English bishops before the year 1292 to create eleven notaries,[2] and four more examples of direct appointment in the Curia.[3] Secondly, there is the evidence of documents left behind, in original or in copy, by English notaries public employed by English bishops. As early as 1282 the *acta* and *processus* of an important ecclesiastical suit in the north of England were being committed to writing *manu publica*.[4] All told, by the death of John Pecham notaries public were active in more than half the dioceses of England. They did not all derive authority from the pope: Robertus filius Petri, notary by imperial authority, prepared for the bishop of Winchester in his manor of West Wycombe the record of a presentation to a benefice on 31 March 1285.[5]

In Scotland the notary public appeared about the same time. One Robert de Garvalde (perhaps taking his name from Garvald, East Lothian) and William de Horsboch (? Horsburgh, co. Peebles) acted at Edinburgh in a suit before the official of the bishop of St. Andrews, on 4 December 1287, and other public instruments drawn up by Robert (a notary by apostolic authority) date from 1298 and 1305.[6] Meanwhile, the bishop of

[1] In 1275 it was said that in Zürich 'non est usus legalium tabellionum' and in 1278 that in Salzburg 'in oppido memorato tabelliones publici non [habentur]' (F. Martin, 'Zum Salzburger Urkundenwesen des 13 Jahrhunderts', *MIöG*, Erganzungsband, 1929, p. 285). For the introduction of the notary public by papal or imperial authority into the Low Countries see H. Nélis, 'Les origines du notariat public en Belgique, 1269–1320', Ketner, 'Vestiging', and R. C. Van Caenegem in *Ius Romanum Medii Aevi*, pars v, 5b (Milan, 1966), 17–18; for Germany, Koechling, *Untersuchungen*; for central Europe cf. p. 23 n. 3 above. See also in general Bresslau, *Handbuch*, i. 632–3, and R. Heuberger, *Allgemeine Urkundenlehre für Deutschland und Italien* (Leipzig, 1921), pp. 54–5.

[2] *Cal. Papal Letters*, i. 490, 515, 523, 539, 542, 543. For Irish and Scottish bishoprics see faculties granted in the same period, ibid. i. 470, 481, 490, 491 (Baumgarten, p. 43), 521.

[3] *Cal.*, i. 468, 482, 528, 545. They were Mr. Thomas de Cardolio (dioc. Carlisle), Walter le Noreys and Elias de Coutona (dioc. York), Bartholomew Thome Everard (dioc. London).

[4] Brentano, *York Met. Jurisdiction*, pp. 239–48.

[5] *Reg. Pontissara*, i. 311.

[6] *Carte monialium de Northberwic* [ed. Cosmo Innes] (Bannatyne Club, 1847), p. 24, no. 23; *Liber ecclesie de Scon* [ed. Cosmo Innes] (Bannatyne Club, 1843), p. 89 no. 124; *Facs. of National MSS. of Scotland*, part ii (1870), no. xii: this is an

Dunkeld had received from Pope Nicholas IV (28 May 1288) a faculty to appoint as notary public one fit clerk of his diocese;[1] and on 30 April 1291 a notary by imperial authority, Nicholas dictus Campion, practised at Roxburgh.[2]

During the next fifty years or so English ecclesiastical records become far more copious than before. They permit the assertion that English bishops of the fourteenth century habitually employed at least one notary public on a permanent footing, paid by benefices or by a salary, although the precise *quid pro quo* is seldom seen. It is only from a suit in the Court of Arches, for breach of contract or wrongful dismissal, that we learn that in 1299 John Salmon, bishop elect of Ely, engaged Stephanus quondam Roberti de Schelfengre, 'tabellio publicus auctoritate sedis apostolice', at an annual salary of 20 shillings with clothing.[3]

The advance of bureaucracy, if only as yet in its early stages, meant a greater demand for exemplifications of title-deeds and for written records of legal processes. Title-deeds of all sorts might have to be exhibited on many occasions at home or abroad. It was convenient to have authentic copies of them prepared by the hand of a *persona publica*, for this obviated the risks involved in handling originals, sometimes of great antiquity. And the notarial instrument was less vulnerable to the hazards of travel than an exemplification authenticated by a fragile wax seal. As early as November 1280 Archbishop John Pecham, when he visited the cathedral priory of Norwich, demanded that the monks should produce for his inspection the titles for their appropriated churches and other ecclesiastical property. They brought the documents to him at Holy Trinity, Ipswich, in March 1281 as he proceeded on his canonical visitation of the diocese; and because some of their deeds were very

original instrument with the notary's sign manual, from P.R.O. C 47/22/8(1). All three documents are cited by W. Angus in *An Introductory Survey of the Sources and Literature of Scots Law* (Stair Soc. Publications, vol. i) p. 289. For an appearance of Mr. Robert at Carlisle in 1284 see Brentano, p. 239.

[1] Reg. Vat. 44, f. 15ᵛ, *Cal. Papal Letters*, i. 491. Faculties had not yet become standardized in form, though the preamble 'Ne contractuum memoria' (cf. below, Appendix II, nos. 1 and 3) was already in use. This one began with the words: 'Volentes tuam honorare personam'.

[2] *Liber S. Marie de Melros* [ed. Cosmo Innes] (Bannatyne Club, 1837), i. 315–17.

[3] *Reg. Winchelsey*, i. 465–6, ii. 750, 780.

ancient and the seals of others had been broken in the recent attacks by the citizens upon the cathedral priory, they asked the archbishop to 'renew and publish' the documents.[1] This he did on a lengthy roll, which begins by recounting the circumstances and then introduces authentic copies: 'As an immediate precaution and for a future memorial we have decreed that the documents be copied and published by a public person, word for word, with his signs, so that by this means the exemplification shall have the same authority as the originals, of which instruments the tenor is as follows: . . .' Despite its production by a *persona publica* named as John de Beccles 'our notary', the archbishop added his seal, but the archbishop's corroboration clause is followed by the notarial eschatocol and sign manual. The notary also drew his sign across the seams where the three membranes of the roll were sewn together.[2] Twenty-three years later Pecham's successor came on his metropolitan visitation to Norwich and called upon his notary, Master Hugo Hugonis de Musele, to verify the titles of the prior and convent. For certain appropriated churches Hugh examined original deeds and endorsed them with his sign manual, but the roll of 1281 covered some of the principal privileges, and Hugh put his sign on the back of the roll.[3]

[1] Below, Appendix II, no. 7. It is dated at Lambeth, 15 May 1281, although the inspection of the documents took place in March at Ipswich. On the same circuit Pecham inspected title-deeds of Spinney Priory (O.S.A., Cambs.) at Burwell (Cambs.) on 23 April, and John Alani de Beccles authenticated an *inspeximus* that survives as a draft or copy, not in the hand seen in John's other instruments, but with a faded sign resembling John's: Canterbury, D. & C. Archives, Chartae antiquae N. 24. This may be an example of a notary's 'private' hand used in preparing a draft (cf. below, p. 104). For a notarial certificate for Plympton Priory, 1335, by Robert de Peyk, see B.M., Add. ch. 67571; it also bore the seal of the bishop of Exeter and was copied, without the notary's eschatocol, in the bishop's register (*Reg. Grandisson*, ii. 775–6).

[2] Richard de Brenchesle or Brenchley made a roll for Westminster Abbey in May 1308 'in hiis novem peciis pergameni consutis et signo meo signatis': Westminster Abbey, Mun. 9496 m. 9 (ad fin.). For other examples see P.R.O., E 135/15/17 (a.d. 1297) and E 30/1208 (a.d. 1299), Purvis, *Notarial Signs*, pls. 1 and 4 (1308 and 1311), and below, Appendix II, no. 7. The rolls of the 'Great Cause' of Scotland are thus marked, Cadomo's twenty-eight times, Tange's thirty-five.

[3] For the sign see *Reg. Winchelsey*, i, p. xix, with references, to which may be added Lambeth Palace, Chartae misc. v. 119 and Cambridge, Christ's College Archives, Creake Abbey chs. 32, 33 (I owe the latter reference to Mrs. D. M. Owen). Hugh de Musele or Mursley was made notary by papal authority in 1291,

A couple of years earlier the place of the notary in visitations of monasteries was defined by a papal decision. He no longer merely inspected and exemplified title-deeds: he was to record the quasi-judicial inquests of the visitor. In May 1300 the bishop of Durham had run into opposition when he went as visitor to his cathedral priory.[1] The monks objected to the bishop's introduction of a horde of laymen and secular clerks into their chapter-house and to the revelation of chapter secrets to outsiders. Bishop Antony Bek was not a man to treat the resistance lightly. After much trouble, culminating in an appeal to Rome, Pope Boniface VIII delivered judgement on 23 July 1302.[2] He ruled that the custom which the monks claimed to obtain in the church of Durham, whereby the bishop was obliged to enter the chapter-house *solus*, with one of the monks to act *loco notarii*, was unacceptable, for reasons which he specified. He declared that the bishop might take with him into the chapter-house of his cathedral 'two or three upright (*honestos*) clerks of whom one at least should be a Benedictine monk, together with a clerical notary'. This decision was eventually incorporated into the *Extravagantes Communes*, I. 7. 1 (Debent superioribus); but before that it was taking effect elsewhere in England. In 1303 a new bishop of Worcester proposed to begin his primary visitation in the cathedral priory. 'His clerks and ours', says the monastic reporter of the event,[3] 'discussed a certain new constitution which the pope had recently put forth, respecting the entrance of a bishop for

was apparently a simple *tonsuratus* until ordained acolyte, 1295, with letters dimissory from the bishop of Lincoln (*Reg. Sutton*, v. 80, 98), and was in Winchelsey's service, 1293 (*Reg. Winchelsey*, ii. 1263, 1270–1, 902). He was made subdeacon (1295) by the archbishop's order, and when ordained deacon (1297) and priest (1298) was described as Mr. Hugh de Musele, rector of Harbledown, a church in the archbishop's gift (ibid. 907, 920, 922).

[1] Dr. Constance M. Fraser details the story in *A History of Antony Bek* (Oxford, 1957). She prints notarial documents recording the visitation and its aftermath in *Records of Antony Bek*, pp. 57–8, etc.

[2] *Reg. Boniface VIII*, iii. no. 4730. For texts at Durham see *Records of Antony Bek*, p. 86.

[3] Worcester, D. & C. Mun., Liber Albus, f. 16ᵛ, transl. by James M. Wilson, *The Worcester Liber Albus*, pp. 36–7, quoted in C. R. Cheney, *Episcopal Visitation of Monasteries* (Manchester, 1931), p. 69, where it is misdated 1302. For the composition with the bishop about bringing seculars into the chapter-house (1224) see William Thomas, *Survey of the Cathedral-Church of Worcester* (1737), Appendix, pp. 74–6.

making a visitation. And since it was doubted whether that decretal was common or special, general or local, the prior declared that he would admit the bishop this time with two clerks and one notary, always, however, saving our composition if the constitution was not a general one. The bishop made a like declaration. And the clerks who entered and were with the bishop in the said visitation were Master Walter of Wootton, archdeacon of Huntingdon, Master John of Rodborough, and Master John Caleys, notary public.'[1]

At almost the same time as the visitation of Worcester, Archbishop Robert Winchelsey visited his cathedral priory and conducted inquiries in the chapter-house with the help of his chaplain and of his clerk, Master William de Chadeleshunte, doctor of civil law. On the request of the convent, he sent his clerk out of the room when the time came to make correction. There is no sign that Winchelsey brought a notary public and no evidence that the Durham case was mentioned; but at some time later in the century the prior of Christ Church, Canterbury, sought a legal opinion on whether the *constitutio Bonefaciana* was general or special in its application.[2] Boniface VIII's decree in the Durham case might apply to other monasteries but not to non-monastic churches; although the presence of a notary public might be less distasteful to secular visitands. At Lincoln Cathedral in 1440 it was agreed that the bishop, visiting his chapter, might bring into the chapter-house 'his own notary and a clerk of his choice, upright men and unmarried'.[3]

Besides normal visitatorial business, exceptionally important ecclesiastical lawsuits called for public instruments. An early example in England is the process against the Order of the

---

[1] Mr. John Caleys was appointed *tabellio* by Bishop William de Geynesborough by papal authority (22 April 1303), and remained in the bishop's service (*Reg. Geynesborough, passim*). In 1310 he left this bishop's successor, Reynolds, to serve the bishop of Ely as registrar and chancellor, 1310–16 (*Reg. Reynolds*, p. 88, and Emden, *BRUC*, p. 117). In view of his early career and profession (cf. below, p. 89), his connection with the University of Cambridge must be considered doubtful.

[2] *Reg. Winchelsey*, ii. 1304–6; *Literae Cantuarienses*, ed. J. B. Sheppard (RS, 1887–9), i. 301.

[3] *Lincoln Cath. Stat.*, iii. 277. In fact, the bishop's registrar at this time was a married man (cf. below, p. 81).

Temple. This dragged on through the years from 1309 to 1312. Provincial councils, of both Canterbury and York, received reports from inquisitors of the examination to which individual Templars had been subjected. The replies of the Templars to interrogatories were drawn up by notaries public,[1] and proceedings of the councils where sentences were delivered and penances imposed were also drawn up in public form. This is not always obvious from the surviving digests; those who copied some of the matter into episcopal registers spared themselves and their readers trouble by omitting the common form of notarial eschatocols.[2] But at least one roll, which describes the proceedings in sessions held at York in 1311, written at the command of Archbishop William Greenfield and his commissary and attested by Henricus Willelmi de Erdeslawe, an imperial notary, is now preserved in the Vatican Archives.[3]

We have seen that from the mid thirteenth century the papal tax-gatherers had brought notaries public from Italy to England to help with their work.[4] When the business of assessing and levying papal taxes was imposed on English prelates, this provided an additional incentive to them to take notaries public on to their staff. In 1291 Oliver Sutton, bishop of Lincoln, was appointed one of the principal collectors of the sexennial tenth laid on the English clergy by Pope Nicholas IV. On 29 March 1297 the dean of Hereford complained against errors in assessment of his revenues and those of the dean and chapter, and he did so in the presence of the bishop's clerks at the Old Temple, London. His appeal was incorporated in a public instrument drawn up by Johannes Roberti de Clippeston, a member of the bishop's household whom he had created notary by apostolic authority a few years earlier.[5] More records relating to assessments in the diocese of Hereford

---

[1] *Councils and Synods*, ii. 1332.

[2] Ibid. ii. 1298, 1307–17, 1333 n. 1. Cf. p. 101 below.

[3] AA. Arm. D. 221, cf. *Councils and Synods*, ii. 1324, 1335–9. This notary's sign manual is in Purvis, *Notarial Signs*, Pl. 9.

[4] Above, p. 24.

[5] *Taxatio Ecclesiastica Angliae et Walliae* (Record Commission, 1802), p. 177. For John's appointment in 1293 see *Reg. Sutton*, iii, p. lxxxiv, and iv. 130–1; cf. ibid. ii. 162 and note; and below, pp. 74–5.

were notarialized by other notaries in 1301 and 1309; in 1309 it was done in the presence of the papal nuncio and collector of arrears, William de Testa, who added his seal.[1]

When English prelates used their licences to appoint notaries, they probably tended to show preference for clerks who already had some training in the law and some acquaintance with the court of Rome. There is evidence that many English clerks with leanings to the law went to Bologna to improve their education, and there they saw the notarial system at work. Direct appointments of English notaries in the Curia and licences granted to Englishmen by imperial delegates abroad point the same way. We may suppose that in the early days after the institution was introduced into England a majority of the notaries had some continental experience.

[1] Hereford, D. & C. Archives, no. 1077.

4. Notarial Activity in the English Church in the Mid Fourteenth Century

INCREASINGLY, in the first half of the fourteenth century the usefulness of a trained notariate was being recognized in English ecclesiastical circles. The bulky episcopal register of Ralph of Shrewsbury, bishop of Bath and Wells from 1329 to 1363, shows what wide variety of normal diocesan business came the way of notaries public and was authenticated by them.[1] Even though the seal was as well established in the tradition of English church government as it was in the practices of the English Common Law, it was now in competition with a sophisticated rival. The seal itself must be known for it to be acceptable, and its probatory force was seriously weakened if named witnesses could not be produced. The seal of an official could only be accounted authentic if its holder was acting within the field of his jurisdiction.[2] Seals were stolen and forged and their impressions were easily broken. So the notary public was useful for drafting any documents which might figure in litigation at the Curia, for certificates of admission or rejection of providees, resignation of benefices, bonds for debts, receipts, letters of proxy.

A few examples of what might happen in the pre-notarial age will make this clear. When a bishop received the presentee to a benefice from distant parts, he required proof that the letter of presentation was genuine, just as he required evidence of the man's ordination.[3] In 1228 the bishop of Lincoln insisted that the prior elect of St. Andrew's, Northampton, bringing a sealed letter from the prior of La Charité-sur-Loire, should

---

[1] Calendared in *Reg. Shrewsbury*.

[2] Statutes of Archbishop John Stratford for the Court of Arches (Wilkins, ii. 694*b*). Cf. above, p. 8.

[3] As proof of ordination letters dimissory were demanded (cf. *Dict. de Droit Canonique*, iv (1949) s.v. Dimissoire, and for the very queer early safeguards in the shape of *epistolae formatae* (which substituted Greek letters for numerals on a system explained by Liddell and Scott) see Giry, *Manuel*, p. 811).

establish the authenticity of the seal. The bishop's registrar solemnly recorded details of the 'probatio signi litteris supra-dictis impressi' by four witnesses, and described it in full.[1] Likewise, when a bishop received a letter of presentation to a benefice allegedly vacated by death or resignation, he must have proof that the last incumbent really was dead or had resigned in due form. Both the legates Otto and Ottobuono, by their canons against intruders into benefices, show how important were the means of proof in the conditions of those times, and how scrupulous bishops must be before they in-stituted new incumbents.[2] In 1263, before notaries public were common in England, one Nicholas of Durham, rector of St. Mary Binewerk, Stamford, sent to the diocesan bishop his letters patent, sealed with his seal, to signify his resignation. But because Nicholas's seal was unknown to the bishop of Lincoln, he refused to accept the resignation without some authentic seal; whereupon the rector prepared another letter sealed by both the prior and the archdeacon of Durham, as well as by himself.[3] It must have involved a tedious journey. A case a few years later shows like trouble over the use of seals. In 1276 a priest came to the bishop of Hereford with a letter of presentation to the church of Acton Scott, sealed with the seal of the patron. His lordship inquired whether he had suf-ficient proofs of the seal. The presentee could only produce one witness whom the bishop rejected as insufficient. Another day was appointed, a fortnight thence, to produce proof.[4] A generation later than this it would be possible, and indeed usual, for letters of presentation and resignation to be drawn up by notaries public in *publica forma*. When Adam of Orlton, bishop of Hereford, was at the Curia in 1319 and secured the renunciation of a claim by John of Ludlow to the church of Madeley, given him by papal provision, he did not have recourse to foreigners to record the fact. An instrument was drawn up in his lodgings at Avignon by an apostolic notary public of Orlton's own diocese and household, Master Richard

[1] *Rot. Welles*, ii. 145–6.
[2] *Councils and Synods*, ii. 249–50 (London, 1237, c. 11), 759–61 (London, 1268, c. 10).
[3] *Durham Annals*, pp. 177–8.
[4] *Reg. Cantilupe*, p. 81. On private seals, cf. above, p. 8.

of Eastnor, and was additionally certified with the sign manual
of Master Richard Hervy, notary public by imperial authority,
also a Hereford man.[1] Other sorts of renunciation were prepared by notaries. On 4 July 1382 William de Overton, notary
public by apostolic authority, was called upon by the abbot of
Ramsey to prepare a public instrument whereby a monk of
Ramsey, Roger de Raundes, resigned all possible rights and
claims which he might have as a professed monk of the abbey;
the occasion was his withdrawal from this Benedictine house
to enter a stricter Order.[2]

The demand for notaries public in the English Church is
revealed in the petitions to the pope for their appointment.
In 1339 the bishop of Rochester, writing to the pope on behalf
of a 'poor clerk' of his diocese, alleges that in many parts of the
country, and especially in the little diocese of Rochester, there
is such dearth of notaries by apostolic authority that in trials
and in other actions at law ecclesiastical business suffers and
truth succumbs to falsehood through lack of adequate testimony.[3] Four years later the bishop asks for leave to create two
notaries public, there being only two in his diocese.[4] Only
a year before the bishop of Rochester first supplicated for the
faculty to appoint a notary public, the University of Oxford
was pulling strings with Roman cardinals to get for its bedel,
Robert de Appelby, the notarial title; it was claimed that few
notaries were found in the university while a lot of business
arose in which notaries were needed.[5] There are examples, too,
of applications from monastic prelates for the faculty of creating
notaries public, although it is impossible to say that these men
were going to find their main employment in the service of
the monasteries.[6]

---

[1] *Reg. Orleton*, p. 110.
[2] Madox, *Formulare*, p. 15, no. xxvii.
[3] *Reg. Hethe*, i, p. xxxix, on behalf of Mr. Hamo atte Brok de Brenchesle.
[4] Ibid. ii. 718.
[5] *Oxford Formularies*, i. 98–101. Robert was only appointed 29 Aug. 1343
under a faculty to the university chancellor's commissary (*Cal. Papal Letters*,
iii. 143). For his activity as notary in Oxford see Emden, *BRUO*, i. 41.
[6] Cf. below, p. 67. For faculties to monastic prelates see below, pp. 44, 78
(Canterbury and Westminster), *Cal. Papal Letters*, v. 113, vii. 542 (St. Bartholomew's, Smithfield, and St. Frideswide's), *Reg. Worcester sede vacante*,
p. 134 (Worcester).

In this period it is becoming usual for a bishop to choose as registrar or *scriba* a clerk who is entitled to style himself notary public. The episcopal register—the archival glory of the medieval English bishops—is now commonly prepared under the eye of a notary, if not by his own hand. In a good many cases his handwriting is identifiable in the register, and he sometimes adds his *signum consuetum* or else a less conspicuous but equally personal paraph.[1] The Canterbury register of Archbishop William Courtenay provides an exceptionally good example. At the foot of folio 1 recto it bears a note by its principal scribe, William Hornby, accompanied by his notarial sign. Hornby, a clerk of the diocese of York and notary public by apostolic authority, declares: 'hoc registrum eiusdem domini archiepiscopi diversis temporibus et locis pro magna parte propria manu scripsi et per alios scribi feci et publicavi ac in fidem et testimonium singulorum contentorum in eo hic me subscripsi et signum meum apposui consuetum'.[2]

In the metropolitan see of Canterbury one branch of administration comes, by the middle of the fourteenth century, to make frequent use of notaries public. This is the Court of Canterbury, or Court of Arches. The statutes issued by Archbishop Robert Winchelsey in 1295 have little to suggest that the notary public played a large part in the court's proceedings. But in Archbishop John Stratford's far more comprehensive statutes of 1345 it is assumed that the registrar of the court is himself a notary public.[3] Moreover, there are other clerks of

---

[1] See, for Worcester, Haines, *Administration*, pp. 134–6 and *Reg. Bransford*, pp. iv–vi; for Lincoln, D. M. Williamson, 'Sede Vacante records of the diocese of Lincoln', *Soc. of Local Archivists' Bulletin*, xii (1953), 15 for the registers of Thomas Bek and the following vacancy, and *Reg. Repingdon*, i, pp. xvi, 166; ii. 223; for York, Purvis, *Notarial Signs*, pl. 5 and *passim*; for Coventry and Lichfield, *Reg. Stretton*, ii. 144–5; for Salisbury, *Reg. Martival*, i, p. xv. Good Canterbury examples are in Lambeth, *Reg. W. Courtenay*, f. 240ʳ (Henry Broun's sign and eschatocol, 7 Aug. 1391) and f. 337ʳ (Robert Hallum's surname and paraph, Feb. 1391).

[2] *Reg. W. Courtenay*, f. 1ʳ. Cf. the work of John de Aldefeld, *scriba* of William Zouche of York in that archbishop's register (Purvis, *Notarial Signs*, pl. 20).

[3] *Stratford*: 'ut possit idem registrarius notarius publicus super his si opus fuerit facere publica documenta'. The second chapter following refers to the registrar's *signum* (Wilkins, ii. 690b, 691a). I am obliged to Dr. Edwin Welch for letting me see his edition of the Statutes in an unpublished University of Southampton thesis.

examiners, who write down responses, positions, interrogatories, depositions: they are to be *notarii publici*.[1] It is assumed that the clerks can supply copies of documents to the parties in lawsuits *sub manu publica vel privata*, and that the proceedings in a case may have to be drawn up in *forma publica* for transmission to other judges.[2]

Although the records of English church courts have not been thoroughly explored, it may well be that the activities of the English notary public were directly or indirectly concerned with the courts much more than with other ecclesiastical administration.[3] Here his activity was unimpeded. In other fields there were strict limits to the utility of a deed *sub manu publica*: it was of no use in the Common Law courts. And since the Common Law claimed jurisdiction over almost every kind of contract, it was not wise to depend upon a notarial instrument where a transfer of land or goods or money was in question. It is instructive to contrast the standard formula of papal faculties for the appointment of notaries public with the reasons alleged by English prelates for requesting them. From the third quarter of the thirteenth century to modern times[4] the preamble used in the papal Chancery ran: '*Ne contractuum memoria deperiret, inventum est tabellionatus officium, quo contractus legitimi ad cautelam presentium et memoriam futurorum manu publica notarentur. Hinc est quod* . . . (etc.).'[5] When we look at English petitions, lying behind these faculties, they are less concerned with contracts and more with court proceedings. This was the chief concern of Henry of Eastry, prior of Christ

---

[1] Wilkins, ii. 690*b*. They swear before the clerk of the register of the court to make accurate copies signed with their proper signs. If they do not do the work properly, they will be replaced and deprived of the status of *persona publica* in that court. When the prior of Winchester admitted John Bennebury with the usual papal oath for a notary public (1351), John also swore never to conspire against the prior or church of Winchester (*Winchester Cath. Chartulary*, p. 157). Cf. below, p. 90 n. 3.

[2] Wilkins, ii. 690*a*, 691*a*.

[3] Mrs. Norah Gurney tells me that notarial instruments figure largely among the archiepiscopal Cause Papers at York, from which Canon Purvis drew many of his examples of signs. Luschek remarks on the penetration of the officiality of Breslau by notaries public (*Notariatsurkunde*, pp. 137–42).

[4] Baumgarten, pp. 43–4.

[5] Tangl, *Kanzleiordnungen*, p. 329, formula cxxxii (italics mine). Cf. below Appendix II, nos. 1 and 3.

Church, Canterbury, when he petitioned the pope for a faculty to create two notaries.[1] Likewise, the words used by Pope Nicholas III, in his faculty to John Pecham, after the standard preamble, show that the archbishop was not mainly concerned with the writing of contracts. He had told the pope that in England there was a dearth of persons qualified to draft in public form legal contracts, judicial proceedings, and other documents of this sort.[2] The formula of Nicholas III reappears in the grant of the bishop of Winchester's petition in 1291 and in a second faculty for the archbishop in 1292.[3]

The nature of the work which notaries public did for their ecclesiastical employers guaranteed that the profession would attract at least some men of ability and ambition and that it might upon occasion open the way to high posts in the Church. At this point it may be well to observe that, in theory at least, and in the Italian tradition, the notary public was more than a mere scribe, slavishly copying or setting down with familiar clichés whatever came his way. He ought to have some know-ledge of legal matters. The Bolognese Salatiele son of Martino Papa subscribes himself in a public instrument 'imperiali auc-toritate notarius ac humilis artis notarie professor et doctor'. His *Ars notarie*, a substantial treatise, implies an acquaintance with the civil and the canon law, especially those sections which bear on testaments and contracts.[4]

A full-dress study on the lines of Dr. Emden's biographical registers of the universities might yield interesting results; but the material has yet to be assembled. When this has been done, it may be possible to say something about the class of people recruited for the profession, the relationship of notaries with like names, and so on.[5] For instance, John Alani de Beccles may well have been a relative, however distant, of Master Alan de Beccles, a well-known scholar and ecclesiastical official

---

[1] Below, Appendix II, no. 2. [2] Below, Appendix II, no. 3
[3] Baumgarten, p. 45, and *Reg. Vat.* 46, ff. 189ᵛ–190ʳ (*Cal. Papal Letters*, i. 557). The formula was used for the patriarch of Jerusalem in 1288 (Baum-garten, p. 45).
[4] See below, p. 76.
[5] Dr. J. K. Hyde's *Padua in the Age of Dante* (Manchester, 1966), pp. 154–75, has a valuable account of the social status and family connections of civic notaries in Padua; but it would be unwise to assume that the profession of notary public in England showed similar characteristics.

of the first half of the thirteenth century.[1] John Erturi de Cadomo was probably connected with a known family.[2] Robertus Ade de Derlington, notary public, set his sign to an act in the archdeacon's chapter at Durham in December 1316 when Master Adam de Derlington, an advocate of the chapter, was also present.[3] Both Robert and William le Dorturer, both of Selborne, practised as notaries public in the first decade of the fourteenth century;[4] and Henry Ade de Lyndeseye may have been the son of Adam filius Ade de Swayny de Boterwik dictus de Lyndeseye.[5]

Meanwhile, one may learn a little about the profession as a whole by observing the personal memorials of a few dignified or successful men, prominent among the more numerous sedulous clerks who did patient secretarial work for decades on end. They include men who spent years at a university, probably in the study of the laws, men who became archdeacons and officials and even bishops. Hamilton Thompson sketched the career of such a one: Master William de Doune.[6] He was born in Devonshire early in the fourteenth century, an illegitimate child. Apparently he started his clerical career as a 'domicellus literatus' of the great John de Grandisson, bishop of Exeter, by 1332. He was a Master of Arts when he witnessed the election of a dean of Exeter in 1335, and in 1343 was scholar in canon and civil law at Merton College, Oxford. He became notary public by apostolic authority in 1340. After serving Grandisson as *scriba*, he became official of the bishop of Lincoln (by 1354), and died as archdeacon of Leicester in 1361. Master Doune's will survives. Among his legacies he mentioned complacently 'a volume covered outside with white leather containing commissions made out in the court of Rome, letters apostolic, the procedure and terms used in causes in the court of Rome, propositions, articles and much other useful matter written almost entirely in my own hand, and containing

---

[1] Emden, *BRUO*, i. 145.   [2] See below, Appendix I.
[3] Durham, D. & C. Mun., Locellus XIII, no. 1.
[4] They appear together in Hereford, D. & C. Archives, no. 1077, 2 Nov. 1309.
[5] See below, p. 88.
[6] A. Hamilton Thompson, 'The will of Master William Doune, archdeacon of Leicester', *Archaeological Journal*, lxxii (1915), 233–84, and a brief notice in Emden, *BRUO*, i. 587–8.

a parchment section in which are written letters or copies of letters of commission and other letters of bishops and certain other things which I got together in the days of my youth, when I was in the service of my lord of Exeter'.

William Doune's formulary or letter-book has never been discovered; but we have others of the fourteenth and fifteenth centuries, composed by bishops' registrars and ecclesiastical lawyers who were notaries public, in part for practical purposes and in part to minister to their vanity as evidence of their skill in rhetoric. Master John de Bononia's teaching had not fallen on barren ground in England. In the fourteenth century he was remembered here as a stylist, worthy to be mentioned along with such exponents of *dictamen* as Peter of Blois and Peter de Vinea.[1] But he also represents the changing pattern of popular legal literature, both treatises and formularies, towards the end of the thirteenth century. The change was produced by new conditions in church government, particularly in the fields of papal provisions and taxation.[2] The contrast between formularies and letter-books of the pre-notarial era (that is, in England, before about 1280) and those of later times is striking. A highly professional book like the *Summa Aurea* of William of Drogheda, which virtually provided a formulary for English ecclesiastical lawyers about 1240, devoted no space to the public instrument and shows no trace of the dictaminal efflorescence of the later exponents of the *ars notarie*.[3] It cannot have been of much use to later English practitioners, who drew on John de Bononia and other manuals of continental origin.

The same contrast is seen in the less systematic anthologies of forms and letters.[4] In the fourteenth and fifteenth centuries

---

[1] *Reg. Pal. Dunelm.*, iv. 427.

[2] See Barraclough, 'Praxis beneficiorum', and Stickler, in *Dict. de Droit Canonique*, vi. 1138–43, on the later 'Ordines iudiciarii' and 'Summae artis notariae'; cf. above, pp. 13–14.

[3] The *Summa aurea* was edited by L. Wahrmund (Innsbruck, 1914).

[4] For thirteenth-century English formularies and letter-books see Cheney, *English Bishops' Chanceries*, pp. 119–30, 'Gervase of Prémontré', and 'Letters of William Wickwane'; J. E. Sayers, 'A judge-delegate formulary from Canterbury', *BIHR*, xxxix (1962), 198–211; F. D. Logan, 'An early thirteenth-century papal judge-delegate formulary of English origin', *Studia Gratiana*, xiv (1967), 73–87. For the literature of twelfth-century collections see Giles Constable, 'Medieval letter collections', introducing his edition of *The Letters of Peter the*

collections of a new sort show us how the notarial profession was developing. One letter-book compiled about 1381–1406, a paper book on forty-two leaves, now in the Bodleian Library (MS. Bodley 859, ff. 1–42), was the work of a notary by apostolic authority named Master Gilbert Stone.[1] He was registrar and chancellor successively in three dioceses (Salisbury, Bath and Wells, Worcester) between 1375 and 1407. As registrar and chancellor of Worcester, in 1404, at the request of Archbishop Thomas Arundel he drafted in high-falutin' language ('rudi modo concepta', he says, with mock modesty) a provincial canon 'ad orandum pro episcopis defunctis'.[2] Gilbert Stone compiled his book mainly because he was proud of his epistolary style, but most of the elegant epistles concern serious business, even when it is stated with intolerable verbiage. Professor Jacob points out[3] how many are 'addressed on behalf of his masters, especially the subtle politician, Richard Clifford, to the Holy See. They point to the need for every bishop to have a registrar who could impetrate in the best curial style, and solicit whatever cardinal was his special protector. There was a good practical reason behind these local works on the *dictamen*. The favour of a friendly cardinal was half the battle, and it was advisable to approach him in the most ingratiating manner. A suit in the Court of Rome was prepared and reinforced by an immense amount of extra-judicial solicitation. Happy was the prelate who had a Gilbert Stone to do it for him.'

Somewhat later than Stone's collection is a vast anthology of a different kind preserved in All Souls MS. 182. Its com-

---

Venerable (Harvard, 1967), ii. 1–44 and R. W. Southern, *Medieval Humanism and other Studies* (Oxford, 1970), pp. 86–132.

[1] The date was proposed by E. F. Jacob in 'Verborum florida venustas', *BJRL*, xvii (1933), as reprinted in his *Essays*, p. 204. Much of this essay (pp. 196–206) deals with collections of this sort. For Stone see also Emden, *BRUO*, iii. 1787–8. Some of Stone's compositions appear in the letter-book of John Prophet, B.M., MS. Harl. 431 (cf. below, p. 63). Systematic formularies were compiled in the fourteenth century for the use of notaries public practising in the papal Curia. Barraclough calendars one completed *c.* 1327 in *Public Notaries and the Papal Curia*, and refers to other texts and earlier literature. See further, for earlier productions, Herde, *Beiträge*, p. 163.

[2] C. R. Cheney, *English Synodalia of the XIII Century* (Oxford, 1941, 2nd edn., 1968), pp. 49–50.

[3] *Essays*, p. 206.

pilation, *c.* 1420, has been plausibly assigned to its owner, Master John Stevens, a comfortably beneficed clerk of Exeter diocese, whose career extends from 1406 to 1459, and who served Archbishop Thomas Arundel as a notary public in the early part of the century. The manuscript contains little to do with the notary's task of preparing public instruments, and is an eclectic assemblage of letters both in Latin and in French. Its author, says Mr. Richardson, was 'omnivorous, indiscriminate, and unmethodical'.[1] Among its many features of interest one deserves underlining in the present context. John Stevens, or whoever compiled the book, thought it worth while to transcribe a considerable proportion of the letters contained in the archiepiscopal register of John Pecham at Lambeth.[2] As Trice Martin observed, 'the object of the copyist was no doubt to obtain a collection of forms of letters, and this was more important to him than their historical interest'.[3] Here, surely, is evidence of the enduring influence of John de Bononia and his circle in English ecclesiastical chanceries.[4]

It would be possible to multiply examples. Ecclesiastical officials who were notaries public seem to have been prone to make collections of letters: sometimes their own letters, sometimes other people's, sometimes for the practical purpose of recording frequently needed formulas of everyday business, which satisfied all the lawyers' requirements for precision, sometimes for the sake of perpetuating a pretty trope or an eloquent outpouring.[5] What we do not find is the notarial

[1] *EHR*, lviii (1943), 225, in the course of discussing the manuscript on pp. 222–30.

[2] See C. Trice Martin in his preface to *Reg. Ep. Peckham*, i, pp. xliv–xlvii. For the manuscript as a whole see Jacob and Richardson, as above, and for its French section M. D. Legge's edition, *Anglo-Norman Letters and Petitions* (Anglo-Norman Text Soc., 1941).

[3] *Reg. Ep. Peckham*, i, p. xlv.

[4] Other instances occur of revived interest in old records during the fourteenth and fifteenth centuries. Not only did the famous literary figures (e.g. Peter of Blois) come up for re-copying of letters; the official letters of Robert Grosseteste only survive as a collection in late manuscripts.

[5] e.g. the letter-books of William Swan, a notary public who spent much of his life in the papal Curia: see Emden, *BRUO*, iii, and Jacob, 'To and from the court of Rome'. More prosaic and pedestrian formularies and letter-books of the fourteenth century and after, for the most part anonymous (and not always the work of notaries), are to be found in various ecclesiastical repositories and the great libraries.

register of the Mediterranean sort, which as an authentic record
of particular transaction was laid up in public archives.[1] This
only serves to emphasize that the notary public in the service
of an English bishop was not fully employed in recording the
processes of an ecclesiastical court *sub manu publica*, or in preparing public instruments. He was called on to draft and write
many other documents: for instance, episcopal letters patent
which would be authenticated by the bishop's seal. Much
ecclesiastical business was not clothed in notarial form and did
not depend on notarial attestation. The notaries public in the
service of English bishops never belonged to a close corporation,[2] to be treated differently from other clerical and legal
servants of the Church. But they were numerous. The number
has probably been underestimated in the past, because it is
only during the last fifty years or so that many episcopal
registers of the fourteenth and fifteenth centuries have become
available in print, while the surviving ecclesiastical court-books
and formularies still demand thorough exploration. Moreover,
much of the notary public's activity is concealed by the incomplete form in which episcopal registrars abstracted documents:
attestations and eschatocols are omitted and have to be inferred
from the fact that a document begins with an invocation or in
other particulars betrays some of the usual features of notarial
draftsmanship.[3] Again, the notary public is not often described

---

[1] Doehaerd, *Les Relations commerciales entre Gênes, la Belgique et l'Outremont*
contains (i. 22–60) a survey of the Genoese notarial records 'tant au point de vue
de l'archivéconomie que de la diplomatique'. A further volume of texts, 1400–40,
'd'après les archives notariales' was edited by R. Doehaerd and C. Kerremans in
1952. A summary inventory of *Cartolari notarili Genovesi 1–149* is in the Pubbli-
cazioni degli Archivi di Stato, vols. xxii, xli (Rome, 1956–61). See also Petrucci,
Notarii: Documenti per la Storia del Notariato Italiano (with 85 texts and plates) and
his edition of *Il Protocollo Notarile di Coluccio Salutati, 1372–3.* The value of
Italian notarial records for commercial and industrial history has been illustrated
recently by Elisabeth Santschi in 'Contrats de travail et d'apprentissage en
Crète vénitienne au xive siècle, d'après quelques notaires', *Schweizerische Ztsch.
für Geschichte*, xix (1969), 36–74. For the *protocollum* in England cf. below,
pp. 95–102.

[2] Bresslau, *Handbuch*, i. 635 remarks the absence of notarial corporations in
Germany; cf. P. Bonenfant, *Cours de Diplomatique*, ii (Liège, 1948), 113. Redlich
(*Privaturkunden*, p. 228) attributed the absence of a collegiate organization among
notaries to their overwhelmingly clerical status.

[3] e.g. *Reg. Ep. Peckham*, i. 147–50, 161–2; *Reg. Swinfield*, p. 33; *Reg. Reynolds*,
p. 16; *Reg. Woodlock*, i. 334, 633. Cf. above, p. 28 n. 2, p. 35 n. 1, and p. 38.

as such, except when the occasion demands it.[1] It should be added that modern legal writers in England have usually shown little interest in a medieval institution which the English Common Law eschewed. The common attitude is exhibited in the footnote of H. C. Gutteridge near the beginning of his essay on the origin and historical development of notaries. 'In order', he says, 'to avoid complication it is thought well to refrain from dealing with the history of Ecclesiastical Notaries. . . . The Ecclesiastical Notary is an officer of the Courts of the Church, and can hardly be described as a legal practitioner.'[2]

[1] e.g. John de Beccles and John de Lewes, Pecham's employees, are only described as notaries when they act as such. In other cases the printed calendar conceals the evidence.

[2] Loc. cit., p. 124 n. 2.

5. The Notary in Civil Employment

THIS leads inevitably to the question whether the notary public by apostolic or imperial authority had any *raison d'être* in medieval England beyond the limits—strictly limited—of ecclesiastical jurisdiction. There certainly was never a possibility that the notary public would acquire that influence over legal procedure in the secular courts which he enjoyed in Mediterranean lands. The English Common Law did not recognize him or his works. When Master John de Bononia dedicated his *Summa* to Archbishop John Pecham he remarked that 'sollempnis vestra curia et regnum Anglie quasi totum' lacked clerks properly instructed in the notarial art; he hoped that his book would be useful 'vobis et curie vestre totique regno'.[1] But if in using the word *regnum* he referred to the civil government of England, in fact he recognized practical limitations by providing no formulas for anything beyond the competence of the ecclesiastical courts. By now the civil courts had their own formularies, their registers of writs, and in the eyes of the Common Law a notarial authentication was as nothing. 'A writing without a seal is not a deed.'[2] It has been observed already that the non-contentious jurisdiction of the Crown was very extensive.[3]

So, it seems, the atmosphere was not favourable to the growth of the notariate or the use of notarial public instruments in secular affairs. Indeed, the idea has arisen that the English royal government of the fourteenth century disliked the existence of this alien institution. At various times during the century we hear of notaries public coming into collision with the civil power for their activity in derogation of the Crown's rights. About 1305 Master William de Rothwell pre-

---

[1] *Summa*, pp. 603, 604.

[2] T. F. T. Plucknett, in *TRHS*, 4th series xxxii (1950), 150. Cf. Tout, *Chapters*, i. 123: 'England ever remained emphatically a land of seals'. Cf. Redlich, *Privaturkunden*, p. 231, on Germany.

[3] Above, p. 9.

pared appeals detrimental to the king's rights to take to the papal Curia.[1] On several other occasions the king's court condemned the introduction of a notary public into its proceedings with a view to making a record *manu publica* for later use in the court christian.[2] But a transaction of this sort was, after all, only incidental to a process which would anyhow have attracted a writ of prohibition if the defendant wanted one. The notary was inculpated as the agent of the plaintiff. Condemnation of him did not imply condemnation of the whole tribe of notaries public; and Luke of Thaxted, who in 1329 was imprisoned during the king's pleasure for daring to notarialize proceedings in the Court of the Exchequer, was very soon pardoned at the request of the bishop of Lincoln and next year was drawing up letters of proxy for the Dean and Chapter of St. Paul's in public form.[3]

One document, indeed, has often been quoted which appears to point to official opposition. King Edward II, in a writ of 26 April 1320, forbade the employment in England of notaries who held their authority from the emperor.[4] This was reiterated by public proclamation on Ascension Day (8 May) in Westcheap Market.[5] Nobody has ever discovered a special political reason for the prohibition at this particular time. But the oath which a notary public swore when he was appointed by imperial authority contained the words: 'nunquam ero contrarius Romanae ecclesiae *nec imperio*';[6] and the royal order was avowedly a demonstration that the king of England 'habet imperium in regno suo'. Its preamble spoke of our realm of England as 'exempt and free from subjection to the empire (*subiectione imperiali*) since the beginning of the world'. Edward II

[1] *Sel. Cases King's Bench*, ii, p. liv.

[2] Ibid., iii, p. lxxxii (1329), cf. *Cal. Pat. Rolls 1327–30*, p. 418; *Cal. of Inquisitions, Misc.*, iii (HMSO 1937), 39, no. 116 (before Aug. 1352).

[3] See above, note 2, and cf. St. Paul's Cathedral, D. & C. Mun., A/77/2062 (9 Feb. 1330). The instrument also bore the seal of the dean and chapter.

[4] Directed to the archbishop of Canterbury and others: Rymer, II. i. 423 (cf. *Cal. Cl. Rolls 1318–23*, p. 186); *Reg. Martival*, iii, no. 209; Somner, *Antiquities of Canterbury* (1703), part 1, app. p. 60; Lambeth Palace, Reg. Archbishop Walter Reynolds, f. 96ʳ. Baumgarten (op. cit., p. 55) opined that the prohibition lasted at least to the time of the Great Schism.

[5] *Chron. Edw. I and II*, i. 288.

[6] Below, Appendix II, no. 4b. J. Selden *Titles of Honour* (2nd edn., 1631), pp. 431–2 (3rd edn., 1672), pp. 343–4.

acted in line with French policy declared somewhat earlier by his father-in-law, Philippe le Bel.[1] But Edward's writ of 26 April 1320 should not have been described by Gutteridge as 'one of the measures taken by him to assert royal prerogative against papal encroachments'.[2] The English king did not proceed to authorize a new sort of notary public to practise in England, as the French king established in France a royal notariate.[3] Nor did his order impinge in the least on the practice of notaries by papal authority. On the contrary, both Edward II (in this very year 1320) and Edward III, through their ambassadors at Avignon, supplicated for faculties for English bishops to create new notaries by papal authority.[4]

---

[1] The arguments of thirteenth- and fourteenth-century polemicists and jurists on this matter are very fully examined by Prof. Walter Ullmann in his important study, 'The development of the medieval idea of sovereignty', *EHR*, lxiv (1949), 1–33, though he does not touch specifically on English evidence.

[2] Loc. cit., pp. 126–7, citing Brooke, who probably owed the misconception to W. Prynne's use of this writ, which he printed in *Brief Animadversions . . . on the Fourth Part of the Institutes of the Lawes of England* (1669), epistle dedicatory to King Charles II, as an example of anti-papalism. A greater scholar than Gutteridge confused the matter. Stubbs wrote in 1882: 'The creation of notaries by the *comites palatini* of both pope and emperor was an abuse against which the legal and professional instincts of Englishmen rebelled' (*Chron. Edw. I and II*, i, p. lxxix).

[3] See Giry, *Manuel*, pp. 827–9. Baumgarten (p. 25) cited a French notary public by royal authority who in 1343 (after practising for twenty years) sought apostolic authority as well. Cf. a notary public in 1324 'auctoritate regia . . . in regno Francie et eius pertinenciis ac resorto': *The War of Saint-Sardos*, ed. P. Chaplais (Camden 3rd series lxxxvii, 1954), p. 38. In 1297 it was claimed that the kings of France had their *tabelliones* at Lyon 'a tanto tempore de cuius contrario non est memoria': *Acta Imperii, Angliae et Franciae, 1267–1313*, ed. Fritz Kern (Tübingen, 1911), p. 205, cf. p. 199. As duke of Aquitaine the English king created notaries in his lands in southern France: see Chaplais in *Le Moyen Âge, livre jubilaire* (1963), p. 467 n. 66. In 1289 Edward I issued letters to one clerk to exercise *officium tabellionatus* with validity for his instruments throughout the duchy, and to two other men to draw up instruments within the Entre-Deux-Mers (*Rôles Gascons*, ed. C. Bémont (Collection de Docts. inédits, Paris, 1885–1906), ii, nos. 1084, 1636–7). For a vernacular deed drawn up by a 'notari public du dugat de Guiayna' dated in Latin 'xiiᵃ die exitus Februarii a.d. mcccxxxiv' see B.M., Add. ch. 59784 (and cf. 59785–6). A large group of Aquitanian notarial documents, 1311–1404, is in Manchester, John Rylands Library, Phillipps charters 147–174.

[4] *Reg. Sandale*, p. 574 from Reg. Vat. 71, f. 189 (21 Dec. 1320) = *Jean XXII: Lettres Communes*, ed. G. Mollat (École française de Rome, 1904–46), iii, no. 12759 (*Cal. Papal Letters*, ii. 210). Cf. faculties answering royal requests 29 April 1322, 18 May 1323, *Jean XXII*, iv, nos. 15367, 17335 (Baumgarten, p. 55).

These requests may at first seem to show remarkable complaisance by the English monarchs towards the episcopate, considering (as we have seen) that the English Common Law had no use for notarial public instruments. But the notary public did find employment under the Crown and his acts were acceptable for certain purposes to the royal Chancery and other civil departments. That the Chancery should turn to notaries upon occasion is not, after all, very surprising. To realize how natural it was one need only recall that during the whole of the thirteenth and fourteenth centuries the chancellorship was held for most of the time by clerics who were bishops or on the road to bishoprics, who at the least held archdeaconries, and who were one and all experienced in the world of ecclesiastical administration, where the notary public was becoming a familiar figure and the notarial act a standard form. During the fourteenth century several chancellors and dozens of other important civil servants were themselves notaries public.

The courts, it has been said, did not treat notarial instruments as valid evidence.[1] But this did not apply in all cases. In 1307 a dispute between Pietro Ispani, cardinal bishop of Sabina, and Walter Bedwin came before the King's Council. The council accepted evidences in the form of public instruments prepared by notaries public in England and in France. One of these documents was an exemplification of a bull of provision of Boniface VIII, made on 18 November 1297. The eschatocol reads: 'Et ego Adam de Louther Karliolensis diocesis sacri imperii publicus auctoritate notarius ac in presenti notarius venerabilis capituli beati Petri Eboracensis . . . presens interfui et eam scripsi, publicavi, meoque signo signavi rogatus.'[2]

A fairly frequent occasion for admitting notarial documents arose in the course of ecclesiastical proceedings against excommunicates. When an English bishop invoked the secular arm against a contumacious excommunicate and sought a writ out of Chancery to the sheriff for the man's arrest, the excommunicate might impede its issue or execution. If he appealed

[1] 'These notaries were not recognised by the law of England', Gutteridge, loc. cit., p. 124.
[2] *Sel. Cases before the King's Council, 1243–1432*, ed. I. S. Leadam and J. F. Baldwin (Selden Soc., 35, 1918), pp. 24–5. For further references to this case over the treasurership of York see Clay, *York Minster Fasti*, i. 28–30.

to the pope from the sentence of the ordinary, the latter must halt his proceedings and must ask the Chancery to follow up its writ *de excommunicato capiendo* by a writ to supersede it. For 'just as the pope could not request the capture of an excommunicate, so too he could not request supersedence'.[1] But early in Edward I's reign it already happened that the Chancery would entertain a request from the appellant himself to supersede the writ *de capiendo*. The bishops protested that unlawful appeals were accepted by Chancery as grounds for supersedence; and in 1309 they requested of the Crown that 'when their subjects who have been excommunicated claim that they have appealed from their ordinaries and sometimes produce notarial instruments on these appeals, greater credence should be given to the letter of the ordinary than to their assertion'.[2] 'Although', says Dr. Logan, 'an instrument of appeal as such did not prove that the appeal had been sent to the superior court or that it had been accepted by that court or *a fortiori* that the excommunicate had been absolved, it was none the less accepted in Chancery as proof of appeal.' Dr. Logan shows that the complaint of the bishops in 1309 had substance, that notarial instruments, as well as letters of judges delegate and papal bulls, might be exhibited in Chancery and admitted in proof of appeal.[3]

Not only were notarial instruments admissible, notaries might themselves be used by the civil government to prepare public instruments: to exemplify documents, or to record legal proceedings, or both.[4] For the making of straightforward authenticated copies, the notarial instrument was in the fourteenth century a competitor with the *inspeximus* or *vidimus* of royal and ecclesiastical chanceries. The first quarter of the century saw great activity by English civil servants in organizing and duplicating of archives.[5] The miscellanea of the

---

[1] Logan, *Excommunication and the Secular Arm in Medieval England*, p. 121.

[2] *Councils and Synods*, ii. 1272 (gravamina of 1309), cl. 3. Notarial instruments had not been mentioned in the clergy's complaints of 1285.

[3] Logan, op. cit., p. 124, cf. pp. 124–6.

[4] For their employment by German kings and emperors see Bresslau, i. 662–4.

[5] The loss of the records of Bordeaux in 1294 entailed a lot of copying; see V. H. Galbraith, 'The Tower as an Exchequer Office', in *Essays in Medieval History pres. to T. F. Tout*, ed. A. G. Little and F. M. Powicke (Manchester,

Chancery and Exchequer in the Public Record Office furnish plenty of examples of notarial instruments. The office of the Wardrobe was perhaps specially inclined to make use of notaries public when authentic copies were needed in quantity and when there was no need or desire to have recourse to the Chancery for the use of the Great Seal. An incident in 1305 which attracted Tout's attention will serve as an example. The Annals of London (which their editor, Stubbs, associated with the well-informed city fishmonger, Andrew Horn) have this entry under the year 1305:[1] 'VII^{mo} kalendas Novembris novem tabelliones, et die sequenti quatuor tabelliones, et tertio die proxima sequenti septem tabelliones fuerunt in garderoba domini regis Angliae et ad scribendas bullas et privilegia domini regis Angliae sub manu publica, et publicarunt XLV bullas.' Tout noted this activity and also a record in Exchequer Accounts 369/11, f. 34 of a payment made between 23 November and 17 December 1305 'ad faciendum transcribere bullas et privilegia a summo pontifice temporibus retroactis regi concessa'.[2] He opined that 'there were always a certain number of professed notaries, both in the Chancery and the Wardrobe, to deal with such matters', and says, with reference to the London annals: 'It is hard to believe that all these "tabelliones" were "papal notaries" of the ordinary type, and they may well have been simply clerks of Chancery, a certain proportion of whom were always notaries.' Had Tout looked a little further he would have found more details which confirm the annalist's precise accuracy in one particular, in the surviving papal bulls in the Public Record Office. For these include eleven instruments exemplifying papal bulls, drawn up and witnessed by

1925), pp. 234, 244. Cf. G. P. Cuttino, 'An unidentified Gascon Register', *EHR*, liv (1939), 293–9. On this occasion copies were not notarialized. For archival activity in the early fourteenth century, see Cuttino's edition of the Gascon calendar (p. 59 below) and *Antient Kalendars and Inventories of the Treasury of H.M. Exchequer*, ed. F. Palgrave (Record Commission, 1836), vol. i.

[1] *Chron. Edw. I and II*, i. 143, cf. pp. xxii–xxviii. Under the same year the writer recorded the birth and death of Andrew Horn's baby (p. 137).

[2] *Chapters*, ii. 70 n. 1. In the next year's account (f. 63d) he found a payment of 20 marks 'magistro Willelmo de Maldon notario publico et quibusdam aliis notariis publicis transcribentibus et in publicam formam redigentibus iiii^{xx}xvii bullas de quibusdam privilegiis regis Londoniis per ordinacionem consilii regis, mense Octobris anno presenti xxxiv [1306]' (ibid. 70 n. 2).

various notaries public and dated between 22 October and 6 November 1305. All told, the exemplified documents amount to thirty-one.[1] Those exemplifications dated 26 October only number four, but they show precisely nine notaries at work, verifying and attesting each other's instruments. Most of the same men write at least once again during the next ten days, and one new name appears on 28 October. As regards Tout's conjecture that not all were 'papal notaries', it can be said that all were notaries public, a majority of them by imperial authority. A more thorough prosopographical study might reveal their standing as freelance notaries or regular employees of the Crown. At present it is only possible to confirm that four of the ten men could be described as king's clerks in a general sense.[2] Most of these instruments are dated by their writers *apud Westmonasterium iuxta* or *prope London'* or *apud Westmonasterium*, but Andreas quondam Guilielmi de Tang' uses the formula *exemplavi London' in garderoba domini regis*.[3] The reason for the preparation of these copies in 1305, as in 1304, is not obvious, though some of the documents transcribed suggest a connection with the king's campaign against Archbishop Robert Winchelsey in the Curia.[4]

The so-called Gascon Calendar provides more evidence of official transcripts of this kind and of the reason behind their making. This calendar records documents stored in the

---

[1] Several exemplifications include up to six bulls apiece, and a few bulls are repeated in different exemplifications. Many, but not all, of the originals remain. See 'List of Papal Bulls' in P.R.O. *Lists and Indexes*, xlix (revised repr. 1963), 277–8. Probably some of the copies made at this session have strayed and the timetable does not agree perfectly with the annalist's note. Four notaries are named on copies of 28 Oct. (none is dated 27 Oct.) and six are named on the latest copies of 6 Nov.

[2] They are William de Maldon, William le Dorturer (employed on work of this sort in 1304 and in later years), Andrew de Tange, and Henry de Colchester. Cf. below, p. 67.

[3] Below, Appendix II, no. 9. This exemplification alone has witnesses whose status as notaries public is not stated and has not been verified: they were John de Wynton' and Geoffrey de Stok', clerks.

[4] The privileges of royal clerks are protected by bulls copied in SC 7/18/22 (Potthast 20615, 1 Oct. 1272) and SC 7/36/2 (Potthast 14722, 27 Sept. 1252), and a mandate of Innocent IV to Eng. prelates (Potthast 12174, 22 June 1246) to relax sentence of excommunication on the king's servants is copied in both SC 7/36/3 and SC 7/36/4; but the other exemplifications do not seem particularly relevant to the state of affairs in 1305.

Treasury and the Wardrobe in 1322; and under the heading of 'Indenture de diversis instrumentis liberatis extra garderobam et postmodum restitutis . . .' we read '[2029] Indentura de transcriptis trigenta sex bullarum, sub manu pupplica, transmissis ad episcopum Cestrie, euntem una cum . . . aliis domini regis Edwardi Anglie nunciis, ad dominum summum pontificem contra diem coronacionis sue apud Viennam' [Pope Clement V, 14 November 1305].[1]

The Crown might also call upon notaries public to make an original record of legal or quasi-legal proceedings, especially when asserting its prerogative *vis-à-vis* the Church. Two examples of this practice may be given. In summer 1297, in the midst of the constitutional crisis over confirmation of the charters, the bishops reaffirmed their inability to pay the king an aid, but undertook to seek the pope's leave to do so. Then the archbishop ordered the bishops that each bishop in his cathedral church, on 1 September, should utter excommunication on any who seized church property without leave. The Worcester annalist reports that the king, faced with this threat, 'in every cathedral church, publicly, before notaries public as witnesses, appealed against it'.[2]

Recurrent occasions for a royal protest arose when the pope inserted an offensive phrase in his bulls of provision to bishoprics. Boniface VIII introduced into the formula words which purported to grant administration of the temporalities as well as the spiritualities of the see. This became part of the standard form, and the royal Chancery developed a standard form for countering it. For the English king did not admit the papal claim to dispose of the temporalities. He not only claimed

---

[1] *The Gascon Calendar*, p. 160. See also p. 16 no. 96: 'Instrumentum per manus Johannis Busch' de dispensacione super matrimonia contrahendo inter E. regem Anglie et Margaretam sororem regis Francie.' The dispensation, dated 1 July 1289 (*Cal. Papal Letters*, i. 576–7) was exemplified by John Bouhs, or Busch, at Alverton, 30 Nov. 1299 (P.R.O., SC 7/40/1). He had witnessed at Westminster, 15 April 1299, a notarial instrument on the submission by Edward I and Philip IV of their dispute to the pope (14 June 1298) and the pope's award (30 June 1298) (P.R.O., E 30/1208, whence Rymer, I. ii. 896–7). Cf. *Gascon Calendar*, nos. 98, 109, 131, 159–68, 415–77 *passim*, 2030. Still earlier, in 1292, he had been paid for transcribing and drawing up in public form Nicholas IV's bulls which authorized the king to take a sexennial tenth from the clergy (*Issues of the Exchequer . . . Henry III to Henry VI*, ed. F. Devon (Record Comm., 1837), p. 105).

[2] *Councils and Synods*, ii. 1173.

the right himself: he actually took possession of the temporalities of all bishoprics at every vacancy, and insisted that
incoming bishops should receive them from his hands. From
the days when Boniface VIII first made his claim to confer
temporalities in 1299, the Crown always reacted sharply.[1] The
bishop was called upon to make abject renunciation of all and
sundry words relating to temporalities which were prejudicial
to the king or the right of his Crown. On 29 September 1307,
in the presence of the king in his chamber in Lenton Priory,
when Walter Jorz O.P. presented his bull of provision to the
archbishopric of Armagh, he renounced the offending words
orally ('sub verborum sententia') 'ipsaque temporalia predicta
non virtute literarum apostolicarum set ex vestra regia gracia,
cui me submitto totaliter in hac parte, me fateor recepturum'.
The declaration and a narrative of the proceedings were
promptly embodied in a notarial instrument: 'Et ego Rogerus
de Staunford clericus Lincolniensis diocesis publicus auctoritate Romani imperii notarius premissis omnibus cum dictis
testibus presens interfui, et ea omnia scripsi, et in hanc publicam formam redegi, meoque signo consueto signavi rogatus.'[2]
Thereafter, bulls of provision always had the same reception.
The royal officials who determined the form of the documents
were probably influenced by the consideration that, sooner or
later, they might be needed in a dispute in the Roman Curia,
where authentication by a notary public would give the record
credit. But it cannot be excluded that the form was regarded
first and foremost as a convenient way of duplication for
internal departmental purposes. Three copies of the renunciation by the new bishop-elect of Winchester were prepared in
1320, to be deposited respectively in the Chancery, the Wardrobe, and the Treasury in the care of the chamberlains.[3]

Above all, the king's government made use of notaries public in its diplomacy. During the thirteenth and fourteenth
centuries the claims of England in Scotland and Ireland, the

---

[1] *Councils and Synods*, ii. 1226–7.

[2] P.R.O., SC 7/44/22, whence Rymer, II. i. 7. I have found no other reference
to this notary.

[3] *Reg. Sandale*, pp. 567–9; Rymer, II. i. 422. For other instruments of renunciation with the relevant bulls see P.R.O., SC 7/44/11 (3 Jan. 1314), SC 7/56/5
(4 May 1317), SC 7/56/17 (30 June 1324), SC 7/42/2 (25 July 1337), etc.

endemic hostility of the Capetian and Angevin monarchies, the dynastic marriages of King Henry III and his successors, all complicate the international scene. There was more correspondence of a legal sort with foreign parts, which needed to be validated by an agreed method of authentication. This the notarial instrument provided. It did not, of course, exclude other means of validation. The pope continued to issue his privileges and indults under the *bulla*, solemn treaties between England and foreign powers bore the great seals of the rulers. Much diplomatic correspondence passed *sub annulo piscatoris* and under the privy seals of kings and princes. But when title-deeds and *acta* had to be produced as evidence by litigants in the Curia or by the negotiators of a treaty, it was desirable—sometimes necessary—to make authentic copies. When, for instance, in 1354 the Commons expressed their unanimous agreement with the project for a perpetual peace with France, the chief English negotiator 'directed a notary to embody this opinion in an instrument drafted in public form' which he could take with him to Calais.[1]

The preparation of public instruments about the 'Great Cause' of the succession to the throne of Scotland, 1291–6, shows how legal and diplomatic proceedings could be recorded *sub manu publica* at royal command.[2] When the king of England wanted a digest of the happenings and the documents in this case, the notarial form was adopted: a narrative was prepared, long after the event, which gave an account, somewhat biased in favour of the king's authority. The two notaries by apostolic authority who prepared long rolls of the process were John Erturi de Cadomo, a servant of the Crown, part-time at least, for many years past, and Andrew 'quondam Guilielmi de Tange', who was one of the notaries called in to the Wardrobe in 1305 to exemplify papal bulls. These rolls incorporated some of the copious dossiers to which the case had given rise. John de Cadomo's 'Great Roll', composed *c.* 1296, gave an authenticated account of events of 1291–3. Andrew de Tange's 'Great Roll', which carried the story down to 1296, was only

---

[1] Tout, *Chapters*, v. 30.
[2] See references to Prof. Stones's important work on this subject below, pp. 121–2.

composed *c.* 1315–18. Again, the procedure which was adopted reflects the archival activity which distinguished the early part of the fourteenth century in English government. The roll was prepared for retention by government departments, and remained of some practical importance for nearly a hundred years more. Tange's roll survives in triplicate (not verbally identical), which 'were probably intended for deposit in the Chancery, the Exchequer, and the Wardrobe'.[1]

The notary public came into his own in all the negotiations between England and France, and between England and the Low Countries, during the Hundred Years War. Whenever truce or treaty is in question some of the most important documents in debate are drafted or transcribed and certified by permanent officials. They are, or later become, superior clerks of the royal Chancery or Wardrobe. Often they have studied law in a university. They draw up public instruments by virtue of apostolic authority or they claim both apostolic and imperial authority.[2] For in the second half of the fourteenth century (despite Edward II's prohibition of 1320) the dual authorization is becoming common in England as also on the Continent. It is indicative of the importance of the notariate in secular affairs that, while many notaries public get their reward for services to bishops in the shape of benefices in the bishops' gift, so others enjoy throughout their careers livings in the king's patronage. Some of them are civil servants of great wealth and repute. It was a notary and chancery clerk, Master John de Branketre, who drafted the Anglo–French treaty of 1359.[3] At the end of the fourteenth century a prominent notary public in royal service was Master John

---

[1] Stones in *SHR*, xxxv and xxxix and in *Archives*, ix. Cf. *Issues of the Exchequer*, p. 117, for the deposit of three rolls of 35 membranes by Andrew de Tange in the three offices, 7 June 1306.

[2] Tout, *Chapters*, iii. 28 n. 1, 212, 226, 229.

[3] Stones in *SHR*, xxxii. 50–1 and J. H. Le Patourel in *TRHS*, 5th series x (1960), 28–30, 36 n. 6. For John's career in the Chancery see Tout, *Chapters*, and Wilkinson, *Chancery under Edward III*. P.R.O., E 30/194, a declaration in French by John, duke of Brittany, about his treaty with Edward III, is sealed by the duke but is drawn up in public form by 'Johan de Branketre clerc de la deocese de Norwycz par les autoritez du Pape et de Lempereur tabellien poubliqz', with the whole eschatocol in French. It was dated at the palace of Westminster, 7 July 1362, indiction 15, 10 Innocent VI.

Prophet. He had acted as notary public by apostolic authority as early as July 1376, in certifying at St. Paul's, London, a singularly important ordinance for the University of Oxford. It resulted from a petition by the Oxford lawyers to the king against the chancellor, proctors, and regents of the university, and it was drawn up by authority of the king and parliament by four bishops. The bishops added their seals to the ordinance, and it was the subject of an *inspeximus* enrolled on the Patent Roll. But the bishops refer to their document as 'has litteras nostras seu presens publicum instrumentum', and among the witnesses preceding John Prophet's eschatocol are three other notaries public, including Gilbert Stone. By 1382 Prophet was registrar of the Court of Canterbury and in 1384 was secretary of the archbishop of Canterbury. Thence he passed into royal service, becoming successively clerk of the council (before 1392), king's secretary (1402), and keeper of the Privy Seal (1406). He was very richly beneficed.[1]

Notaries of this calibre might even aspire to bishoprics. Walter Skirlaw died in 1406 as bishop of Durham, Benedict Nicholl in 1433 as bishop of St. David's.[2] The most remarkable 'success story' is that of Master John de Thoresby. He was proctor for Archbishop William Melton of York at Avignon in 1323–4, and by 1330 was acting in the Curia on the king's behalf. In 1336 he was being paid an annual salary of forty marks for 'his services to the king in Chancery and also in his office of notary'. Next year, as a notary public by apostolic authority, he recorded Simon de Montacute's renunciation of the offensive words in his papal bull of translation.[3] He was

---

[1] For the Oxford ordinance see *Cal. Pat. Rolls 1374–7*, pp. 290–3, *1396–9*, p. 109, and *Collectanea*, iii (Oxford Hist. Soc., xxxii, 1896), p. 140. For Prophet's career see Otway-Ruthven, *King's Secretary* and Brown, *Clerkship of the Council*, pp. 8–16. He was first described as clerk in 1392 but was acting in 1389. For his 'journal' of the Council see below, p. 139. B.M., MS. Harl. 431 is a letter-book of his; for its contents see the table in *Cat. of the Harleian MSS.* (1808), i. 251–5 and cf. Jacob, *Essays*, pp. 73–4. John's benefices fill two columns of Emden's *BRUO*, iii. 1521–3.

[2] Walter Skirlaw, described by Tout (*Chapters*, iii. 439) as 'a notary of Chancery', attests as notary by apostolic authority in 1353 (sign manual in Purvis, *Notarial Signs*, pl. 21). For Benedict Nicholl see Emden, *BRUO*, iii. 2200–1.

[3] *Cal. Pat. Rolls 1334–8*, p. 329, *Cal. Close Rolls 1337–9*, p. 144. Tout describes him as 'King's notary', *Chapters*, v. 15. An example of his sign manual would be welcome.

a trusted diplomatic agent of King Edward III, keeper of the Privy Seal (1345), chancellor (1349), bishop of St. David's (1347) and Worcester (1349), and archbishop of York from 1352 to 1373.[1]

For convenience of presentation we have treated separately the activities of notaries in offices of Church and State. But such convenience as this all too often falsifies history. There were no two distinct classes of notary public. Where individual careers can be studied it becomes clear that the borderline of the two employments was often crossed. This was likely to happen when many important offices of State were in the hands of prelates of the Church. It is a situation not unfamiliar in the earlier history of royal and episcopal clerks.[2]

This said, the problem remains to what extent English notaries public looked to kings and bishops and ecclesiastical corporations to provide them with their whole livelihood. Were there freelance notaries public? And if so, were they subject to public control? The contrast with southern Europe is marked. The same conditions did not apply. In the south many notaries public were commonly restricted to a local practice, and they were much occupied in drafting and enregistering contracts for private individuals. By the time that notaries appeared in England, the acts and registers of their brethren in the south had acquired a certain public character. Notaries were servants of the public, and their registers became municipal archives. In England, as we have seen, this particular need did not exist. The scope for the production of public instruments was less than in southern Europe. The English notaries' work for private persons has left much less trace than those activities in the service of the Crown and the Church which have been described already. Here they could perhaps find more or less permanent employment on the same terms (variable and uncertain) as other clerical assistants, with the

---

[1] For his career see Tout, Wilkinson, and Emden, opp. cit. See also his biography in W. H. Dixon and J. Raine, *Fasti Eboracenses* (1863).

[2] Cheney, *Eng. Bishops' Chanceries*, p. 19, and, on the activities of Peter the Scribe and others in the mid twelfth century, see T. A. M. Bishop, *Scriptores Regis* (Oxford, 1961) and H. A. Cronne and R. H. C. Davis, *Regesta Regum Anglo-Normannorum*, iv (Oxford 1969). Cf. Brentano, *York Met. Jurisdiction*, p. 82.

extra advantage of being qualified to draw up public instruments when required.[1] Perhaps just because in England this special task only came their way occasionally, and because their corroboration of a contract had no validity in the eyes of the Common Law, the local authorities did not demand that they should have local licence to pursue their calling. They did not, *qua* notaries public, take oaths over and above the oath they swore when they were licensed by apostolic or imperial authority, and (at least in the thirteenth and fourteenth centuries) they were hardly ever described as *notarii iurati*.[2] They kept no official registers of their acts after the fashion of the Italian and Provençal municipal notaries and the *échevins* of the Low Countries.[3]

Nevertheless, if there is little positive evidence of private practitioners among English notaries of the thirteenth and fourteenth centuries, in the present state of knowledge the possibility must not be excluded that many notaries public rubbed along without regular employment either by the civil administration or by prelates of the Church. Throughout the period notaries public are paid occasionally by private individuals to draw up and certify public instruments.[4] When they record *sub manu publica* proceedings in court christian it is not always possible to say whether they were appointed by the court or by a party in the case. The unhappy litigant in the Court of King's Bench in 1329, who got into trouble for introducing a notary public into court (to make a record with a view to later action in court christian),[5] was certainly employing the man as a private individual.

But these facts do not prove the existence of a large class of private practitioners to be contrasted with those in government employment. They simply underline the fact, often noted, that the civil service of the Middle Ages (and of much later days, too) was an ill-defined body of men, whose activities were not limited to the Crown's service. Tout observed that 'the permanent civil service' was a phrase first applied to

---

[1] Cf. Thoresby's salary in 1336 and onwards, above, p. 63.

[2] See below, pp. 90–1.   [3] See below, pp. 97–101.

[4] Notarial instruments produced in Chancery by excommunicates to prove that they had appealed provide a whole category of examples (p. 56 above).

[5] See above, p. 53.

government employees in England in 1853.[1] In the Middle Ages, he said, 'there were few public servants who did not take advantage of their position to do a good deal of business on their own account',[2] and he did not speak only of illicit activities. Again, their 'direct pay was inconsiderable and irregular'.[3] For many of them the rewards consisted less in fixed stipends of an office under the Crown than in fees, benefices, gifts in kind, expectancies. The Crown made no exclusive demands on them. So, in common with other 'royal' clerks, notaries may have divided their time between public and private activities, just as in the medical profession today those are to be found who act as private consultants while they draw salaries and fees from the National Health Service; already at the end of the twelfth century (as Mr. Richardson observed long ago)[4] Exchequer clerks sometimes acted as scriveners or notaries and wrote private deeds. Colour is given to this conjecture by the fact that dignified members of the legal profession could simultaneously hold office under the Crown and draw pensions and retaining fees from religious houses.[5] Compare the names

---

[1] T. F. Tout, *Collected Papers*, iii (Manchester, 1934), 193, in a lecture on 'The English civil service in the fourteenth century', published first in *BJRL*, iii (1916–17), 185–214. The words 'civil service' and 'civil servant' first came into use in relation to British rule in India, in the reign of George III.

[2] Ibid., p. 209.　　　　　　　　　　　　　　　　　　　[3] Ibid., p. 207.

[4] *TRHS*, 4th series xv (1932), 65, cf. 83. Prof. Peter Acht shows that in the same period in Metz one finds a scribe primarily in the service of the bishop who also writes for others (*Die Cancellaria in Metz* (Frankfurt, 1940), pp. 46, 86–91). For the dual occupation of Italian notaries public in the service of bishops and cities see R. Brentano, *Two Churches*, pp. 295–6.

[5] e.g. G. O. Sayles, 'Medieval judges as legal consultants', *Law Quarterly Rev.*, lvi (1940), 247–54; R. A. L. Smith, *Canterbury Cathedral Priory* (Cambridge, 1943), ch. 5: 'The prior's council'; E. H. Pearce, *Walter de Wenlok, Abbot of Westminster* (1920), pp. 88–92; W. A. Pantin, *The English Church in the XIV Century* (Cambridge, 1955), p. 33, and in *Essays in Medieval History pres. to Bertie Wilkinson* (Toronto, 1969), p. 199. Andrew de Tange, sometimes employed by the Crown, also worked for the convent of Durham who paid him a pension between 1292 and 1303 (see below, Appendix II, no. 22). Accounts of the Dean and Chapter of Lincoln for 1305/6 show payments of 53s. 4d. to Willelmus Johannis Costard, notary by apostolic and imperial authority, 'pro labore suo et sollicitudine circa negocia capituli per totum annum impensis', and of 40s. to Roger Roberti Bartholomei de Geytingtone, notary public by imperial authority—here described as *notarius domini episcopi*—'pro labore suo' (Lincoln, D. & C. Archives, B i/2/4). Mr. Henry de Cantuaria, notary public and royal clerk (below, p. 73 n. 4) was also a monastic pensioner (*Cal. Pat. Rolls 1313–17*, pp. 12, 375).

of those notaries public who were called into the Wardrobe at Westminster to exemplify papal bulls in October 1305 with those who were engaged at Westminster Abbey in 1306–7 in producing instruments on the serious domestic disturbance between the abbot and the prior. One finds that three employed at the abbey were among the ten who worked in 1305 in the Wardrobe: William le Dorturer of Selborne, Henry de Colchester, William de Maldon. William le Dorturer had worked for the abbey in 1303, and copied instruments for the Crown in 1304, and in 1308 he was again working for the abbey. Both Henry de Colchester and William de Maldon were used by the Crown before and after 1306–7 sufficiently to qualify for the description of civil servant (if the title is permissible at all).

Just as the employees of the Wardrobe in 1305 include some notaries not found on other occasions, so among the notaries at Westminster Abbey we encounter names we do not meet with again. Until the records have been combed more carefully, it is impossible to be sure whether all normally made a living in or around the palace of Westminster. All the notaries in the records under discussion in the last paragraph received special reward for their professional services. This does not preclude the possibility that some of them were more or less permanently employed by the king or the abbey. On the other hand, some notaries public may have formed a reservoir of casual secretarial labour.

Colour is given to this idea when one encounters notaries at work in their own homes. On 1 September 1384 one Richard Upton, clerk of the diocese of Coventry and Lichfield, recorded in public form the admission by proxy of Mr. Thomas Lansel to the chantry ('nuncupatam vulgariter Helle') in St. Paul's Cathedral founded for the souls of William de Chadeleshunt and Piers Gaveston.[1] Upton, who was a notary by apostolic authority, did this business 'in hospicio habitacionis mei . . . in vico nuncupato vulgariter Pater noster Rowe in parochia ecclesie sancte Fidis virginis London' situato'.[2] A little later,

---

[1] For William and his chantry see Emden, *BRUO*, i. 382 and R. Newcourt, *Repertorium Ecclesiasticum Parochiale Londinense* (1708–10), i. 207 note *k*.

[2] St. Paul's Cathedral, D. & C. Mun., A/75/1995. Upton did not write the instrument himself, but added his sign and eschatocol, in which he approved certain 'dictiones interlineatas et rasuras'.

one John Hall, a priest of the diocese of Llandaff, notary public by both apostolic and imperial authority, executed a document in his dwelling-house at Bristol.[1] Both of these instruments seem to be commissioned by private persons, presumably with the idea that they may be needed for production in the court christian. Half a century earlier two London laymen had recourse to a notary public to record the oath sworn by one of them that he would make no claim on the other by reason of any contract or agreement made between them 'from the beginning of the world until the day of making these presents'.[2]

If notaries public were employed by private persons in secular affairs, despite the unfriendly attitude of the common lawyers, it is not difficult to imagine that unattached notaries might practise in various parts of England, and that they might include men with dubious credentials. A mandate of Bishop Kellawe of Durham as early as 22 November 1312[3] and the royal writ of 26 April 1320 already mentioned[4] could be interpreted in this sense. The bishop ordered his official to suspend from their functions in his diocese certain persons who claimed to be notaries public by imperial authority and who drew up *soi-disant* public instruments; the notaries and their documents were not to be accepted until their *bona fides* had been established. The royal writ was more sweeping. It complained that 'although our realm of England is entirely free from subjection to the Empire', imperial notaries, engaged in dealing with matters of which cognizance belongs to the king and with other matters, have increased to the diminution of the Crown's rights and to the damage of the people. Sheriffs and prelates are told to give no credence to their acts. This is couched in such general terms as to make the real object of the order doubtful. It does, however, suggest that notaries public who claimed imperial authority were not regarded as profitable to the established authorities in the country.

Why the king's objection did not apply to notaries by apostolic authority is not altogether clear, for notaries of both

---

[1] On 26 June 1386. Hereford, D. & C. Archives, no. 570. The sign is reproduced by Emanuel, Fig. 31.

[2] Below, Appendix II, no. 18. Any such claim would as a result expose the claimant to an action for perjury in the court christian. Cf. no. 19.

[3] *Reg. Pal. Dunelm.*, i. 119, 253.   [4] See above, p. 53.

sorts served identical needs. The discrimination may have been purely on political grounds or may have had something to do with the methods of appointment, a subject which must be considered next. For the moment it is enough to reiterate the fact that notaries public by apostolic authority survived after 1320; indeed, the banning of the imperial title directly resulted in their increase. The survival and increase are all the more remarkable since most of the services for which a notary public was used by private persons in southern Europe lay outside the range of the English Common Law. Notaries public in England never justified their existence as a corporation of scribes for private citizens, to whom recourse would automatically be made for general scribal work.[1] Professional scribes were needed, no doubt, and existed, though we know little about them. In London, and probably elsewhere, they already formed a lay guild of scriveners by the mid fourteenth century.[2] But these must be distinguished as a class from the notary public. Among the early matriculands in the London guild, towards the end of the fourteenth century, only a few of those who inscribe their names in the 'Common Paper' also draw a sign manual in the margin and write beneath it 'notarius publicus'.[3]

The notary public remained a person of consequence in England throughout the fourteenth century. The Common Law did not want him, and his employment in other departments was more a matter of custom than necessity. But the occasions on which he appeared and framed instruments in notarial form were numerous. They were not confined to what may be described as normal legal proceedings. Any happy or untoward event might produce a notarial instrument,

[1] See above, p. 50.
[2] For the London scriveners see Jenkinson, *Later Court Hands in England* and Steer, *The Scriveners' Company Common Paper, 1357–1628*. Jenkinson opined that 'most large towns probably had similar gilds' (op. cit., p. 30). For scriveners at York in the XIV cent. see *The Layfolks' Mass-Book*, ed. T. F. Simmons (Early Eng. Text Soc., 71, 1879), pp. 400–1.
[3] E. Freshfield, 'Some notarial marks in the "Common Paper" of the Scriveners' company', *Archaeologia*, liv (1895), 239–54, and Jenkinson, op. cit., plates 1–3, 7. Freshfield thought it 'probable that a large proportion of the Scriveners' Company consisted of notaries' (p. 240); but he does not apply this conjecture specifically to the medieval period.

if legal proof were likely to be needed later on. Thus, William de Walton summoned the notary Henry of Great Sugnall to his house in Lichfield in March 1344, to certify that his daughter had been born in wedlock.[1] Still more remarkable is the incident at Canterbury in March 1297 when, as a result of the prior and chapter's compliance with *Clericis laicos*, the king's officials sequestrated the priory's stock of wheat and the wheat became rotten and overheated. The monk who was *granetarius* summoned Henry de Tichefeld, notary public, to bear witness that he was denied proper access to the grain. The main door of the granary being bolted, the two men climbed into a loft whence the notary could see some hundred measures of wheat lying on the floor, which workmen were trying to spread and to ventilate; for it was hot enough to warm cold hands and was steaming. Then the king's sequestrators arrived, and stopped the workmen and turned them out, despite the *granetarius*. All this was solemnly recorded and repeated by the notary in his eschatocol: 'predictum bladum sic putrefactum vidi et palpavi, dictosque custodes intrare et exire ut premittitur, et ipsos operarios operantes circa ipsum bladum similiter vidi, et omnia premissa prout superius conscribuntur ad rogatum dicti granetarii in publicam formam redegi meoque signo et nomine roboravi.'[2]

Finally, we should not overlook the atmosphere of dignity and ceremonial associated with the appearance of the notary public at great public events. He appeared, says Holdsworth, 'on occasions of more than ordinary solemnity'.[3] He was present when John Balliol swore fealty and renounced fealty to Edward I.[4] He was present when peace terms were agreed with France and with Castile.[5] Notaries witnessed the Irish chieftains' acts of submission to Richard II in 1395,[6] and two

[1] Below, Appendix II, no. 19.

[2] Canterbury, D. & C. Archives, Chartae antiquae C. 169 (cf. *HMCR*, v. 433*a*).

[3] Holdsworth, *Hist. of English Law*, v (1924), 114.

[4] Rymer, I. ii. 781, 836–7.   [5] Cf. Tout, *Chapters*, iii. 226, 28 n. 1.

[6] For notarial instruments prepared then see E. Curtis, *Richard II in Ireland, 1394–5*. Some ten of the original submissions are in P.R.O., C 40/10/25. They were all copied on 17 membranes of Exch. K.R. Memo. Roll 18 Richard II, whence Curtis prints, with translation, pp. 57–201. He gives the facsimile of an original for frontispiece.

notaries were of the commission which went to the Tower of London on Michaelmas Day 1399 to hear that king renounce his title to the crown.[1] The official account of the proceedings, though not a notarial instrument, has features reminiscent of one.[2]

[1] *Rot. Parl.*, iii. 416b, as noted in Brooke's *Treatise* (8th edn.), p. 12. For the concern in these affairs of one of the notaries, Mr. William de Feriby, see M. V. Clarke and V. H. Galbraith in *BJRL* xiv (1930), 150–3 (pp. 28–31 of offprint), and for his career Emden, *BRUO*, ii. 678–9. His colleague was Denis de Lopham, who was in practice in London as early as 1390 (St. Paul's Cathedral, D. & C. Mun., A/75/1975).

[2] G. E. Caspary has called attention to the canonistic and civilian influences in its drafting: 'The deposition of Richard II and the canon law', *Proceedings of 2nd Intern. Congress of Medieval Canon Law*, ed. S. Kuttner and J. J. Ryan (Monumenta Iuris Canonici, Series C: Subsidia 1, Vatican City, 1965), pp. 189–201.

6. The Appointment of Notaries Public

THE foregoing discussion of the activities of notaries public in England has thrown some light on the circumstances in which they acquired their title and the sort of career for which they qualified. Now it may be well to look more closely at the manner of appointment, the qualifications demanded, and the control exercised over them. The matter is obscure but calls for tentative remarks, even though they are necessarily scrappy and incomplete.

The appointment of individual English notaries public by apostolic authority is often recorded, in the papal registers in the case of direct appointment, and in the registers of English bishops when the bishops have received faculties to make notaries. The bishop recites the papal letter in the common form used by the papal Chancery, together with the standard oath which the new notary has taken.[1] One point the English evidence makes plain. The pope never delegated the right of creating notaries in unlimited numbers at any one time, or gave the right permanently to any particular office in the English Church. From Pecham's time onwards the archbishops of Canterbury often got faculties to create one or more;[2] but this did not exclude other arrangements. On 21 December 1320 Pope John XXII granted to the bishop of Winchester the faculty to grant 'tabellionatus officium singulis personis quas singuli diocesani regni Anglie et terre Wallie predictorum tibi duxerint nominandas'. At the same

---

[1] Tangl, *Kanzleiordnungen*, pp. 50, 329 (formulas cxxxii–cxxxiii); for the oath see below, Appendix II, no. 3; further, Baumgarten, pp. 64–8, and examples in English registers, *Reg. Sutton*, iii. 170–2 (1291), *Reg. Orleton*, pp. 147–9 (1320), *Reg. Trillek*, pp. 10–12 (1344), and Purvis, *Notarial Signs*, pp. ix–xi (1379, from Reg. Alex. Neville, York). For the background and practice of appointments Baumgarten gives the fullest general picture.

[2] Lambeth Palace, Reg. W. Courtenay, f. 186ᵛ, contains a faculty to create as many as twelve (29 March 1386).

time he allowed him to grant the office to six nominees of the king.[1] About the same time the University of Oxford asked the pope to empower its chancellor to appoint a limited number of notaries public.[2] Gutteridge misconceived the situation when he wrote that 'originally the power of appointing notaries was vested in the Archbishop of Canterbury as the Pope's representative in England'.[3]

When an individual received his commission in the Curia, we cannot always tell whether this was his unaided enterprise or whether he had outside support. Petitions of all sorts from comparatively humble people commonly went to the Curia under eminent patronage. They sometimes show the support given to candidates for the notariate. King Edward I himself asked Pope Boniface VIII to appoint a clerk in 1300.[4] A more unusual case is recorded in 1344 when the bailiffs and citizens of Canterbury support the application of Tristrandus de Cantuaria.[5] In a few early instances of curial appointment, the notary was later at pains to state his credentials in the documents he drew up. Thus Edmund de Verduno, on 26 August 1281, writes: 'Require registrum domini pape in clxxxvi [*recte* clxxxviii] capitulo, tempore Pape N. tercii, vel privilegia penes mercatores de Scala in curia Romana.'[6] In 1297 Walter le Noreys refers to his title 'in registro felicis recordacionis

---

[1] *Reg. Sandale*, pp. 573–4. Requests by the bishops of Worcester (1321) and Hereford (1324) for action on this faculty occur in *Reg. Cobham*, p. 109 and *Reg. Orleton*, pp. 277–8. Cf. above, p. 54 n. 4.

[2] *Oxford Formularies*, i. 75–6, cf. i. 98, 100, ii. 442–3 and above, p. 42.

[3] 'Origin', p. 134. Nor were King's College, Cambridge, and Eton empowered to create notaries (Denholm-Young, 'The cursus', p. 86, H. G. Richardson, *Oxford Formularies*, ii. 443). King's College statutes provided that the oaths of scholars, fellows, and provosts should be recorded in a public instrument, and the earliest surviving 'Liber protocollorum' shows that the college employed notaries public by apostolic authority for the purpose. I am obliged to Mr. John Saltmarsh for showing me this book.

[4] He wrote on behalf of Henry de Cantuaria (*Reg. Corbridge*, i. 36, cf. 29). Henry appears repeatedly in later records as a royal clerk. Cf. above, p. 66 n. 5.

[5] *Cal. Papal Petitions*, i. 34; granted in *Cal. Papal Letters*, iii. 143 (25 Jan. 1344). Other examples of outside support may be found in the registers of petitions.

[6] Brentano, *York. Met. Jurisdiction*, pp. 202–6. Perhaps his faculty was in pawn with Italian bankers. Hostiensis discusses the case of the notary who loses 'instrumentum de tabellionatu suo', *Summa*, f. 103rb (De fide instrumentorum, § 2).

domini Honorii pape iiii centesimo x°iiii capitulo de anno
primo pontificatus sui registratus'.[1] Early in the fourteenth
century Richard de Brenchley entitles himself 'publicus sacrosancte Romane ecclesie apostolica, per litteras domini pape
vera bulla plumbea bullatas, et imperiali auctoritate notarius'.[2]

Whether the candidate went in person to the Curia or relied
on the papal faculty granted to a local prelate, he had to undergo
examination. At the Curia in the thirteenth century the
examiner was usually a papal chaplain, named in the resultant
commission to the notary.[3] Once a cardinal deacon, Peter de
Piperno, formerly vice-chancellor, acted in this capacity.[4]
Later on, the vice-chancellor was often charged with the
business. The commission which states the notary's duties ('ut
illud prudenter et fideliter exequaris et cum necesse fuerit ad
te in hiis que ad officium ipsum pertinent recurratur') is un-
informative about the nature of the test; it states simply : 'fuisti
repertus ydoneus'. English prelates are seldom more explicit
when they act on papal faculties to create notaries. It is not
clear whether they conduct the required examination themselves or what tests have been applied. Bishop Oliver Sutton
of Lincoln provides more than usually full statements when
he uses the faculty of Nicholas IV to grant the office to two
men. Addressing John de Feriby (17 December 1291) he
suggests that he has personal knowledge of his 'pericia et
mores commendabiles' and that careful examination has shown
John to have 'sufficientem literaturam'.[5] His letter to John de

---

[1] P.R.O., E 135/15/17 m. 4, referring (correctly) to Reg. Vat. 43 f. 34ʳ. Cf.
Hugh de Musele (13 Feb. 1293) 'in registro felicis recordacionis domini Nicholai
pape iiiiᵗⁱ CCC° secundo capitulo de anno quarto pontificatus sui registratus'
(*Reg. Winchelsey*, ii. 1263, cf. *Reg. Nicolas IV*, no. 5429); Matthew de Alvine-
cherche dictus de Asshebarewe (11 March 1321) 'in sacrorum registrorum volu-
mine quinti anni sanctissime memorie domini Clementis pape quinti, sub capitulo
centesimo septuagesimo tercio registratus' (*Reg. Martival*, i. 204, cf. *Reg. Clem. V*,
iii. 18*b*, no. 5186).

[2] Westminster Abbey, Mun. 5415 (26 Jan. 1308). He did not regularly mention
the papal letters (ibid., Mun. 9496 m. 9 ad fin., of 17 May 1308).

[3] Above, p. 31; also *Cal. Papal Letters*, i. 482 and Reg. Vat. 41, f. 127ᵛ,
46 ff. 5ʳ, 124ʳ. Cf. Tangl, p. 329, formula cxxxii, and Baumgarten, pp. 30–7.

[4] Below, Appendix II, no. 1. For Cardinal Peter see Baumgarten, pp. 83–6,
and R. Fawtier, *Reg. Boniface VIII*, iv, p. ix.

[5] *Reg. Sutton*, iii. 170–2. A notary public appears among the witnesses of the
creation. The faculty recited is that contained in Reg. Vat. 46, f. 108ᵛ (*Reg.
Nicolas IV*, no. 6136).

Clipston (23 October 1293) declares that his 'peritia et circum-
spectio, fidelitas et morum honestas ex familiarium et iuratorum
nostrorum ac aliorum fidedignorum testimonio te nobis multipliciter recommendant'. In his oral grant of office to John de
Clipston he tells John that he has found him 'ad nominatum
officium in literatura et aliis in hac parte requirendis per
diligentem examinationem idoneum esse'.[1] In these cases the
men were probably already on the bishop's staff of clerks; and
phrases like 'per diligentem examinationem' and 'idoneum
reperientes' do no more than repeat the terms of (and show
compliance with) the papal faculty. Later creations by bishops
of Hereford do not go beyond these generalities, but the
notaries who draw up the records state that they have been
present at the examination.[2] Not much more light is thrown on
the qualities expected of the notary by letters which relate
to an application from the University of Oxford for its bedel,
Robert de Appelby, in 1337–8. They define *idoneum* as 'probum,
pudicum et sobrium, et honestis undique moribus adornatum,
literatum, intelligentem, egregieque scribentem, et omnino
nostre communitati perutilem et fidelem', and again as 'com-
petentis literature, bene scribentem, discretum, providum et
maturum'.[3]

A little more can be inferred about the nature of the examination by considering the oath which notaries swore at admission.
But it must be remembered that the formula remained unchanged for centuries; bishops exacted it in the form in which
it was transmitted to them in their faculties; it was not adapted
to English conditions. The oath binds the notary to draw up
contracts and instruments according to the wishes of the parties
or party, adding and subtracting nothing; nor shall he prepare
instruments recording enforced or fraudulent contracts. He
shall prepare a protocol and be ready to draw up a public
instrument on the basis of the protocol for the proper fee,
when required. This at least tells us that the notary public was
expected to display a modicum of legal science besides scribal
competence and probity. It is difficult to say more.

---

[1] *Reg. Sutton*, iv. 130–1. The ensuing document is drawn up and 'published'
by a notary.
[2] See p. 72 n. 1 above.   :See above, p. 42.

Where had the notary public acquired the basic educational grounding for his work? The grammar school and apprenticeship in a bishop's chancery or consistory may have sufficed for some; others, as has been seen (pp. 45–8), studied in the law faculties of the universities and were men of learning. But in between the lowly and most exalted members of the profession there were others who had received some systematic training of a vocational kind in, or on the fringes of, a university.[1] In Italy, the original home of the *tabellio*, Bologna provided courses which did not lead to an academic degree but which specifically provided instruction in the *ars notarie*. They included a grounding in grammar and *dictamen*, directed to practical ends.[2] Teachers in these courses were themselves practising notaries public, like Salatiele, 'artis notarie professor et doctor', who wrote a manual for students. In his *Ars notarie* (above, p. 45), he insists on the qualities and legal training required of a notary public. His admonitions begin: 'Debet autem observare notarius in primis ut singula que sibi scribenda occurrunt in iudicio sive extra prius teneat in pectore quam ore, ut mens eius facti preambula quod sit negotium secum studiose considerans discernat utrum ea que rogatus sit scribere sint verba tantum que dicantur vel facta que fiant, vel tam verba quam facta que simul dicantur et fiant, item utrum sint verba que dicantur vel facta que fiant ab una parte tantum alteri parti vel etiam que vicissim; secundo ut omnia que gratia sui officii in scriptis redigit fideliter et caute conscribat sine cuiusquam lesione et preiudicio seriem non mutando et iuris subtilitates et vincula innectendo; tertio ut negotii qualitatem coram hiis quos negotium tangit et testibus vocatis intelligibiliter proferat, et ut renuntiationes pertinentes ad iuris subtilitates et vincula enucleat et renuntiantibus aperiat; quarto ut tales adhibeantur testes et tot qui a iure non prohibeantur ferre testimonium . . .'.[3]

[1] The last chapter of Istvan Hajnal's *L'Enseignement de l'écriture* (rather misleadingly so called) has valuable discussion of this vocational training, despite some incautious conjectures.

[2] Hastings Rashdall, *Universities of Europe in the Middle Ages*, ed. F. M. Powicke and A. B. Emden (Oxford, 1936), i. 110–11 and notes. The intimate connection between grammar and rhetoric with juristic studies which had existed in the classical Roman period has recently been stressed by Peter Stein, *Regulae Iuris* (Edinburgh, 1966), especially ch. iii.

[3] *Ars Notarie*, ii. 11–14 (second recension, c. 1242–56).

By the year 1304 the statutes for the guild of notaries of Bologna provided for a lengthy period of instruction, first in grammar for four years and then for two years or more 'in documentis notarie sub ordinario doctore ipsius artis, cive Bononie'. A successful examination in grammar, latinity, and the notarial art, at the end of this course, allowed a student to obtain his licence to practise as a notary in the city and county of Bologna.[1] The Bolognese guild and similar guilds in other Italian cities could not grant their members the right to authenticate documents *ubique terrarum*, though they might encourage guildsmen to acquire this right. The object of the prescribed examination was to regulate the local practitioners. Nevertheless, the course of training they devised for their own members may well have served the foreigners who flocked to Italian university cities, hoping to return home with better qualifications for a clerical career and with the licence of a notary public to practise *ubique terrarum*. In the northern countries schools were less likely, perhaps, to provide a course dedicated to the notarial art. It would be unwise to press analogies between the needs of the Italian civic notary and those of the notary by apostolic or imperial authority operating in England.[2] None the less, from the thirteenth century onwards, business and government in northern Europe made increasing demands on a professional clerkly class.

What is beyond question is the existence of teachers at Oxford from at least the middle of the fourteenth century who purveyed the sort of instruction which would be useful in the clerical work of commerce and estate management. Mr. Richardson has pointed out 'the looseness and originality of twelfth-century deeds in marked contrast to the growing uniformity and technicality of those of the thirteenth and later centuries, and expert guidance was necessary if the many

---

[1] *Statuti delle società del popolo di Bologna*, ed. A. Gaudenzi (Fonti per la storia d'Italia), ii. (1896), 41–4: Società dei Notai, 1304. For the concern of the civic authorities of Bologna in the education of notaries see also Gina Fasoli, 'Giuristi, giudici e notai nell'ordinamento comunale e nella vita cittadina', *Atti del Convegno Internazionale di Studi Accursiani*, ed. Guido Rossi (Milan, 1968), i. 27–39; also G. Orlandelli, '"Studio" e scuola di notariato', ibid. i. 73–95.

[2] For one thing, the Italian city authorities had a prejudice in favour of notaries who were laymen, and therefore subject to civic jurisdiction: see *Statuti*, ii. 41.

legal transactions which required to be in writing were to be put in proper form. It is inconceivable that the necessary expertness could be acquired without formal instruction, and we can point to at least one place in England where this formal instruction was given, the University of Oxford.'[1] Such teaching as this, in Oxford, was not directed primarily to the needs of the notary public, but it must have introduced the student to some basic legal principles, to some of the vocabulary of the learned law, to some useful procedural safeguards, and to the forms of notarial instruments used in ecclesiastical courts. Young Englishmen with this training, even if they had not been to Bologna, might make a passable showing when they applied for licence to act as notaries public.

Whatever was demanded by way of qualities of character and intellect and learning, questions of age and status arose. The common form preserved in the papal Chancery ordinances laid down the condition that the candidate should have completed the twenty-fifth year of his age.[2] If this was enforced it would at least allow for experience of clerical work and some background of legal training. Baumgarten seemed to think that it was a well-established rule, despite the fact that it was not prescribed in surviving faculties until the fifteenth century. He cited the petition of the abbot and convent of Westminster (11 August 1349) for faculty to create six notaries, of whom three, being clerks of eighteen years of age, might be promoted to a benefice apiece.[3] At this rate, the minimum educational requirement cannot have been high. Baumgarten was satisfied on slender evidence that the Curia took the examination seriously, but observed that in the provinces there was no guarantee of a common standard.[4]

As regards clerkly status, Pope Innocent III had in 1211 forbidden a bishop to allow clerks in holy orders to act as *tabelliones*. The place which this prohibition came to occupy in the Decretals of Gregory IX shows the reason. It was put under the title 'Ne clerici vel monachi secularibus negotiis se

[1] *BJRL*, xxiii. 446–7; cf. his remarks in *Oxford Formularies*, ii. 333–9, and *American Hist. Rev.*, xlvi.

[2] Tangl, p. 329, formula cxxxiii.

[3] Baumgarten, pp. 10–11, citing *Cal. Papal Petitions*, i. 171.

[4] Baumgarten, pp. 30–7.

immisceant'.[1] Under the same title went canon 18 of the Fourth
Lateran Council, which ordered clerks in holy orders and
beneficed clergy to avoid secular office and cases of blood.
Faculties granted by the popes to English prelates during the
thirteenth century do not mention this or any other condition
regarding the status of the candidate;[2] but in view of Innocent
III's decretal the Common Law rule may have been thought
to be a sufficient directive. The point may also have been
covered for a short period by a clause inserted in faculties
which required bishops to appoint 'iuxta formam quam
Romana ecclesia servare in talibus consuevit'.[3] In the mid
fourteenth century the prohibition was linked in the formularies with a new restriction which became even more usual.
A limiting clause had been introduced into faculties apparently
for the first time under Pope John XXII: 'dummodo dicte
persone non fuerint coniugate'.[4] The object was presumably
to ensure that notaries public should not endanger their
privilegium fori and should be justiciable in the court christian.[5]
Under John XXII the Chancery extended its new clause to
read: 'dumtaxat personis clericis non coniugatis nec in sacris
ordinibus constitutis'.[6] With the same pope a clause 'clericus
non coniugatus nec in sacris ordinibus constitutus' was introduced into the oath the notary swore.[7] Under Clement VI both

---

[1] Migne, *Patrologia Latina*, ccxvi. 486–7; *Compilatio IV*, 3. 19. 1; *Extra*,
3. 50. 8.

[2] e.g. *Reg. Sutton*, iii. 170, iv. 130, *Reg. Orleton*, p. 147.

[3] e.g. Reg. Vat. 41, f. 151ᵛ; 43, ff. 13ᵛ, 58ᵛ, 168ʳ, 169ʳ; 44, ff. 15ᵛ, 43ʳ (cf.
Baumgarten, p. 45). The formula seems to have been dropped early in the pontificate of Nicholas IV. Its omission from some earlier direct appointments and
faculties may be explained by the presence of the petitioner in the Curia: e.g.
Archbishop John Pecham's faculty of 25 March 1279 ('In nostra proposuisti
presentia constitutus'), below, Appendix II, no. 3.

[4] 21 Dec. 1320 (*Reg. Sandale*, pp. 573–4). Faculties granted by this pope,
21 March and 4 July 1317 (Baumgarten, pp. 46–7) and 15 Jan. 1320 (*Reg. Orleton*,
pp. 147–8), show no such restriction.

[5] This may explain the insistence on the clerical status of notaries described
as 'cum unica et virgine coniugatus' (Baumgarten, pp. 10 n. 2, 33). 'Bigamist'
clerks forfeited their privilege. De Boüard quotes 'N. bigamus auctoritate
apostolica et imperiali notarius' (1411, *Manuel*, ii. 196).

[6] Baumgarten, pp. 55 (1322) and 47 (1325, cf. ibid. 1332); cf. Tangl, p. 329,
formula cxxxiii.

[7] Baumgarten, p. 47. Cf. *Benoît XII: Lettres communes*, ed. J. M. Vidal, i (École
française de Rome, 1903), 142, etc.

faculty and oath contain the restriction.[1] Even so, there was room for doubt about the law. In the time of John XXII the prior of Canterbury sought advice from the Curia. He quoted the current form of oath: 'Ego N. clericus non coniugatus nec in sacris ordinibus constitutus iuro' etc., and wished his correspondent to ask the wise men of the Curia whether notaries so appointed, if they subsequently married or proceeded to holy orders, might retain and exercise the office of notary. 'Some who account themselves wise men in England say Yes, but others say No.'[2] What reply the prior got we do not know.

How strictly were the rules observed? Dispensations from the ban on married men and clerks in holy orders were sometimes granted,[3] but it is doubtful whether they cover most of the breaches of the rules. English evidence shows that the decretal which forbade notaries public to be in holy orders was not observed. When Bishop Oliver Sutton made his appointments he noted on each occasion that the man was in minor orders.[4] But the need to provide these men with livings, combined with new rigours of the law against beneficed clerks in minor orders, meant that the Church did not interpret very strictly *Extra*, 3. 50. 8. From Archbishop Pecham onwards, English prelates were prepared to appoint even a priest as notary, or to ordain a notary to holy orders.[5] The married notary is much less in evidence. If he existed, he and his employer understandably did not flaunt his marital status. Until the fourteenth century he committed no offence by marriage, so long as he remained in minor orders. Nevertheless, maybe we owe the revelation that Pecham's John of Beccles was *uxoratus* to an unfriendly Hereford scribe; for John had forsaken Hereford to serve the bishop of Hereford's legal opponent, the archbishop.[6] Other references to married notaries in England are

---

[1] e.g. 26 April 1344, *Reg. Trillek*, pp. 10–11.

[2] *Literae Cantuarienses* (RS), i. 301–2.

[3] Baumgarten, pp. 18–19. When Urban VI authorized the archbishop of Canterbury to create twelve (above, p. 72 n. 2), he granted 'etiam si sex earum [personarum] in sacerdocio constitute vel coniugate fuerint'. Boniface IX allowed the bishop of Hereford to appoint six clerks as notaries 'eciam si . . . in sacris ordinibus constituti aut . . . coniugati' (19 Nov. 1389; *Reg. Trefnant*, pp. 27–8).   [4] See above, p. 74.

[5] Of Pecham's clerks William de Holaym was subdeacon and John Lewensis priest (*Reg. Pecham*, i. 116) and John de Bononia (?) was a subdeacon in 1288

scarce. The prior of Winchester admitted a married clerk, John Bryan, to the office (9 April 1356) on the strength of a faculty from Pope Innocent VI.[1] Robert de Foxton, who was registrar of the Ely Consistory between 1373 and 1384, was a notary public and a married man.[2] On 22 January 1391 the bishop of Lincoln admitted a married clerk in the person of John Makesey, who was in the service of his successor in 1405.[3] By this time bishops clearly had no qualms about employing notaries who were married. For most of the first half of the fifteenth century a married clerk, Thomas de Colston, served the bishops of Lincoln as registrar.[4] In 1476 the archbishop of York admitted John Haryngton to the office of notary by apostolic authority as 'clericus cum unica virgine coniugatus'.[5] By the fifteenth century the pope was even prepared to license a layman for the notarial office.[6]

If evidence about papal appointments is not very good, imperial appointment of English notaries is a yet more obscure matter. Before Edward II laid his embargo on imperial notaries in 1320, they were common, perhaps commoner than notaries by papal authority. For the forty years since their first arrival we can name at least forty or fifty, and probably there were many more. But records of their appointment are extremely rare. The silence of episcopal registers, our main source outside the papal registers for apostolic authorization, suggests that English bishops did not welcome the imperial title or themselves seek faculties from the emperor or his somewhat mysterious delegates.[7] In contrast to papal practice, the

(i. 77). On the other hand, Edmund de Verduno remained in minor orders until he became rector of Snargate, 1290 (ibid. ii. 23, 29). Cf. *Reg. Sutton*, i. 196; v. 100, 101–2. Hamo atte Broke, priest in 1333, may be the Mr. Hamo atte Broke of Brenchley recommended to the pope for the notariate six years later (*Reg. Hethe*, i. 514, xxxix).   [6] See above, p. 29.

[1] *Winchester Cath. Chartulary*, p. 157, no. 366.   [2] Emden, *BRUC*, p. 241.
[3] Lincoln, Ep. reg. XII (Buckingham, Memoranda), f. 379[v] and XIV (Repingdon, Institutions), f. 210[v].
[4] Emden, *BRUO*, i. 470. He was a notary public by 4 Dec. 1408 (*Reg. Repingdon*, i. 139). In 1421 Archbishop Chichele dispensed him from his statute, 'Cum ex eo clerici coniugati' (Lyndwood, *Provinciale*, p. 129), to enable him to act as scribe and registrar although married 'cum una sola et virgine' (*Reg. Chichele*, iv. 215). His notarial sign is reproduced in *Lincoln Cath. Stat.*, i. 154.
[5] Purvis, *Notarial Signs*, p. xii.   [6] Baumgarten, p. 10.
[7] Bresslau, *Handbuch*, i. 629–31, de Boüard, *Manuel*, ii. 189–94. Cf. Mikucki on

emperor sometimes delegated the right of creating notaries in perpetuity, and of creating notaries public who would have licence to practise *ubique terrarum*. Naturally, English and French bishops did not get imperial licence, but it was sometimes given to bishops within the emperor's dominions. The archbishops of Embrun enjoyed this privilege, as was noted by Hostiensis (himself archbishop of Embrun), who contrasted it with the rights of the counts of Provence and Savoy, who could appoint notaries public only for their own territories.[1] The Emperor Charles IV gave the right to the archbishops of Prague in 1358.[2] Hostiensis also noted that the counts of Lomello enjoyed this right in heredity.[3] English records, as will be seen, show the families of Alliate and Monte Florum exercising the right in the fourteenth century; and in 1370, according to Du Cange's *Glossarium* (s.v. Comes), Charles IV granted the right in heredity, with other rights and the title of 'sacri Lateranensis palatii comites', to Amizinus de Bozullis (*legum doctor et miles*) and Johannes de Bozullis, citizens of Pavia.

The earliest record of an appointment of an Englishman as notary public by an imperial delegate is from the act-book of Beverley collegiate church.[4] It takes the form of an instrument prepared by an English notary (by imperial authority) and witnessed by English clerks at Lyon, in the cloister of the Friars Minor, on Christmas Day 1305 ('anno nativitatis domini m ccc vi'). In it Rogerus de Monte Florum dei gracia Comes Palatinus speaks. After a formal preamble ('Sagax humane nature . . .') he inclines to the personal petition of Ricardus Botemound de Sutton, clerk of the diocese of York, and confers upon him the privilege of the imperial notariate. He declares that the candidate has been examined and found suitable and has personally sworn the usual oath of fealty to the most holy Roman Church and the holy Roman Empire 'necnon etiam . . . tabellionatus officium fideliter et legaliter exercendi'. The count has invested Richard with the badges of

Poland: 'Nous ne savons rien de certain sur la création des notaires impériaux chez nous', 'Essai', p. 340.

[1] *Summa*, f. 103ʳ*b* (De fide instrumentorum § 2).   [2] Mikucki, p. 340.

[3] Cf. G. C. Bascapè, 'I conti palatini del regno italico e la città di Pavia', *Archivio stor. lombardo*, lxii (1936), 281–377, esp. pp. 287–8.

[4] *Memorials of Beverley Minster*, ed. A. F. Leach, i (Surtees Soc., 1898), 177–9.

his office and given him the kiss of peace. Monastic registers yield further evidence, in the shape of requests by priors of three English monastic cathedrals for the right to act as subdelegates in this matter. In a fourth case, Roger de Monte Florum delegated the creation and investiture of an individual applicant to the prior of Durham (below, Appendix II, no. 4a). On 5 March 1306, in the cathedral of Lyon, Bassianus de Alliate,[1] describing himself as of Milan, Count Palatine by the grace of God, granted the petition of Henry of Eastry, prior of Christ Church, Canterbury, for a faculty to create three public notaries.[2] The faculty was witnessed by the count's son and by a clerk of the diocese of Milan, and was written and signed by an English notary. After the formal preamble ('Sagax humane nature . . .') the faculty requires candidates to be examined and ceremonially invested. The oath to be taken is rehearsed. This, interestingly enough, is more precise in stating the scope of the notary's duties than the papal formula. In the same year 1306 the prior of Winchester turns to Roger de Monte Florum, Count Palatine, for a faculty to appoint two clerks as notaries by imperial authority. Again the form of oath is recited in full. This grant is dated at Bordeaux in the cloister of the Friars Preachers, on 22 November 1306.[3] A curious feature of these comital acts is that they were issued in the cities in or near which the court of Pope Clement V was then established. A third imperial faculty on record was probably later in date and came, like the Canterbury one, from Bassianus de Alliate. On 27 May 1315 the prior of Worcester Cathedral acted upon it to appoint John de Maddeleya, clerk, as notary public.[4]

[1] For the privileges of the counts palatine of Alliate see Bresslau, *Handbuch*, i. 630 and for formulas used by them see the fourteenth-century formulary calendared by Barraclough, *Public Notaries*, p. 221, nos. 299–300.

[2] Below, Appendix II, no. 4b.

[3] Selden, *Titles of Honour* (2nd edn., 1631), pp. 431–2 (3rd edn., 1672), pp. 343–4, calendared in *Winchester Cath. Chartulary*, p. 223, no. 527. The preamble is that used by the count of Alliate. Much of the rest is similar and, although the form of oath is shorter, it details many duties of the notary. Cf. Barraclough, op. cit., p. 222, no. 300c for the 'comes palatinus de Monte Florentie'. Clerics of the Monte Florum family gained interests in England early in the fourteenth century: see the indexes to Le Neve, *Fasti 1300–1531*, xii (1967), Tout, *Chapters*, vol. vi, and *Accounts rendered by Papal Collectors*, ed. W. E. Lunt (Philadelphia, 1968).   [4] Below, Appendix II, no. 6.

Among the notaries by imperial authority who practised in England before 1320 at least six claimed a commission from the prefect of Rome. Whatever the prefect's power in Rome at this period, and whatever the actual process of delegation may have been, these English examples suggest the probable answer to a question which Bresslau was obliged to leave open: Did the prefect derive his title to grant faculties from the emperor or from the pope?[1] On 23 February 1288 and after, Willelmus Johannis de Anlauby, clerk of the diocese of York, subscribed as 'auctoritate imperiali et alme urbis prefecti publicus notarius'.[2] On 19 October 1289 and after, Adam filius Ade Swayny de Boterwik dictus de Lindeseia, of the diocese of Lincoln, often ended his subscription with the words 'ac alme urbis prefectorie dignitatis publicus auctoritate notarius'.[3] Another notary who claimed both apostolic and imperial authority, Willelmus de Maldona, of the diocese of London, used the formula without the word 'ac',[4] while two more, Willelmus filius Willelmi dictus le Dorturer de Selebourne, of the diocese of Winchester, and Walterus le Noreys filius quondam Roberti Lawys de Killum, of the diocese of York, came near to the same form with 'sacrosancte Romane ecclesie et sacri imperii ac alme urbis prefecti publicus auctoritate notarius'.[5] Slightly later, in 1309, Rogerus Roberti Bartholomei de Geytingtone, clerk of the diocese of Lincoln,

---

[1] Bresslau, *Handbuch*, i. 631 n. 2. Giry had assumed that the pope had conferred the prerogative on the prefect (*Manuel*, p. 827 n. 2). Later writers on the office of prefect, which had settled in the family of Vico, mention this prerogative without speculating on the source of authority: see L. Halphen, *Études sur l'administration de Rome au Moyen Age* (Bibliothèque des Hautes Études, 1907), pp. 77–80, and A. de Boüard in *Mélanges d'archéologie et d'histoire*, École française de Rome, xxxi (1911), 303–5 and *Le Régime politique et les institutions de Rome au Moyen Âge, 1252–1347* (Bibl. des Écoles françaises d'Athènes et de Rome, 1920), pp. 133, 157–8.

[2] Lincoln, D. & C. Archives, D ij/62/1/3, 4, 5, and 8.

[3] Westminster Abbey, Mun. 22932 (19 Oct. 1289, damaged); Purvis, *Notarial Signs*, Pl. 2 (1303); P.R.O., SC 7/36/3 (22 Oct. 1305) and SC 7/64/22 (6 Nov. 1305).

[4] Emanuel, loc. cit., p. 6, from Hereford, D. & C. Archives, nos. 1855 (4 Oct. 1303) and 1851 (1 July 1308); ibid., no. 1077 (20 Sept. 1301); *Echt-Forbes Charters*, Fig. 39, from P.R.O., C 47/15/1/1 (1312).

[5] P.R.O., E 135/15/17 m. 4 (1297), Hereford, D. & C. Archives, no. 1077 (20 Sept. 1301), and Westminster Abbey, Mun. 12732 (1303). William le Dorturer later uses 'prefectorie dignitatis' for 'prefecti' (1317, *Reg. Martival*, ii. 189).

subscribed as 'imperiali ac alme urbis prefectorie dignitatis publicus auctoritate notarius'. On 6 January 1320 Willelmus Johannis Costard, clerk of the same diocese (who in 1312 had subscribed as 'publicus auctoritate apostolica et imperiali notarius') styled himself 'publicus auctoritate apostolica imperiali [ac al]me urbis prefect' notarius'.[1]

In all cases the prefectorial title follows the imperial and seems to be linked with it. In two other cases these two titles are merged in one (as in that of Willelmus de Maldona): Nicholaus de la Gare and Robertus Gilberti de Wysebeche claim no apostolic authority; they entitle themselves respectively 'publicus auctoritate imperiali alme urbis prefecti notarius'[2] and 'publicus sacri imperii alme urbis Romane prefectorie dignitatis auctoritate notarius'.[3] In no case is the prefectorial title found by itself. It is not easy to see why these notaries, if already possessed of imperial authority, should seek a separate commission from the prefect of Rome. So perhaps we may legitimately conclude that they claimed imperial authority because they had received their commission at the hands of the prefect as representative of the emperor. Curiously enough, those modern authorities who mention the prerogative of the prefect in this matter seem to be unaware that the notary public outside Rome and central Italy ever claimed to hold the prefect's licence.

Swayny, Maldon, le Dorturer, le Noreys, and Costard are only five out of at least twenty English notaries before 1320 who claim both apostolic and imperial authority; and other countries show the same combination of titles. How did this come about, and why? Some of the earliest who practised in England (John de Bononia included) have already been noted as being of the company. The question is difficult to answer because comparatively few of the English notaries public of this period have left any clue to the date of their appointment by either one or the other authority, while still fewer hint at the order of double appointment. In one case at least the order

---

[1] Lincoln, D. & C. Archives, D ij/62/1/10–12.

[2] Nicholas is of Canterbury diocese: *Reg. Winchelsey*, ii. 1319 (22 Feb. 1298).

[3] Robert is of Ely diocese: P.R.O., SC 7/36/7 (6 Nov. 1305), Westminster Abbey Mun. 9496 m. 6 (13 July 1307).

is clear. Adam de Louther, of the diocese of Carlisle, 'sacri imperii publicus auctoritate notarius', prepared a public instrument certifying a papal provision on 18 November 1297. Less than three years later the archbishop of York appointed him notary public by apostolic authority.[1] In the case of Ricardus natus quondam Henrici de Ganyo, a clerk of Bishop Antony Bek of Durham, we simply have the evidence that in 1300 and in 1303 he called himself notary public 'sacri Romani imperii auctoritate', whereas in and after 1307 his style was 'apostolica et imperiali auctoritate'.[2] It must be inferred that he added the papal to the imperial commission between 1303 and 1307. A third case is a little more complicated. Johannes Thome de Barneby super Done, clerk of the diocese of York, was nominated by the bishop of Worcester for appointment as *tabellio* by the bishop of Winchester in 1321, in virtue of the faculty lately received by the bishop of Winchester from the pope.[3] Many years later, in 1336, John de Barneby (whom the bishop of Worcester had described during the intervening years as his registrar and household clerk) styled himself notary public by apostolic and imperial authority. Since it is most unlikely that he would seek the imperial licence after 1320, one may assume that he already held it then, and that the royal ban on imperial notaries led him to obtain the papal title in 1321.[4] With Master Philip of London we meet a notary who had by 15 October 1320 dropped the title 'sacri Romani

---

[1] See above, p. 55, and *Reg. Corbridge*, i. 28–9 (23 July 1300). In *Reg. Greenfield*, v. 97 (29 May 1311) he is described simply as 'auctoritate apostolica'. The Italian notary Thomasinus Petrigoli uses the imperial title in 1283 and the papal in 1290 (Brentano, *York Met. Jurisdiction*, pp. 220, 225).

[2] Cf. *Records of Antony Bek*, pp. 202, 90 and *Reg. Pal. Dunelm.*, i. 529 with *Records*, pp. 127, 149, 164.

[3] *Reg. Cobham*, p. 109, quoted by Haines, *Administration*, p. 134 n. 8. Cf. above, pp. 72–3.

[4] Purvis, *Notarial Signs*, Pl. 18 (from Reg. W. Melton, 1336). Another of his instruments with the double title (1340) is in *Reg. Pal. Dunelm.*, iii. 488 (cf. 490, 493). The appearance of the double title in other cases may be explained by the same order of events: William de Wrelleton (Purvis, Pl. 18, 1336), Richard de Scholdone (*Reg. Roffense*, ed. John Thorpe (1769), p. 554, 1346). John de Chaill, created notary by apostolic authority, 1326, may be the John Cheyle 'notarius' who witnessed a document of the bishop of Salisbury, 1318 (*Reg. Martival*, ii. 207). In 1320 Martival's registrar was notary by imperial authority only; he had to fall back on the seals of his superiors to authenticate documents (see below, pp. 90–1).

imperii auctoritate publicus et auctenticus notarius' which he had used in earlier years, and had substituted 'sacrosancte Romane ecclesie auctoritate apostolica notarius'.[1] The problem of double appointments *before* 1320 remains unsolved.[2] Why were both titles sought? Did the imperial title always come first? Was the imperial notariate open to literate laymen and the apostolic reserved for clerks? Were higher standards of literary or legal competence demanded of the notary appointed by apostolic authority?[3] What were the Counts Palatine doing in the neighbourhood of the Roman Curia? All these questions about notaries with the imperial title evidently concern Europe as a whole and cannot be answered only from English material.

The question of the appointment in this period of laymen to be notaries, whether by papal or by imperial authority, must remain an open one, for the material is very hard to interpret. It does, however, call for some brief observations here. The most useful evidence is the notary's own eschatocol; but we have the names of many notaries public without any instrument which they have formally subscribed. And the evidence of the eschatocol itself is not clear. Beyond doubt, the majority of English notaries who practised in the thirteenth and fourteenth centuries were clerks, for they declared their status (usually with the name of a diocese) when they put their sign and name to instruments. But some failed to do so. This is true of all the earliest practitioners in England, both English and foreign. Not until John Alani de Beccles do we encounter an English notary who adds the name of a diocese to his own name. He never claimed the title of clerk, and was—as we have seen— once described as *uxoratus*. But can we assume that those who

[1] Hereford, D. & C. Archives, no. 2871 (Emanuel, Fig. 7), 9 Feb. 1307. He acted in the Wardrobe Oct.–Nov. 1305 (P.R.O., SC 7/18/22, SC 7/36/1 and 2, cf. *Echt-Forbes Charters*, Fig. 34). His new title, with his old sign, appears on 15 Oct. 1320 in St. Paul's Cathedral, Mun. A/75/1987 (below, Appendix II, no. 16). In 1328 he acted as executor of Andrew Horn (*Cal. of Letter Books London, E*, ed. Sharpe, p. 216).

[2] Mikucki records in fourteenth-century Poland 44 imperial notaries, 5 apostolic, and 6 with both titles ('Essai', p. 339). In Silesia relatively few bore the apostolic title; these were mostly foreigners or were educated in Italy (Luschek, p. 15). Cf. de Boüard, *Manuel*, ii. 196.

[3] I find no support in Baumgarten, pp. 19–20, cited by Herde, *Beiträge*, p. 11 n. 72, for the idea that apostolic notaries underwent a more severe test and were therefore better qualified than imperial notaries.

did not call themselves clerks were laymen? Apparently not so. Walterus le Noreys filius quondam Roberti Lawys de Kyllum Eboracensis diocesis is proved to have been in minor orders at the time of his appointment by an entry in the papal register. Again, John Erturi de Cadomo, who never mentions in eschatocols his status or diocese of origin, is described elsewhere as 'clericus' and held many ecclesiastical benefices while acting as notary public. So in this respect the argument from silence in the eschatocols is of no use. It has been shown that commissions granted by the popes generally provided for notaries to be unmarried clerks in minor orders, though the rule was not universally observed by English bishops (above, p. 81). Of the notaries by imperial authority who practised in England the majority can be shown to be clerks. That laymen were sometimes appointed remains a possibility. One pointer, though inconclusive in itself, may be cited. In the witness-list of the act of the archdeacon of Westminster in 1325 five names are followed by the description 'clericis', after which come 'Gilberto de Lutgarshale, Henrico de Lyndeseye notariis publicis, et aliis testibus in multitudine copiosa'.[1] The natural inference (though dogmatism would be out of place) is that Gilbert and Henry were laymen. Gilbert is found elsewhere acting as a notary for the royal Chancery. As for Henry, he must be the Master Henricus Ade dictus de Lindeseye employed by the dean of St. Paul's proctor in 1320.[2] This suggests that he was the son of Master Adam filius Ade de Swayny de Boterwik dictus de Lyndeseya, the notary by apostolic and imperial authority of the diocese of Lincoln, well recorded between 1289 and 1305; and this in turn suggests that Master Adam himself was either a layman or a *clericus coniugatus*.[3]

It still remains uncertain what the reference to a diocese meant. Assuming that there *were* lay notaries, did it mean the same thing for laymen and clerks?[4] Was it the man's diocese

---

[1] Westminster Abbey, Mun. 5965.

[2] *Reg. Martival*, ii. 304.

[3] Adam subscribes as 'Lincolniensis diocesis', not as '*clericus* Lincolniensis diocesis'; but this in itself proves nothing, as the case of Walter le Noreys shows.

[4] Luschek tries to make a distinction in the case of Silesian notaries public, lay and clerical (*Notariatsurkunde*, pp. 13–14).

of origin, or the diocese where he received minor orders, or whence he came with letters dimissory for ordination, or the diocese where he received his notarial appointment? All that can be said is that where the notary's name is formed from a place-name, the place is usually found to be in the diocese which is named in his eschatocol.

Whatever the authority by which the notary public was admitted, papal or imperial, the oath which he took was probably accompanied by a formal investiture. Baumgarten, to be sure, found little positive trace that the Curia demanded a solemn investiture, but produced pointers in that direction.[1] The bishop of Hereford, in creating a notary in 1344 in virtue of a faculty from Clement VI, declares: 'te de eodem officio per calami, atramenti, et carte tractacionem presencialiter investimus, ut idem officium prout pertinet ubique locorum fideliter exerceas in futurum cum super hoc congrue fueris requisitus.'[2] The investiture of Richard Botemound de Sutton, at the hands of the Count Palatine Roger de Monte Florum in 1305, was 'per pennam, calamarium, atque cartam quae tunc in manibus nostris tenebamus', and the prior of Canterbury used the same form for the ceremony in 1306.[3]

When a man was appointed notary public he seems to have enjoyed the honorific title of *magister*. It is impossible to prove this, and the title was not regularly used—never in the notary's own formal eschatocol. True, a great many of the profession at some stage in their career studied in universities and qualified themselves, especially in law faculties, by graduation. But the mastership is so commonly credited to those notaries public who have left no trace in a university that it probably came into use here as in certain other offices and crafts in the later Middle Ages to signify a certain status, without an academic connotation. In support of this conjecture one may note that the chief clerks of the English royal Chancery were styled *magistri* and that curial formularies explicitly gave

[1] Baumgarten, pp. 38–9.

[2] *Reg. Trillek*, p. 11 (cf. p. 53). The bishop of Chichester used a similar formula 1404 (*Reg. Rede*, i. 180–1). In 1313 the bishop of Durham, acting on papal authority, invested Willelmus natus Petri de Colby 'per pennam, calamarium, atque cartam' (*Reg. Pal. Dunelm.*, i. 565).

[3] *Memorials of Beverley*, i. 178; cf. below, Appendix II, nos. 5 and 6.

the title to members of the College of apostolic notaries and to other papal officials irrespective of any academic background.[1]

Once the English notary public had received investiture, it seems, as already noted, that he was free to draw up public instruments anywhere, at the request of a public authority or a private person, provided—a large proviso—that he did not involve himself in business within the competence of the king's courts. Only if he assumed the office of royal Chancery clerk, or clerk of a cathedral chapter, or registrar of an ecclesiastical court, would he be called upon to take an additional oath to the local authority. He did not do so then *qua* notary public. Notaries in the royal Chancery in the mid fourteenth century swore an oath, but so did other Chancery clerks.[2] Likewise, notaries public employed by certain cathedral chapters took oaths not to reveal chapter secrets; but the oath was incidental to their general tasks and was unconnected with the status of notary.[3] The title of *notarius iuratus* is practically unknown in England, and one exception to the rule is instructive. Master John de Barwe (Barrow on Humber), finding himself deprived by the king's writ of 26 April 1320 of the right to use his imperial title, clung nevertheless to the name of notary. He even continued to use his customary sign manual. He introduced it into instruments which he framed during 1320 as registrar of the bishop of Salisbury. He was recording a protracted legal process which started with a session of the bishop's commissary on 17 March 1320 and continued before the bishop on 17 April; but the instruments drawn up as record can only have been completed and sealed some months later, for the king's prohibition was already known and documents dated in June were included. The phrase *notarius iuratus*

---

[1] See Bresslau, *Handbuch*, i. 549 n. 2, Herde, *Beiträge*, p. 49, and Herde in *Archiv für Diplomatik*, xiii (1967), 234 n. 44.

[2] 1346: *Statutes of the Realm*, i (Record Commission, 1810), 306.

[3] See p. 44 n. 1 above, and K. Major, 'The office of chapter clerk at Lincoln in the Middle Ages', pp. 163–88. The clerk of the register of St. Paul's Cathedral was 'ad hoc iuratus' (*Reg. Stat. S. Pauli*, p. 73). Mr. John de Broadwas, *clericus* and *tabellio*, was admitted into the household and service of Godfrey Giffard, bishop of Worcester, and took an oath, but this did not concern his notarial work specifically (Haines, *Administration*, p. 90 n. 1). For Canterbury see *Literae Cantuarienses* (RS), i. 314.

is explained in the final clauses of the text of each instrument. In the first one they read :[1]

Acta sunt hec . . . in presencia magistri Johannis de Barwe registrarii [*sic*] dicti patris et notarii publici ac in officio registratoris dicti patris et ad alia acta iudicialia dicti patris et commissariorum suorum conficienda [*ms.* conficiendorum] et in scriptis fideliter redigenda iurati, ac magistri Willelmi de Wynterborne notarii publici, Roberti de Farendon' clerici et aliorum in multitudine copiosa. Et quia notarii publici auctoritate imperiali non audent nunc suum notoriatus [*sic*] officium exercere, propter quandam factam in ea parte prohibicionem regiam hiis diebus, ac sigillum meum pluribus est ignotum, [sigillum] subdecanatus Saresbiriensis hiis actis nostris predictis apposuimus et ea consueto signo registratoris et notarii dicti patris in testimonium consignavi [*ms.* consignari]. Sigilla eciam venerabilis patris domini Rogeri dei gracia Saresbiriensis episcopi et officii discreti viri . . officialis eiusdem ad mei rogatum presentibus sunt appensa. Et nos Rogerus permissione divina Saresbiriensis episcopus et . . officialis predicti sigilla nostra presentibus apposuimus ad predicti commissarii instantiam personalem in testimonium premissorum. Et ego Johannes de Barwe super Humbr' Lincolniensis diocesis clericus dicti patris registrator et notarius iuratus omnibus et singulis supradictis dum coram dicto commissario et per eum agerentur prout supra scribuntur una cum testibus prenominatis interfui eaque sic ut premittitur fieri vidi et audivi ac de mandato predicti commissarii hiis me subscripsi et signum quo utor in officio memorato apposui consuetum.

John de Barwe's reluctance to drop his title and sign is understandable, but he had produced an anomalous and exceptional term, which does not seem to have been common. Others in his position probably acquired papal faculties sooner or later, as John de Barneby did in 1321.[2]

There were formal requirements for the notarial office; but how strictly were they observed? And how much control was

---

[1] Salisbury, Reg. Martival, vol. ii. f. 298ᵛ. The whole *acta* begin on f. 298ʳ with recital of citation, etc., and continue over several more pages in records of contumacy and eventual submission. The *acta* of the second sitting, on 17 April, before the bishop and Mr. Henry de Soppeleya, D.C.L., has Master John's eschatocol in the same form *mutatis mutandis* (f. 299ʳ). I am obliged to Dr. Kathleen Edwards for bringing this case to my notice and to Mrs. D. M. Owen for lending me a microfilm.

[2] See above, p. 86,

exercised by English authorities over these men, who might be entrusted with responsibilities *ubique terrarum*? In England, as abroad, both civil and ecclesiastical powers were concerned at the activities of persons who styled themselves notaries illicitly.[1] But a striking feature of the notarial system (or should one say, lack of system?) is the failure of the authorities to control those they had created. For those notaries public licensed by English bishops, maybe, the fact of creation was easily verifiable: maybe registrars did enter into the episcopal registers the record of every creation and oath taken. For those notaries public who had been directly appointed by papal letters the fact could in the last resort be verified in the papal register, provided (as seems likely) that all faculties were enregistered.[2] But for the notary who was appointed on the faculty of an imperial delegate verification would probably be much harder. What was conspicuously lacking in fourteenth-century England was an official list of the Italian sort, a *matricula* of notaries public, which would have furnished evidence of their titles, handwriting, and signs manual.[3]

On 6 June 1396 Pope Boniface IX addressed a mandate to the archbishops of Canterbury and York, to counteract abuses in the practice of the notariate.[4] This presumably answered a petition from Courtenay and/or Arundel. Nothing, however, seems to have been done about it for a while, for the times were not propitious. Arundel was on the point of leaving York for Canterbury after Courtenay's death; his successor at York, Robert de Waldeby, died in the winter of 1398–9; meanwhile Arundel lost Canterbury and then recovered it. In October 1399 he presided in convocation of Canterbury at St. Paul's, where a proposal was put forward that bishops should cause

---

[1] See above, p. 68.   [2] See above, p. 72.

[3] Cf. the 'Common Paper' of the London scriveners (p. 69 n. 2 above). In fifteenth-century Poland the ecclesiastical authority prepared an official *matricula* of notaries public, which contains the oath and sign of every man admitted. For a facsimile of three entries (1441) see K. Górski, *Wojciech z Żychlina* (Prace Komisji historycznej Poznanskiego Towarzystwa Przyjaciol, Nauk ix, fasc. 1, Poznán, 1936), Pl. 1. And cf. de Boüard, *Manuel,* ii. 216.

[4] The text of the bull is contained in Arundel's mandate (below, p. 93 n. 2), but appears to be otherwise unknown, nor had Arundel's mandate been entered into those contemporary English episcopal registers which I have so far examined. Cf. below, p. 131.

notaries public and *tabelliones* to produce the titles of their creation and that the bishops should enregister the names diocese by diocese. The penalty for non-production of title should be suspension from the notarial office.[1] But this proposal was lost in a great series of *gravamina* put up by the prelates and clergy to the bishops. It bore no fruit immediately. A few years later, Archbishop Arundel acted upon the bull of Boniface IX and wrote (18 February 1402) to the bishop of London for its enforcement in London.[2] He proposed that all practising notaries public should be sent for examination by the archbishop or his staff; the names of those approved would be listed (*matriculata*) in the archiepiscopal register, and the archbishop would send a list of notaries to each diocesan concerned. I do not find that this order extended to the whole province of Canterbury. Arundel's registrar recorded his mandate in the covering letter which the bishop of London sent in reply on 14 April 1402. Bishop Robert Braybrooke reported that his officials had published the mandate at St. Paul's Cross on Sundays and posted it in the porch of the cathedral church, and had cited all notaries on specified days to appear within twenty days before the archbishop or members of his staff, produce their titles, and undergo examination. The bishop declared that after twenty days he would not admit notaries to practise (nor permit them to, so far as lay in his power), unless he had received their names under seal from the archbishop as inscribed in the archiepiscopal register. He annexed to his letter a sheet bearing the names of the notaries known to be practising in his diocese. The archbishop's registrar copied into his register this sheet (which Wilkins did not print when he printed Braybrooke's covering letter).[3] The bishop named thirty-five notaries who had responded to his citation within the city of London, headed by the registrar of the Court of Canterbury and the scribe of the acts of that court. Their credentials, presumably, were taken for granted; but against the other thirty-three the registrar noted 'comp*aruerunt* et exhib*uerunt* sufficient*er*', or simply 'exhib'. Then came the names of three practitioners in the archdeaconry of Essex, five

---

[1] Wilkins, iii. 241 (art. 19).   [2] Ibid. iii. 268–9.
[3] Below, Appendix II, no. 21.

in that of Middlesex, five in that of Colchester; only the Colchester names were annotated: 'exhib*uerunt* suffi*cienter*'. The lists were followed by another list: 'These are the names of those who claim to exercise the office of notary public in our city and diocese, who are of ill fame and bad repute, as we are informed, some of whom have been cited in person, others by general proclamation in the aforesaid places by the said commissaries, officials, and assistants. . . .' Thirteen names follow, five of whom had been cited 'personaliter' and eight 'per edictum'. I find no trace of any action taken by the archbishop against the ill-famed as a group; but it is noteworthy that later in the same year one of these dubious characters, Robert Knyght, was one of two defendants in a suit of breach of faith and perjury. They had been excommunicated by the archbishop for contumacy in not appearing to answer summonses; in October and November he sought writs out of chancery against them *de excommunicato capiendo*.[1] It seems, then, that in the diocese of London in 1402 forty-eight notaries public established their bona fides and thirteen others failed to do so.

We are still left without any evidence of a general check on all the notaries public who practised in both provinces of the English Church. The problem was probably more urgent in London than elsewhere, and at Lambeth and in the Court of Arches archiepiscopal authority could most easily be brought to bear upon it. In general the ill effects that might be expected from the want of systematic supervision were perhaps mitigated by the circumstances in which notaries public were commonly employed. We have seen that there may have been many who might be described as 'freelance' notaries; but many were more or less permanently employed in a department of State or an episcopal office, and even those who had no regular employer must have depended much on the patronage and business brought to them by the bishops. Most of them were well known in courts and chanceries.

[1] Lambeth, Reg. Thomas Arundel, vol. i, f. 418ʳ. John Corsere, summoned 'per edictum' among the ill-famed, may be the John Cossier (notary by papal and imperial authority) who made his notarial sign when he entered his name in the Common Paper of the London Scriveners' Company *c.* 1390 (Jenkinson, *Later Court Hands*, Pl. 1 (i)).

7. Diplomatic

BECAUSE the notary public of the thirteenth century had grown up in a legal climate quite foreign to England, his practices in England tended to differ from those of the Italian-based notary. Even when he was engaged in drawing up public instruments—an activity which did not occupy all his time—engrained English customs stood in the way of exact copying of Italian models. No attempt will be made here to compare in a comprehensive way the notarial diplomatic of the two regions. A few points will be noted to show how the imported style imposed itself on English practice, and to provide materials for comparison with notarial practice in other northern countries.

Memoranda and protocols

The notary public in a southern city, called in to record a private contract or judicial process in public form, began by writing on the spot a rough memorandum of the transaction, with the names of the parties and of others present. Whether he wrote this on a scrap of paper or entered it in a notebook was immaterial. He then went away and might put off until another day the composition of the definite record, dressed up with the appropriate legal formulas, the titles of the persons involved, and the full date (of the original transaction). He might at this stage introduce many details not in his note for which he trusted to his memory; he might even record in direct speech words spoken by the parties. This document was entered into a comparatively tidy register or cartulary of the notary's acts, and in course of time it became normal for such books to be deposited as authentic records in public custody. Both the record and—by a natural transference—the register were described by the word *protocollum*. The next stage in the notarial procedure was, in one sense, unnecessary for the completion of the transaction. But it was usual. An interested party

commonly called upon the notary public to prepare an engrossment on the basis of his *protocollum*, and received (in return for
payment) a document on parchment dressed up with invocation, date in the most elaborate form, and a subscription-
clause or eschatocol in the notary's own hand accompanied
by his special sign manual. One may contrast this with the
procedure used by the petitioner in the papal Curia, whereby
he obtained letters of grace or of justice from the papal
Chancery : here it was the engrossment that mattered, whereas
the entry in the papal register (commonly abridged, whether
from the draft or the engrossment) formed no essential part
of the proceeding, but merely additional insurance. The notarial
procedure resembled more closely the modern system of
registering births, deaths, and marriages in this country : here
the official register is the authentic original; interested parties
may buy, if they so choose, certified copies. At the same time,
if notarial instruments are to be critically handled, it is important, as we shall see, to remember what a transmogrification
the original record may have undergone before it took on the
final public form. Durandus warns us to expect change : 'While
the notary sets down briefly a form of contract in the protocol
or minute, he (or the notary who succeeds him in the task) can
afterwards amplify the wording in the public instrument, can
add and change and put in everything useful for the contract,
provided however that the form and substance of the contract
are not changed.'[1]

Early in the thirteenth century and after, a notary public
appointed by apostolic or imperial authority inherited the
tradition of the older notaries who had more closely circum-
scribed powers. The oath which was required of a notary
public when created by apostolic authority makes this clear.
He must swear : 'I will draw up contracts in the form of a protocol (*in protocollum*) and, having drawn one up in a protocol,
I will not maliciously delay to make a public instrument from
it, contrary to the wish of the persons or person concerned,

---

[1] Durandus, *Speculum*, lib. II, partic. ii § 9 (p. 312*a*): 'Licet notarius in protocollo seu abbreviatura ponat sub compendio formam contractus, ipse tamen,
vel is, qui in hoc sibi succedit, potest postea in publico instrumento verba
ampliare, addere, et mutare, et omnia ibi ponere, quae ad contractum sunt utilia,
servata tamen forma ipsius contractus, et substantia non mutata.'

saving my just and customary fee.'[1] In the land where this oath was framed, the protocol was highly important. It was the record which, so to speak, put the seal on the notarial act. It reduced the public instrument, copied from it by or for a notary and confirmed with his sign manual for the benefit of the party, to the position of a secondary document.[2] Thus, when in the 1250s the case between the archbishop of Canterbury and the chapter of Lincoln came before a judge in the Roman Curia at Viterbo, the notary public, Bernardus de Insula Romanus, wrote down the proceedings and then caused them to be transcribed, and, with the help of another notary, made careful collation and correction of the copy 'cum originalibus'.[3]

Casual references show that the English notary public adopted the general procedure and some of the nomenclature used in the south. But because of the different legal traditions of north and south the Italian notarial system of archive-keeping never took firm root in England. Medieval English records refer, as will be seen, to the *protocollum* in a variety of senses, meaning a document which lay behind a signed public instrument: either the original minute or the elaborated draft, whether on a single sheet or in a book. But in England the protocol, useful though it was, did not have the status which it enjoyed in the south. Notaries' minutes, systematically if roughly jotted down in a register 'demeurèrent', to quote de Boüard, 'sans cesse l'article essentiel de la pratique notariale en pays de droit écrit'. Did England resemble in this respect the Mediterranean countries? Was the original minute or the more formal notarial register—the *protocollum* or *cartularium*—regarded generally as an object to be kept for ever?[4]

[1] Above, p. 52, and below, Appendix II, no. 3.

[2] Doehaerd, comparing the Genoese contract in minute and engrossment, observes: 'Sur le plan juridique, cette différence peut s'exprimer comme suit: la minute possède la qualité intrinseque d'être *authentique* par excellence, la grosse possède la qualité extrinsèque d'être *exécutoire*. La première jouit d'une valeur probante complète . . ., seul l'écrit habillé de formalisme vaut en justice' (*Relations commerciales*, i. 31–2).

[3] Above, p. 18.

[4] De Boüard, *Manuel*, ii. 174–81, 205–12. Archbishop Winchelsey's statutes for the Court of Arches (1295) show the first three stages in preparing the *acta*. First, the clerk of the register made a minute, then a *protocollum*, in *schedula*, and finally entered the *acta* in the register, after checking doubtful points with the judge (Wilkins, ii. 208*b*). Cf. below, p. 126.

To arrive at an answer to the question we may examine examples of the use of the word *protocollum*, and some other evidence in English ecclesiastical records. To begin with, in 1283 Edmund de Verduno refused to draw up public instruments for the monks of Durham on the basis of a roll of proceedings in the court of Rome which had been sent home in unauthenticated copies; and he gave his reason: 'pro eo quod protocolla eorum non habebat in publica forma redigere non curavit.'[1] He had good canonistic authority for his intransigence. Chapter I of the title 'De fide instrumentorum' in *Extra* (2. 22. 1) reads: 'Si scripturam authenticam non videmus, ad exemplaria nihil facere possumus.' Notaries were generally careful to insist upon the authenticity of the original record they copied. Thus, when Andrew de Tange prepared a public instrument about legal proceedings of the prior and convent of Durham in 1300, he declared that 'ea inveni cum protocollo in omnibus et per omnia concordare'.[2] Again, on 13 May 1309 Rogerus Roberti Bartholomei de Geytingtone recorded notarially an appeal and the appointment of a proctor by the bishop of Lincoln in a dispute with the abbot of Barlings. The eschatocol of the surviving instrument ends: '[acta] manu mea propria fideliter scripsi, hic inserui, et in hanc publicam scripturam et formam redegi, meoque signo solito signavi rogatus'. After a space, at the foot of the sheet, the notary has written: 'facta est collatio'.[3]

The word *nota* for the original minute, which was common in the south, does not seem to have been much used in England. When Edward II, sitting in the green room at Westminster on 25 November 1313, made a declaration about the transference of the Templars' confiscated lands to the Hospitallers, he called on a southern notary, John Durand, clerk of the diocese of Albi, to record it. John's eschatocol records that 'hoc presens publicum instrumentum in nota recepi manuque mea propria in hanc formam publicam redegi'.[4]

---

[1] Brentano, *York Met. Jurisdiction*, p. 216.

[2] *Records of Antony Bek*, p. 204. Cf. below, pp. 126–8.

[3] Lincoln, D. & C. Archives, D ij/62/1/10.

[4] P.R.O., E 30/1368, printed in Rymer, II. i. 235. A related document by the same hand is in E 135/1/25. They were, as the endorsements read, enrolled at the Exchequer among the records of Hilary Term of the seventh year. Luschek pro-

There are signs that, at least in the early days of notaries in England, some of those employed by bishops to draft public instruments might retain their protocols. Archbishop John Pecham's registrar referred to *acta* concerning the confirmation of the dean of Exeter which were to be found 'in registro Johannis de Beskles publici notarii'.[1] John Alani de Beccles had been in Italy, and perhaps entertained the idea of keeping a special register of his notarial acts; but if so, neither it nor any successor has survived in the archbishops' muniments at Lambeth. In 1295 the bishop of Lincoln ordered two notaries public who were of his household to record in *protocolla* the admission by a rector that he held two churches in plurality.[2] A few years later the archbishop of York's registrar noted that a certain rector's presence in the archbishop's company on a certain day was proved 'testificante Ricardo de Clifton', notario publico, per protocolla sua penes ipsum residencia, in quibus dictum Rogerum testem nominatum invenit'.[3] In 1305 letters of proxy were prepared *manu publica*, 'prout in prothocollo penes J. de Malmesburia remanente plenius apparet'. This note was made by the bishop of Winchester's registrar, and John reappears in the bishop's service in 1307 as 'Johannes Johannis de Gunelode de Malmesburia Saresb. dioc. publicus imperiali auctoritate et nunc venerabilis patris Henrici dei gracia Wintoniensis episcopi notarius et iudex ordinarius'.[4] Later, in Archbishop William Courtenay's time, the 'prothogollum' of letters of institution and induction could be nothing more than a minute of the proceedings, endorsed on the letter of presentation.[5]

If notaries public who were employed by bishops and ecclesiastical corporations commonly retained *protocolla* of the public instruments (or other documents) which they drafted

duces comparable examples of the use of *nota*: 'in notam recepi et deinde rogatus et requisitus presens publicum instrumentum confeci'; 'ad notam statim recepi'; 'per alium clericum et notarium . . ., notula tamen per me concepta' (*Notariatsurkunde*, pp. 51, 53).

[1] *Reg. Pecham*, i. 118. [2] *Reg. Sutton*, v. 110.

[3] *Reg. Corbridge*, i. 299–300 (1302).

[4] *Reg. Woodlock*, i. 42–3, 169–70. In 1303 Thomas de Seleby, employed by the monks of Durham in the Curia, described himself as 'publicus imperiali auctoritate notarius et iudex ordinarius' (Durham, D. & C. Mun., 2. 8 Pont. 1. iv and v).

[5] Churchill, *CA*, i. 23 n. 7.

for their masters, the fact may account for their disappearance. Records of many transactions would not survive in official custody just because they were for the time being preserved in notarial protocols. The boundary between private and official in the matter of records is proverbially vague; in this instance it was probably as often blurred as the doubtful distinction, already noted, between permanent and part-time civil servants. On the other hand, registers of notarial business, supposing them to have been compiled by individual notaries, never acquired any special status. Because the notary public was not indigenous, the English Church authorities relied on other types of record which they had built up during the thirteenth century, just as the departments of State had their chancery rolls, plea rolls, feet of fines, and formularies.

Before 1279, when Archbishop John Pecham brought notaries public into his household, the practice had already developed in at least six English dioceses of keeping official, roughly contemporaneous, registers of the bishops' *acta*. The archbishop of Canterbury followed suit.[1] The English bishop's register, if not unique in medieval Europe, was a highly exceptional archival development. It served both as a record of current business and as a formulary. The latter function is seen by the index which the archbishop of York's registrar made to 172 common forms in his register: 'Kalendarium registri . . . de omnibus formis litterarum cursoriarum contentarum in eo.'[2] Together with *matriculae* (like the French *pouillés*) and some other categories of record, it provided administrators with a rich assortment.

Perhaps notaries habitually kept personal registers of their compositions, and not for one employer only. Reference has been made to the miscellaneous formularies and letter-books of William Doune and Gilbert Stone and John Stevens. But the bishop's registrar or scribe (who was often a notary public) lumped together in the episcopal register notarial instruments

---

[1] It is often said that Archbishop Robert Kilwardby carried off to Rome in 1278 an episcopal register of the usual English sort; but the evidence is far from conclusive.

[2] *Reg. Romeyn*, ii. 179–90, cf. i. 240–2. Miss Reynolds, editing *Reg. Martival*, vol. ii, remarks: 'To a considerable extent the register was kept to serve as a formulary' (p. v).

and other *acta* and memoranda and correspondence. The memorandum by Bishop Oliver Sutton's registrar, cited above, to the effect that the bishop's notaries had prepared protocols, itself had the character of an official, authentic, record, and no more was needed. For this reason, when exemplifications *sub manu publica* were copied into an episcopal register, the notarial eschatocol did not need to be copied.[1] Some registrars might append it, just as some registrars who were themselves notaries adorned the registers with their signs and signatures.[2] But *protocolla*, whether in the form of loose minutes or quires, were likely to be soon discarded. The registrar might just record them in their first rudimentary form, with the notary's signature, if not his sign. The original *nota* or minute of the transaction would then not need to be kept, and our best hope of finding examples is (as in the case of original petitions to the pope) among the book-binders' waste of the Middle Ages. At the back of Register II of Bishop Roger Martival of Salisbury is a seven-line rough note on a narrow strip of parchment which seems to be a notarial minute : it may have been removed with adjacent pieces from an early binding of the register. It records a receipt for the proceeds from Brimpton vicarage during a vacancy, paid to the bishop in his chapel at London in 1324.[3]

A comparable piece is a small and dirty sheet of parchment in the archives of Hereford Cathedral.[4] The face bears an incomplete, undated form of appeal *a gravamine* to the apostolic see and for tuition to the Court of Canterbury, in the name of John ap Harry of the diocese of Hereford, 'coram vobis autentica persona et testibus hic presentibus'. It is roughly written, with a few mis-spellings and interlinings. On the dorse, in another hand, is the notary's minute :

Lata et lecta ista infrascripta provocacio xxi die mensis Augusti anno domini m⁰ ccc^mo nonagesimo octavo, indiccione sexta, pontificatus Bonifacii divina providencia pape noni anno nono, in hospicio sive domo habitacionis cuiusdam Walteri Clerk' de Fowechurche [Vowchurch] Herefordensis diocesis, presentibus

---

[1] Cf. above, pp. 38, 50, below, pp. 138–9.
[2] e.g. *Reg. Sutton*, ii. 159–62.   [3] Below, Appendix II, no. 15.
[4] Hereford, D. & C. Archives, no. 2693, measuring *c.* 24 × 9 cm.

discretis viris domino Stephano ap Howel presbitero Menevensis diocesis et Waltero Clerk' literato Herefordensis (diocesis *interlined*), et aliis testibus, ac me Ricardo Wheelar' notario publico.

A note below is marked for insertion at some point unspecified: 'apud quandam crucem altam prope civitatem Herefordensem situatam in parte boriali que vulgariter nuncupatur Ayleston' Croyse'. The document is evidently the draft of an appeal, perhaps partly prepared by the hand of the literate Walter Clerk and further annotated by Richard Wheeler or le Whylare. He is known as a notary by apostolic authority, of Worcester diocese, active in Hereford between 1385 and 1399.[1] On the basis of the information put together on this sheet it would be possible to prepare a formal instrument at the request of John ap Harry.

The completed instrument

The completed instruments drawn up by English notaries show the same external features as many of those prepared on the Continent in the same period. That is to say, they show a wide variety of shapes and sizes and handwritings. Most of them differ from the usual English episcopal *acta* and private deeds in being longer than they are broad, and many are nearly square. The preference for length was justified by the notary's desire to display his *signum consuetum* to best advantage. It is not unusual for the sign to be 8, 10, or even 15 cm high,[2] and it is generally taller than it is broad. A tall format also encouraged the lengthening of the initial 'I'. On one of John de Cadomo's Great Rolls (E 39/15/2) the 'I' of 'In' is 30 cm high. Notaries public were particularly employed in recording legal processes, often long-protracted. When an instrument exceeded the limits of a single sheet (and a single sheet could be as much as 68 cm square)[3] membranes were sewn end to end to form a con-

---

[1] Emanuel, 'Notaries public', p. 15. Richard acted as proctor of John Prophet, when the latter was a prebendary of Hereford, in 1397 (*Reg. Trefnant*, p. 139).

[2] Two signs 18 cm tall are those of Andrew de Tange (1291) in P.R.O., E 39/16/13 and of William de Syreston (1311) in York Sede Vacante Roll (Purvis, Pl. 1).

[3] This is the size of the instrument of divorce of Joan from Earl William of Salisbury in 1349 (P.R.O., E 30/67). This was probably executed in the Curia, although English notaries were present with others.

tinuous roll, and the notary normally repeated his sign across each seam for greater security. In this period English notaries do not appear to have used the quire or book-form for lengthy instruments.

Attention has already been called to the way in which many English notaries public followed continental usage in stating their patronymic, and to the probability that many had been educated abroad.[1] Not surprisingly, in a few cases (though they *are* comparatively few) during the first decades of notarial activity a continental training was reflected in calligraphic peculiarities. To take John Erturi de Cadomo: both the general style of script and his use of un-English forms of abbreviation make it likely that he had spent some of his formative years in the south.[2] The hand of John Alani de Beccles is distinctly unusual for an Englishman of this period.[3] Andrew quondam Guilielmi de Tange[4] and Adam filius Ade de Swayny[5] have highly idiosyncratic hands, which may owe something to Italian influence. With Helias de Coutona, commissioned in the Curia in 1291, the influence is more definite.[6] Thomas de Seleby, who practised in the Curia, developed a beautiful writing which clearly was modelled on that of the papal Chancery.[7] As late as 1343 an act by Thomas Hamund de Asshewell has a distinctly Italian air.[8] These early notaries (and some others) borrow the southern fashion of *elongata* for the invocation, and occasionally use it for 'Et ego'.[9] Adam de Swayny writes 'ET ⋮ EGO ⋮ ADAM ⋮'.[10] Likewise, elaborate decoration of the initial 'I' in the invocation, far beyond the embellishments on normal English charters, is so common as

[1] Above, pp. 28–9, 76.
[2] Dr. Pierre Chaplais called my attention to his habit of abbreviating 'auctoritate' to 'auctoītate'. Cf. Pl. 5.
[3] See Pl. 2: he writes 'Ricřo' for 'Ricardo'. In Canterbury, D. & C. Archives, Chartae antiquae A. 208 he writes 'Robřo' for 'Roberto'.
[4] A fine example is Pl. 4. See also his rolls of the 'Great Cause' of Scotland (above, p. 62), and Durham, D. & C. Mun., 1. 14. Pont. 14.
[5] e.g. P.R.O., SC 7/64/22, SC 7/36/3.
[6] See an example of 1300 in Durham, D. & C. Mun., 1. 9. Pont. 2.
[7] A fine example is Durham, D. & C. Mun., 2. 8. Pont. 1. v.
[8] Westminster Abbey, Mun. 32652.
[9] e.g. Richard de Brenchley in Westminster Abbey, Mun. 5415, and Robert of Wisbech in P.R.O., SC 7/36/7. For an Italian example see Appendix II, no. 11.
[10] Above, n. 5, and Purvis, *Notarial Signs*, Pl. 2.

to be the rule.[1] All in all, the physical appearance of these early
notarial documents puts beyond question the debt of England
to the Continent in the development of this sort of instrument.[2] Its singularity is emphasized by the fact that several
scribes display a 'private' hand which differs from their 'public'
hand, as witness receipts given by Andrew de Tange to the
bursar of Durham, and notes written at the foot of royal writs
by John de Cadomo.[3] But we do not have to rely on the
evidence of foreign features in the physical appearance of the
original notarial instrument. Its internal features, also preserved
in copies, display its exotic character.

Formulas

The formulas used by English notaries for framing instruments followed various patterns. To some extent form varied,
naturally enough, according to the kind of business; and pre-
vious chapters have illustrated the main sorts of instrument
cast in notarial form in England. The majority were transcripts
(*transcripta, transsumpta, exempla*) of all manner of title-deed
and judicial act. But also were included records of admissions
to office, resignations of benefices, procuratorial instruments,
instruments to record citations and judicial appeals, recognizances and quittances of debt, even a certificate of birth.[4]
Compared with Italian notarial instruments, the English contain
few contracts and records of debt (and most of those involve
at least one ecclesiastical party); wills were comparatively
rarely put into public form.[5] It would be fair to say that in

---

[1] e.g. William le Dorturer in Westminster Abbey, Mun. 12732. The initials
of John de Cadomo's two rolls of the Great Cause are respectively ten and twelve
inches high (P.R.O., E 39/15/1 and 2).

[2] Foreign influences on the diction and handwriting of English clerks (noted
by C. Johnson and H. Jenkinson, *English Court Hand 1066–1500* (Oxford, 1915),
part I, p. xviii) were not of course confined to notarial instruments or the
writings of notaries public.

[3] Durham, D. & C. Mun., Misc. ch. 4136g and 3456; P.R.O., C 81/15/1390
and C 81/16/1465.

[4] A small selection is in Appendix II below.

[5] A Spanish knight gave Edward I quittance for wages by an instrument
drawn up by Andrew de Tange at Carlisle, 20 March 1307 (below, Appendix II,
no. 14). The great collection of wills in *Reg. Chichele*, vol. ii, includes only seven
notarialized wills (three of them being wills of bishops), and four of the seven
bore seals.

England all of these notarial acts could be matched by non notarial examples, and that in some the objective and subjective elements are joined. It should be added that this diversity of usage is found also in other northern lands, where seals and signs were used alternately or conjointly.

Turning to the purely formal aspect of the notarial act, we find at once two main forms. The notary may produce an objective form, that is, he issues the document which he has prepared in his own name, and usually signals the fact very early in the document by the statement: 'in presentia mei notarii subscripti'. Or else he adopts the subjective form in which an individual or group or corporation announces that the making of the present instrument has been entrusted to a notary. In both forms the completion of the instrument lies in the notary's eschatocol, written in the first person (of which more will be said shortly); in both forms this type of authentication may be supplemented by a seal or seals.[1]

Despite the co-existence of these two forms and of the sealed and the unsealed instrument, it may be useful to generalize briefly on the formal pattern of English notarial instruments. This is subject to the provisos that the rules were flexible, that not all clauses were indispensable, and that facts inserted at one point in some instruments appear elsewhere in others.

The nearly invariable opening is an invocation: 'In dei nomine, *or* In nomine domini, amen.'[2] This, with its conspicuous initial and occasional use of *elongata*, marks out the notarial record from most other English deeds of the period. For an invocation was less common in England than abroad.[3] (The only non-notarial document which commonly begins

---

[1] For northern France see de Boüard, *Manuel*, ii. 263. Over two-thirds of the Polish notarial instruments seen by Mikucki bore seals ('Essai', p. 341). The same is found in Silesia (Luschek, *Notariatsurkunde*, pp. 239–91, cf. 44–5). Cf. below, pp. 112–15.

[2] Note the *gaffe* which John de Beccles committed in writing 'In dei nomine domini amen' (Pl. 2). When he prepared the exemplification of Norwich title-deeds, which he drew up as a subjective act of the archbishop, he used a form of invocation seldom used by English notaries: 'In nomine patris et filii et spiritus sancti amen' (Appendix II, no. 7).

[3] Not that the invocation was entirely unknown in English private deeds of the twelfth and thirteenth centuries: e.g. Madox, *Formulare*, pp. 49, 248, 250, 275, 276 (nos. lxxxix, ccccxviii, ccccxxii, cccclxii, cccclxiv).

thus is the last will and testament, seldom notarialized in England.) Even so, a notary might discard the invocation without breaking the rules.[1] The purely objective instrument then normally proceeds to state the date of the acts or words which the notary is recording. The date should give the year of the Lord, day and month, the indiction and the year of the reigning pope. The date includes the place where the business is done, unless this is reserved for an 'Actum (et datum)' clause at the end of the text. Then follows the statement that the business is done in the presence of the notary (who does not normally give his full name at this stage) and of witnesses whose names will be particularized later on in the record. This leads to the statement of the transaction or the rehearsal of the document to be exemplified. The text normally concluded with an 'Actum (et datum)' clause. This gives the place-date, if not previously stated, and refers to the preamble for the time-date ('Acta fuerunt hec apud Westmonasterium in camera viridi dicti domini regis anno, die, mense, indictione, et pontificatu predictis').[2] The witnesses are now named for the first time, usually with the indication that they were 'ad premissa vocati specialiter et rogati' or the like.[3] It emphasizes the fact that deliberate publicity was of the essence of the notary's act: there must be nothing casual or unpremeditated about the presence or choice of witnesses. The notary adds details to show that they are respectable and suitable.

Whatever the substance of the instrument, it is completed by the notary's own authenticating clause, which is the only part of the document which he must write himself. This eschatocol, accompanied by the notary's sign, is essential to the validity of an unsealed instrument. It begins 'Et ego' or

---

[1] This is noticeable in instruments which adopt the opening of letters patent; cf. John de Bononia's form, quoted below, p. 111.

[2] Rymer, II. i. 235.

[3] Below, Appendix II, no. 16; cf. nos. 11, 12, 18–20. In no. 10 the witnesses, being in the presence of the archbishop, are described as 'testibus nominatis', which must amount to the same thing. In no. 13 the phrase is omitted. No. 12 introduces the names of witnesses for the first time in the eschatocol ('ad hoc rogatis'). The special summoning of witnesses is sometimes mentioned at the beginning of the instrument, e.g. 'coram me notario publico infrascripto ac testibus subscriptis ad hoc specialiter vocatis et rogatis': Adam de Swayny at St. Paul's, London, 20 Oct. 1289 (Westminster Abbey, Mun. 22932).

'Ego', and gives the man's christian name, patronymic, and/or nickname. We have already seen (p. 28) that English notaries often follow the Italian habit in describing their parentage. Commonly—but not always in the early days—the notary states his clerical status and diocese (above, pp. 87–9). Then comes the indication of the apostolic or imperial authority which allows him to practise 'ubique locorum'. He then explicitly confirms that he was present at the business in hand, saw and heard it, wrote it and published it. If the copying of documents was involved, he says that he has carefully collated and corrected the copies with the help of named collaborators (more will be said of this below). The notary concludes by saying that being asked ('rogatus' or 'rogatus et requisitus'), he has written or caused to be written this instrument in public form and has signed it with his customary sign.

The eschatocol or *subscriptio* is susceptible to many modifications and amplifications, and a single notary does not stick slavishly to a single form or words. In a simple exemplification the date may appear in the eschatocol instead of the beginning of the instrument. The concluding participle 'rogatus' is almost invariable, for this is the formal indication that the notary is a *persona publica*, authorized to prepare the instrument on demand. In the earliest case where its absence has been noted, the instrument prepared at Leominster by John de Beccles in December 1282, the notary had already named the demandant clearly as the archbishop of Canterbury: 'mandavit michi notario ut super huiusmodi exhibicione et recepcione publicum conficerem instrumentum'.[1] It appears in exemplifications of papal bulls made for the Crown in 1305[2] and it is very common to find the notary, in his eschatocol, enlarging upon the demand which has been made of him. This is often found in instruments of both the objective and subjective sorts, and may occur in instruments which are sealed or unsealed. The following phrases may be cited as random samples. 'De mandato dicti abbatis ac ad preces magistri milicie Templi' (1268);[3] 'peticione dictorum . . . prioris, procuratoris, ac

---

[1] Below, Appendix II, no. 10.
[2] Below, Appendix II, no. 9.
[3] *Reg. Sutton*, i. 80, issued in the name of the abbot, with his seal.

testium' (1281);[1] 'ad mandatum prefati magistri Laurencii et
requisicionem domini Willelmi de Craneford' (1303);[2] 'de
dictorum iudicum mandato' (1308);[3] 'a prefato fratre Waltero
de Woxebrugg' ut predicitur procuratore specialiter rogatus'
(1334);[4] 'de mandato et auctoritate dicti domini officialis [Curie
Cantuariensis]' (1344).[5] The fact remains that the simpler formulas, 'rogatus' and 'rogatus et requisitus', prevailed.[6]

The signum

The *signum* is the most eye-catching mark of an original
notarial instrument; but no attempt will be made here to
comment on the various devices.[7] In the fourteenth century it
became common to use, besides the *signum*, an inconspicuous
paraph at the end of the eschatocol, and the paraph sometimes
serves as the sole mark of a notary's activity in a bishop's
register.[8] Conforming with continental practice the English
notary generally made his mark on the left side of the document
and wrote his eschatocol beside it. Some, however, departed from the rule. John Alani de Beccles put his sign on the
right hand of his eschatocol.[9] When two notaries in Durham
certified the same document in 1316, the first to subscribe,
Nicholas de Stayndropp, put his tall sign on the left, while his

---

[1] Canterbury, D. & C. Archives, Chartae antiquae N. 24, issued in the name
of the archbishop of Canterbury and unsealed. Cf. above, p. 35 n 1.

[2] Ibid., A. 219, issued in the name of the notary and sealed by the dean of
Storrington.

[3] Westminster Abbey, Mun. 9496, issued in the notary's name, unsealed.

[4] Ibid., 21259, issued in the notary's name, unsealed.

[5] Lincoln, D. & C. Archives, D ij/62/1/15, issued in the notary's name, with
the official's seal, recorded in a corroboration clause after the eschatocol.

[6] Often followed by some such phrase as 'in fidem et testimonium premissorum'.

[7] Thirty-six signs, mostly English, are assembled with a useful introduction
which discusses their design, by Emanuel, 'Notaries public'. Purvis, *Notarial Signs*,
reproduces 100 signs, ranging from 1304 to 1723. Bishop Browne included in
Echt-Forbes Charters an account of Scottish notaries, illustrated by 55 signs,
a dozen of them English. Freshfield and Jenkinson illustrate notarial signs of
London scriveners.

[8] Above, p. 43.

[9] Pl. 2. The foreigner, John de S. Dimitrio, put his sign on the right, and put
another device over the invocation of his documents (below, Appendix II,
no. 8). Italian notaries sometimes put their signs before the invocation, e.g.
Salatiele, son of Martin Papa, in 1244 (Salatiele, *Ars Notarie*, vol. i, tav. 1. Cf.
ibid., vol. ii, p. 15 : 'vel in principio vel in fine').

companion, Robert Ade de Derlington, saved space by putting his sign on the right.[1] Occasionally a notary drew his sign after he had written the eschatocol, beneath it, or drew the sign in the middle, below the text of his instrument, and wrote his eschatocol round it.[2]

Multiple subscriptions and signs are not very common, and it is not easy to see the reasons for their occurrence. In some cases a solemn occasion may have caused a second notary who was present to add a separate eschatocol after the notary responsible for the drafting and writing of the instrument had written his. This might explain why John Erturi de Cadomo subscribed the narrative of proceedings of the king in parliament on 5 April 1305 over the provision of the bishop of Byblos to the priorate of Coldingham.[3] The document had been drawn up by John dictus Bouhs; but we are left without explanation why Gilbert de Lutegareshale, the third notary present, did not subscribe in the same way. Maybe the sheet of parchment was not big enough, and Gilbert was the junior of the trio. Other instances of multiple subscriptions occur in ecclesiastical records produced in the northern province during the fourteenth century. They are mostly of a judicial character and are produced at times when official business had congregated in court a group of notaries. Once at York as many as six wrote their eschatocols and made their marks on the roll of *acta* of a process.[4] At York it was common for notaries to set their *signa* in the archiepiscopal register and here, too, cases occur of multiple subscription.[5] The canonist Durandus noted one occasion for the practice. It was proper,

[1] Durham, D. & C. Mun., Locellus XIII, no. 1.

[2] York, Borthwick Institute, Diocesan Records, R vii. E. 2a, b, and d: Robert de Elmuswell (Purvis, Pl. 3).

[3] Pl. 5. Printed in Rymer, I. ii. 969–70, *Rot. Parl.*, i. 178, and *Memoranda de Parliamento*, ed. F. W. Maitland (RS, 1893), p. 300, from P.R.O., SC 9/12, a copy of the instrument. Cf. below, pp. 113, 128, 147. The original instrument is P.R.O., E 39/2/47.

[4] York, Borthwick Institute, Diocesan Records, R vii. E. 7 (Purvis, Pl. 10). An instrument of Archbishop Simon Islip of Canterbury, 6 Oct. 1361, preserved in triplicate (P.R.O., E 30/180, 185, 1497, printed in Rymer, III. ii. 626–7) has three notarial signs and eschatocols, although none of the subscribing notaries wrote the text of the documents. For the 'Mitnotar' in Breslau, see Luschek p. 46.

[5] See Purvis, Pl. 18 (two), 21 (two), 34 (three), 46 (two).

he said, for two or three other notaries to subscribe and sign
the exemplification of a notarial instrument, if you wished to
add an air of solemnity.[1]

Substitute notaries

The notary whose eschatocol and sign authenticated the final
public instrument might not be the person who prepared the
original *nota* or minute; or he might have prepared the original
and left to another scribe the task of writing out the final
instrument, except for the eschatocol which must be the
notary's holograph. As regards the former practice, the canon
law allowed that, under proper safeguards, the *nota* of a deceased
notary might be put into public form by another hand.[2] More
often a notary public subscribed an instrument, presumably
based on his notes (since he always claims to be present at the
business), of which the text had been written by another,
anonymous scribe. Perhaps these occasions became commoner
in the later Middle Ages and point to some advance in the
status of notaries public. An example of 18 December 1397
from St. Paul's Cathedral shows a common form of eschatocol
for such cases:

Et Ego Thomas Cottyngwyth' clericus Eboracensis publicus
auctoritate apostolica notarius premissis omnibus et singulis dum
sic ut premittitur agebantur et fierent [*sic*] sub anno, indiccione,
pontificatu, mense, die, et loco predictis una cum prenominatis
testibus presens interfui eaque omnia et singula sic fieri vidi et
audivi, aliis arduis negociis multipliciter occupatus, per alium
scribi feci, publicavi, et in hanc publicam formam redegi, signoque
et nomine meis consuetis signavi in fidem et testimonium omnium
premissorum rogatus specialiter et requisitus.[3]

The main features, external and internal, of the English
notarial instrument have been outlined. It may be well, however, to say a little more about variations of practice and about

---

[1] Durandus, *Speculum*, lib. II, partic. ii § 4 (p. 287*b*): 'Si autem velis aliquid
amplius solennitatis adiicere, poteris . . . omnibus autem conscriptis, et etiam
nomine notarii originalis, praeter signum eius, quod nullo modo scribere
teneris, adiunge tibi duos vel tres tabelliones cum quibus diligenter auscultatis
ipsum exemplum cum authentico; et si inventum fuerit concordare, unusque
illorum posito suo signo se subscribat, hoc modo . . .'

[2] *Extra*, 2. 22. 15.

[3] St. Paul's Cathedral, D. & C. Mun., A/75/1973.

particular types of instrument before discussing matters of dating, accuracy, and fraud.

Hybrid forms

Among the earliest surviving records of foreign notaries in England we have noted hybrid forms, in which Italian features were combined with English and seals added to signs manual. Variety of form continues to characterize English notarial acts even when they become more common; and this is hardly surprising when one observes the lack of uniformity even in Italian examples. Certainly John de Bononia thought it necessary to provide for the instruction of English clerks a choice of exemplars. He offered an alternative for most of the official acts which a bishop's clerk was called upon to draft. For letters of proxy *ad causas* there are several forms.[1] One begins with the customary invocation: 'In nomine domini amen. Anno domini a nativitate eiusdem etc. reverendus pater dominus J. dei gracia Cantuariensis archyepiscopus tocius Anglie primas in presencia mei notarii et testium subscriptorum fecit, constituit, et ordinavit . . . Actum in tali loco presentibus talibus . . .'; presumably the eschatocol ('Et ego . . .') followed. Another form omits both invocation and date at the beginning. Instead, it opens: 'Universis presens instrumentum publicum inspecturis pateat manifeste quod reverendus pater . . . tenore presencium fecit . . .'. The notary appears (in the first person) only in the last clause of the text: 'promisit mihi notario . . . iudicio sisti . . .'. A corroboration clause follows, recording the attachment of the archbishop's seal. Then comes: 'Actum in tali loco, presentibus talibus testibus anno domini etc.' and the eschatol ('Et ego . . .') written by the notary. Both these forms are drafted *manu publica*; but John de Bononia provided a third proxy drafted *manu privata* with a seal, in the traditional form of letters patent of the archbishop with general address, concluding with a corroboration clause which mentions the seal, and the date introduced by the word 'Datum', not 'Actum'. These may be regarded as typical of the variety found in English practice. Proxies of all three sorts might be cited from the records, sometimes a single proxy in two forms.

[1] *Summa,* pp. 611, 612, 614, cf. 651.

Sealing

The appending of a seal to one of the notarial forms of proxy
is significant. If any action in the civil court was envisaged, an
authentic seal would be desirable. In the court christian either
form of authentication was admitted; and a document from
York of the year 1338 shows that a seal was at least as
acceptable as a sign on the return to a citation. The official of
the Court of York had sent a mandate to Master Hugh de
Corbrig', notary public, to cite Master John de Hirlawe,
defendant in a case in the court; he required a return 'per
vestras patentes litteras harum seriem continentes, sigillo
autentico aut signo vestro publico communitas'. Hugh sent his
return, reciting the mandate and reporting the citation; he concluded: 'In cuius rei testimonium, quia sigillum auctenticum
ad presens habere non potui, signum meum consuetum apposui.
Dat' apud Novum Castrum super Tynam, x^{mo} kalendas Decembris anno domini supradicto.' He set his sign immediately
below, but naturally wrote no eschatocol.[1]

Many of the judicial records for the court christian carried
both sign and seal. A document relating to the case just cited
is a commission and summons from Master John de Hirlawe
(who was commissary of the bishop of Durham's vicar-general),
under the hand of the same notary. John's seal is added to
Hugh's sign.[2] At Exeter in 1284, the office of subdean was
endowed by agreement of the bishop and the dean and chapter.
The foundation deed was recorded *manu publica* with all notarial
formality. But the notary's eschatocol continues after the usual
closing words, 'meoque singno consueto singnavi rogatus',
with an extra clause: 'Ad maiorem autem cautelam et evi-
denciam pleniorem, sigilla domini Exoniensis episcopi et
Exoniensis ecclesie capituli sepius nominatorum superius huic
instrumento publico sunt appensa.'[3] When in 1346 a new

[1] York, Borthwick Institute, Diocesan Records, R vii. E. 35. For the sign see
Purvis, Pl. 19. Purvis supposed that the notary meant that he could not then have
a seal of his own (p. vii); but the emphasis was on 'sigillum authenticum'.
A notary might have a personal seal (cf. below, Appendix II, nos. 22, 23) but
probably not a seal of office which would count as authentic.

[2] Ibid., R vii. E. 35.

[3] *Reg. Bronescombe*, pp. 324–5. The same Bartholomew de S. Laurencio, notary
by apostolic and imperial authority, drew up in public form, a few months

Master was elected and admitted to St. Mark's Hospital, Bristol, a whole dossier of documents was needed. Most of them were authenticated simply by a notary public, John de Chaill; but the final election decree, containing a digest of the proceedings, though prepared and signed by the same notary, received the seal of the dean of Bristol.[1] A few years earlier, in the diocese of Chichester, the bishop's official recorded by the hand of John de Amberley, notary public, his decision in a dispute between the rector of St. Thomas's, Winchelsea, and the vicar of Icklesham, over parochial rights. The notary began with an invocation, but then plunged straight into a narration of the case: 'Cum inter magistrum Johannem . . . (etc.)'. The official caused the record to be sealed with the seal of his office and signed with the notary's sign. It was 'datum et actum apud Bouxle tercio idus Junii a. d. m° ccc° quadragesimo primo, indictione nona, pontificatus domini Benedicti divina providencia pape xii anno vii'. The document concludes with the certifying of an interlineation in the text in proper notarial form, but (in the cartulary copy, at least) there is no notarial eschatocol.[2]

Despite the frequent addition of seals of office, the fact remains that many notarialized *acta* of ecclesiastical courts bore only a sign manual, and certain types of ecclesiastical business in the king's court were treated in the same way. The instrument of 5 April 1305, which records King Edward I's reaction to a papal provision for Hugh, bishop of Byblos, has no seal.[3]

Exemplifications of charters and bulls constitute a category in which the form is not obviously determined by the content or the issuing authority. John de Bononia expected transcripts of papal letters and the like to carry both sign manual and seal.[4] But the pure notarial instrument and the notarial instrument with the seal of the issuing authority are both found in use.

---

earlier, the sentence of judges delegate in a case of appropriation. One of the judges was the bishop of Exeter. Here Bartholomew used a similar eschatocol, adding that the judges had caused their seals to be appended (*Glastonbury Chartulary*, i. 51–5). Bartholomew used the roman calendar for dating.

[1] *Reg. Bransford*, pp. 131–3.
[2] B.M., MS. Cotton Vesp. F. xv f. 71ᵛ. Cf. below, p. 127.
[3] Above, p. 109.
[4] *Summa*, pp. 697–9. Cf. Brentano's remarks, *York Met. Jurisdiction*, pp. 221–3, 240.

Nor can it be said that the difference reflected the preferences of the ecclesiastical and civil authorities. A notary public at Norwell on 21 April 1298 exemplified in purely objective form a dispensation for plurality from Pope Nicholas IV and collated it with the help of two clerics. But this was apparently not enough to satisfy all requirements; for, two days later, at Newark, the bishop of Lincoln inspected the original bull and appended his certificate ('Et nos O. Lincolniensis episcopus . . .') and seal to the notarial transcript.[1] This must have cost the applicant another fee.

A certified extract by Bishop Walter Reynolds of Worcester from the register of his predecessor, Bishop Godfrey Giffard, was written as if by the bishop and set both episcopal and notarial forms of authentication side by side. It concludes as follows.

In cuius rei testimonium publicacionem huiusmodi per manum Gilberti de Secheford' scribe nostri et notarii publici infrascripti in hanc publicam scripturam redigi mandavimus et sigilli nostri appensione fecimus communiri. Act' et dat' apud Bredon in manerio nostro, v idus Maii, videlicet die mensis Maii xi, anno domini m ccc xii, indictione decima, presentibus . . . testibus vocatis et rogatis, pontificatus domini Clementis divina providencia pape quinti anno vii°. Et ego Gilbertus Johannis dicti Hamergold de Secheford Norwycensis diocesis, publicus sacri Romani imperii auctoritate notarius predicte publicacioni per dominum patrem anno, indictione, die, et loco prenotatis facte una cum testibus predictis interfui et ipsam publicacionem sicut premittitur factam in hanc publicam scripturam manu mea scriptam redegi ac signo meo consueto de mandato venerabilis patris predicti cum nomine signavi rogatus.[2]

Here the features of normal episcopal letters patent are incorporated in a notarial instrument. It is both *actum* and *datum*.[3]

---

[1] *Reg. Sutton*, vi. 89–90. The notary, Elias de Cowton, expressed the date in notarial fashion: 'die lune decimo mensis Aprilis exeuntis'. The bishop adopted another (and not his usual) style: 'die mercurii in festo S. Georgii martiris'. Cf. another sealed instrument (1297), ibid. vi. 13–14.

[2] Worcester, County Record Office, Reg. Walter Reynolds, f. 49ᵛ (cf. *Reg. Reynolds*, p. 40). At f. 54ᵛ (cf. p. 46) the bishop grants a dispensation for defect of orders, quoting his papal authority; it is authenticated by both the seal and the notarial eschatocol.

[3] Cf. Bishop Richard Kellawe of Durham, 20 July 1306: 'Presens instrumentum . . . in publicam formam redigi mandavimus et nostri sigilli appensione muniri, Actum et datum . . .' (*Reg. Pal. Dunelm.*, i. 529–30).

It expresses the day of the month in the bishop's and in the notary's ways. Notice, too, that whereas the bishop speaks of his scribe, Gilbert of Seckford, notary public, Gilbert's eschatocol gives the lengthier form of his name and his full notarial title, omitting mention of his office under the bishop.

But the seal, though common on notarial exemplifications, was not necessary. Archbishop John Pecham, in his progress on visitation of the diocese of Norwich in 1281, had his notary John of Beccles draw up records of this sort for Norwich Cathedral Priory and for the Austin canons of Spinney; his seal was put on the former, but not on the latter. The wealthy cathedral convent could afford both forms of insurance; maybe the little priory of canons was deterred by the *sigillator's* fee.[1] More striking is the fact that all the exemplifications of papal bulls prepared in the royal Wardrobe in 1305 were pure notarial instruments, unsealed.[2]

Dating

Something must be said about the notarial system of dating. The traditional Italian method of dating public instruments, as is well known, involved setting down both the year of grace and the indiction, sometimes adding, for good measure, the imperial or pontifical year. One is reminded of Thomas Madox's quaint remark about early English diplomas, which were 'sometimes dated even with a redundancy'. These details were followed by the day of the month expressed in a peculiar fashion, known as the Bolognese style; it reckoned the days of the month forward to mid month, and backward for the second half of the month: thus 'quarto die intrante Junio' (or 'intrantis mensis Junii') equalled 4 June, and 'quarto die exeunte Junio' equalled 27 June. 'Prima die mensis', or 'ultima' or 'penultima die' were also used.[3] To this the notary public by apostolic or imperial authority commonly added the year

---

[1] Above, p. 35 n. 1.

[2] Above, pp. 57–8, and below, Appendix II, no. 9.

[3] Cf. John de Bononia, quoted below. Italians at work in England wrote 'die prima Junii', 'die tertia intrante Junio', 'die xv Junii' in 1277 (*EHR*, xxxii. 72, 74, 76, 77–9) and 'die lune penultima die Januarii' in 1279 (Ibid., p. 83). English notaries sometimes wrote 'ultima die mensis' (*Reg. Pecham*, i. 188 (1282), P.R.O., SC 7/36/1 (1305)).

of the pope, before or after the day of the month. The place-date was often given with utmost precision. This formula differed from all methods current in England when notarial instruments were first introduced into the country. The royal Chancery dated by regnal year and day of the month (reckoning forward from the first). Episcopal documents normally used the episcopal year and/or the year of grace and the day of the month according to the Roman calendar. Other deeds, when dated, bore the year of grace and/or regnal year, and sometimes indicated the day by reference to feasts of the Church. It hardly ever entered the head of an Englishman who was drafting a private deed to refer to the year of the reigning pope or the indiction. Place-dates were briefly stated: 'apud Bukkeden', 'apud Westmonasterium', and the like. By contrast, one of the earliest known notarial instruments drawn up in England by an English notary (as we believe him to have been) 'facta fuit . . . apud Lamehuth' iuxta London', in camera prefati domini archiepiscopi Cantuariensis, ipso archiepiscopo presente et audiente, anno a nativitate domini m°cc°lx° octavo, indictione undecima, die lune xv die intrante mense Octobris, pontificatus domini Clementis pape iiii anno quarto'.[1] John de Bononia's *Summa* provided an example for English use: 'In nomine domini amen. Anno eiusdem a nativitate m° cc°lxxx° iii°, indictione xi, die prima mensis Marcii, pontificatus domini Martini pape iiii anno ii . . . Actum Cantuarie in capitulo . . .'.[2]

A public instrument drafted in England late in the thirteenth century or after commonly follows this form, even when it incorporates a document written *privata manu* dated in English fashion.[3] Minor variants appear, as in Italy. In both countries the Roman calendar is sometimes used for the day of the month, and the day of the week may or may not be mentioned.[4] The feasts of the Church are used rarely to date a notarial document.[5]

---

[1] *Reg. W. Giffard*, p. 142, cf. above, p. 21. For comparison with continental instruments see the convenient collections of Doehaerd and Petrucci, and *Epistolae et Instrumenta*.

[2] *Summa*, p. 607. The printed text reads 1284, but the other elements are consistent with 1283.   [3] Cf. above, pp. 114–15.

[4] Below, Appendix II, no. 12; and cf. P.R.O., SC 7/36/2–4, all of 1305.

[5] 'Memorandum quod die dominica in festo Epiphanie domini, videlicet viii id. Jan. a.d. mccclii finiente': the notarialized record of a pension paid, *Cartulary of Cirencester Abbey*, ed. C. D. Ross (1964), ii. 497, no. 574.

More often the days of the month are counted forwards in one series. It is less common in England than in Italy to find the forms *intrante mense* and the like;[1] and the unknown notary who acted for the bishop of Hereford in 1280 showed an imperfect understanding of the Bolognese style when he wrote 'die lune xxvii mensis Maii exeuntis'.[2]

The English often imitate the Italians in naming precise times and places when they record public proceedings: thus, on 18 September 1307 'about the third hour of the day, being in the conventual church of Osney, near Oxford, in the diocese of Lincoln'.[3] On 24 May 1334 Henry of Colchester dated events in the churchyard of Longdon (Worcs.) 'ante horam eiusdem diei primam', and in the churchyard of Castlemorton 'hora tercia eiusdem diei'.[4] On 19 March 1349 a bull of Pope John XXII was published 'circa horam terciam' by a notary in the choir of the church of St. Mary the Virgin at Oxford.[5] Acts are recorded in the chapel next the church on the south side at the New Temple, London (1282),[6] at Carlisle in the hall of Sir Robert de Cotingham (1307),[7] in the chancel of the parish church of Ratcliffe-on-Soar (1381).[8] They are executed 'at the usual hour of chapter' (1284),[9] or 'after sunset' (1311).[10] Other circumstances may be described: 'the brethren being specially assembled in the chapter-house for this, by the ringing of

---

[1] Elias de Cowton gives the day of the week with the day 'mensis Maii exeuntis', 1300 (*Records of Antony Bek*, pp. 192, 204). John de Cadomo writes 'undecimo die exeunte Junio', 1300 (ibid., p. 74).

[2] *Reg. Cantilupe*, p. 283. Cf. Nicholas dictus Campion at Roxburgh: 'tricesimo die mensis Aprilis exeuntis' (*Liber S. Marie de Melros* [ed. Cosmo Innes], (Bannatyne Club, 1837), i. 315, and a hybrid instrument issued at London 'xx die intrante mense Marcii', 1282 (B.M., MS. Cotton Vesp. F. xv, f. 177ᵛ).

[3] *Reg. Winchelsey*, ii. 1154.

[4] Westminster Abbey, Mun. 21259. This Henry of Colchester is not to be confused with the notary Henry Ricardi of Colchester who was active early in the century (e.g. P.R.O., SC 7/18/22).

[5] *Oriel College Records*, ed. C. L. Shadwell and H. E. Salter (Oxford Hist. Soc., 1926), p. 22.

[6] Rymer, i. ii. 605.

[7] Appendix II, no. 14.

[8] *Cartulary of Burscough Priory*, ed. A. N. Webb (Chetham Soc., 3rd series xviii, 1970), p. 181, no. 181.

[9] Brentano, *York Met. Jurisdiction*, p. 221.

[10] *Reg. Pal. Dunelm.*, i. 108. For dating by the hour cf. de Boüard, *Manuel*, i. 317.

a bell in the customary manner'.[1] When the bishop of Lincoln wished to add a codicil to his will, he summoned knights of his household before him in the clerks' chamber at Theydon Mount, about the middle of the afternoon ('circa medium relevium') and, showing them the sealed document, ordered *tabellio suus* to make a public instrument recording what he had said and done.[2]

Such nicety of dating prompts the questions, what was being dated? and what did the date mean? As for the first matter, the usual word in a notarial instrument for introducing the date is 'Acta' or 'Actum'. This provides a clue. The notary purports to record an event or events, even if the event is simply the presentation or reading of a document. Since his record is in no sense a dispositive instrument the date upon it need bear no relation to the time and place at which he ultimately prepares his engrossment and pens artistically his sign manual.[3] There is one obvious exception to this in simple exemplifications of earlier documents, when the notary puts into his eschatocol the circumstances of his copying and collation. One of the Wardrobe copies of papal bulls made in 1305 will illustrate this:

Et ego Robertus filius Gilberti de Wisebeche . . . predictas literas apostolicas . . . cum magistris Ada de Lyndeseye et Philippo de Londonia notariis publicis anno domini millesimo ccc quinto, indictione quarta, mensis Novembris die sexto, tenui et inspexi ac de verbo ad verbum scripsi ad Westmonasterium prope London, examinavi diligenter et ascultavi . . .[4]

In a case of this sort (unless there are several identical copies) the date may be assumed to be the actual date of writing. But it is otherwise with the records of *acta* where the date occurs, not in the eschatocol, but at the beginning of the instrument

---

[1] This is in a form of proxy supplied by John de Bononia (*Summa*, p. 608); the setting is Christ Church, Canterbury.

[2] *Reg. Sutton*, v. 3, cf. 188–9.

[3] Cf. the Baumgartenberg formulary, ii. 12: 'De differencia inter datum et actum. Datum quidem inportat solummodo tempus in quo datur litera. Actum autem inportat tempus in quo ea facta sunt super quibus litera datur' (Rockinger, *Briefsteller*, p. 778). Mabillon drew attention to the distinction made in the Carolingian diploma between *Datum* and *Actum*: 'quorum unum sit rei transactae, alterum confecti instrumenti signum' (*De Re Diplomatica* (2nd edn., 1709), i. 192).   [4] P.R.O., SC 7/36/7.

and is commonly followed by the words 'in presencia mei notarii subscripti' or the like. For here the recorded transaction purports to have been minuted by the notary public at the stated place and time, and in his eschatocol he commonly says 'interfui'. This offers no guarantee that he wrote more than a rough note, or at the most his *protocollum*, on that occasion.[1] Andrew de Tange provides a simple example. He was present in Brancepeth rectory with the bishop of Durham after sunset on 11 November 1311, when a royal messenger delivered a writ to the bishop. The bishop, we are told, received it respectfully, opened and read it, 'and handed it to me, the aforesaid notary, requesting me to make a public instrument about the serving of the writ on him'. Andrew copied the writ, listed those present at the serving of it, and in his eschatocol declared: 'praemissae porrectioni, una cum dictis testibus interfui, eamque ut praemittitur anno, indictione, mense, die, loco, et hora praenotatis, fieri vidi, rogatus super ea praesens feci publicum instrumentum. . . .'[2] There is no need to suppose that Andrew straightway sat down on a cold winter's night and made the formal instrument adorned with his sign; 'feci' need not be contemporaneous with 'interfui' and 'fieri vidi'. The discrepancy between the time of the transaction and the notarializing of it becomes evident when legal proceedings which extended over months or even years are gathered together in a single notarial instrument.[3]

Risk of misunderstanding a notarial date arises in the reckoning of the year of grace. Among the multiplicity of

---

[1] The date on Genoese instruments was transcribed unchanged from the minute, without regard for lapse of time (Doehaerd, *Relations commerciales*, i. 38–9).

[2] *Reg. Pal. Dunelm.*, i. 108–10. Canonists recommend notaries not to prepare instruments by night. Baldus de Ubaldis, *Super Decretalibus*, 2. 22. 1 (Lyon, 1551, f. 285*r b*) writes: 'Suum officium debet publice exercere cum sit servus publicus, et ideo caveant tabelliones facere instrumenta in media nocte nisi in causa necessitatis.'

[3] Westminster Abbey, Mun. 9496 is a roll of nine membranes recording acts by several notaries and proceedings in a lengthy ecclesiastical suit. After the case was finished, the judges entrusted the whole to Mr. Richard de Brenchley for publication on 27 May 1308. He claims in his eschatocol that 'omnibus premissis actis iudicialibus in prescripto processu contentis dictis diebus et locis interfui presentemque processum ex eisdem actibus iudicialibus pro ut ea fieri vidi et audivi . . . redegi. . . .' Cf. above, p. 91.

styles current in the Middle Ages two were especially apt to become confused in notarial instruments: the style of Christmas and that of Lady Day, or the Annunciation. John de Bononia uttered a warning on this subject:

Anno domini a nativitate dicitur ad differenciam illorum qui incipiunt annos domini ab incarnacione. Unde in terris ubi consuetudo est incipere annos domini ab incarnacione non debet scriba dicere 'anno domini a nativitate' set 'anno domini ab incarnacione', ut servet consuetudinem sue terre. In curia Romana incipiunt notarii 'anno domini a nativitate'; curia tamen in privilegiis incipit annos domini ab incarnacione; et renovat indictionem seu mutat octavo kalendas Octobris, iuxta hos versus:

> Cum redit October, indictio fit nova semper.
> Quatuor atque tribus hiis est prelata diebus.[1]

Despite his recommendation in the *Summa*, John had used the nativity style in his early documents in England, and this although on 19 February 1280 he was certifying proxies dated 14 kal. Marcii and 13 kal. Februarii a.d. 1279 which must both belong to the same year, having been dated according to the custom of the country by the incarnation style.[2] Perhaps experience had taught him, by the time he composed the *Summa*, how much confusion was caused by adherence to the Italian fashion in England.

John de Bononia treated *incarnatio* as equivalent of *annunciatio* (25 March).[3] This equivalence cannot always be taken for granted;[4] but in England, where the annunciation reckoning got the upper hand, it was very common. Even a foreign notary (as we may suppose him to be) adapted himself to English ways in placing 17 March 1279 in 'anno incarnacionis domini m cc lxxviii';[5] but at Westminster on 15 February 1286 a notary named Petrus Passavantis de Vico dated an instrument 'a nativi-

---

[1] *Summa*, p. 610. The verse had been quoted by Hostiensis in his *Summa* (f. 103ᵛ*b*). The Bedan indiction seems to be the rule in England, as in the Curia at this period; but Luschek claims that the so-called 'Roman' indiction prevailed in Silesian instruments (*Notariatsurkunde*, pp. 88–9).

[2] *Councils and Synods*, ii. 861, and *Oseney Cart.*, iv. 455–7.

[3] Calculated by the Florentine method, i.e. 25 March *following* the beginning of the historical year.

[4] Giry, *Manuel*, i. 108–9 and Bresslau, *Handbuch*, ii. 434 n. 4. For *incarnatio* as the equivalent of Christmas see *Epistolae et Instrumenta*, nos. 1*b* (1217) and 2 (1202). [5] *Epistolae et Instrumenta*, no. 33 (above, p. 24).

tate mᵒccᵒlxxx sexto'.[1] English notaries public commonly availed themselves of the liberty to follow local custom which John de Bononia allowed, even when they only specified 'anno domini'. Frequently, like other scribes, they added a warning signal: 'anno domini ab incarnacione secundum cursum ecclesie Anglicane',[2] 'secundum usum ecclesie Anglicane',[3] 'secundum morem et computacionem ecclesie Anglicane'.[4] But the exceptions are numerous enough to keep the student on his guard. Edmund de Verduno wrote 'anno a nativitate eiusdem' in instruments of 1281; but he had changed to 'anno ab incarnacione eiusdem secundum cursum Anglicane ecclesie' by 1284.[5] One of Pecham's native notaries, John de S. Martino Lewensis, used both the form and reckoning 'a nativitate' in 1282.[6] But an Englishman might fall in with the continental fashion in writing 'a nativitate', while he stuck to the English way of reckoning. Thus, John Erturi de Cadomo dated the homage of John Balliol at Newcastle-upon-Tyne, 26 December 1292, as 'anno a nativitate . . . 1292 secundum quod observat ecclesia Anglicana'; in other words, he used the annunciation reckoning.[7] Robert de Londonia and Adam de Swayny used the form 'a nativitate' in 1289.[8] John Bouhs followed a foreign notary's example when certifying with him in April 1299, and again used the 'a nativitate' form when he wrote on his own in November of the same year.[9]

The nativity style of reckoning continued to be used by the prominent English notary, Andrew de Tange. The form in

[1] Westminster Abbey, Mun. 22930. Other foreigners in England may date 'a nativitate' (e.g. Rymer, I. ii. 896, II. i. 235), but the style does not always affect the date and is not discernible.

[2] Worcester, D. & C. Mun., B. 1613 (above, p. 20); Brentano, *York Met. Jurisdiction*, p. 221; *Reg. Martival*, i. 199.

[3] *Reg. Orleton*, p. 186. [4] *Reg. Martival*, i. 202.

[5] Brentano, *York Met. Jurisdiction*, pp. 204, 221.

[6] *Reg. Pecham*, i. 188, ii. 38. Henry de Tichefeld used the nativity style and reckoning on 6 March 1297 at Canterbury (D. & C. Archives, Chartae antiquae C. 169).

[7] Stones, *Anglo-Scottish Relations*, p. 63. John used 'a nativitate' elsewhere, but sometimes wrote 'anno domini'.

[8] Westminster Abbey, Mun. 22931 and 22932. In some later instruments Adam simply wrote 'anno domini': P.R.O., SC 7/36/3 and 7/64/22 and York, Borthwick Institute, Diocesan Records, R vii. E. 2; likewise Edmund de Verduno in 1284 (Brentano, *York Met. Jurisdiction*, p. 255).

[9] Rymer, I. ii. 897, 916.

which Andrew chose to give his name, 'Andreas quondam Guilielmi de Tange', suggests a determination on the part of this Yorkshire clerk not to appear insular or provincial. Master Andrew assigned to 26 December 1293 the act by which he recorded John Balliol's homage of 26 December 1292, unmoved by the fact that he was including a transcript of John's own statement that the homage was paid 'on the morrow of the nativity in the year 1292'.[1] He was also ignoring the usage of the English Chancery for which he was writing the instrument, which reckoned from the annunciation as Balliol did. Andrew seems to have dated consistently from the nativity, to judge by documents of later years from his hand.[2] By contrast, a notary appointed by Henry of Eastry, prior of Canterbury, one Richard Mayeu filius Roberti Mayeu de Nortone, dated an instrument 'secundum cursum ecclesie Anglicane millesimo tricentesimo septimo, indictione sexta, xv kal. Marcii' [i.e. 15 February 1308], undeterred from using this method by the fact that his instrument exemplified a commission from Robert Winchelsey dated at Poitiers (contrary to the archbishop's usual practice) 'quinto kal. Februarii anno a nativitate domini m° tricentesimo octavo'.[3]

In the course of the fourteenth century, as notaries public became acclimatized to England, they came to use more regularly the incarnation style and reckoning which were the mark of official documents of both Crown and Church in England, in contrast to the systems used on the Continent. But foreign notaries might refuse to conform,[4] and Englishmen might behave differently abroad. Professor Stones notes an example of professional perversity in 1328.[5] On one day (17 March) two notaries public drew up two instruments at Edinburgh. One of them, an Italian from Poggibonsi, dated his instrument 'a nativitate' 1328, while an English colleague

[1] Stones, *SHR*, xxxii. 49. Tange's 'Great Roll' was put together so late that this instrument of 1292/3 may not be contemporary with the event. But this is immaterial to the point in question. Cf. below, p. 132.

[2] *Records of Antony Bek*, p. 191 (1300), Appendix II, nos. 9, 14 (1305 and 1307).

[3] Canterbury, D. & C. Archives, Chartae antiquae A. 194. In Reg. Q, as printed in *Reg. Winchelsey*, ii. 1331–2, the year reads 1307.

[4] 'Pour les styles, les notaires ne suivent pas nécessairement l'usage de la région où ils instrumentent' (P. Bonenfant, *Cours de Diplomatique*, ii. 114).

[5] *SHR*, xxix (1950), 44, 49, and cf. *SHR*, xxxii. 50.

dated his 'anno ab incarnacione secundum cursum et computacionem ecclesie Anglicane' 1327. On the other hand, an English notary public who drew up an instrument in the Roman Curia might use the curial 'nativity' style and reckoning: Richard de Midelton, clerk of the diocese of York, notary public by apostolic and imperial authority, did so when on 19 February 1351 he dated an instrument in the dwelling of William de Bergeveny, S.T.P., at Avignon.[1]

Civilian vestiges in notarial instruments

At various points in the common form of English notarial instruments one is reminded of the fact that we are not dealing simply with the importation of Italian dictaminal fashions. These forms, inculcated by thirteenth-century Italian teachers of the *ars notarie*, have a longer lineage, and are impregnated with the notions and phrases of the civil law.[2] The *Invocatio*, which formed the opening of nearly all notarial instruments, had been borrowed from continental models in the earliest Christian Anglo-Saxon documents, but had practically ceased to be used in England when the diploma went out of fashion. In Italy, on the other hand, it had a continuous existence from early times in private deeds. Again, in English notarial instruments the invocation is followed, as we have seen, by an elaborate dating clause. This was in accord with *Novella* 47, cap. 1 of Justinian, which required documents drawn up by *tabelliones* to open with the full statement of the year of the reign of the most holy augustus and emperor, the name of the consul of that year, and in the third place the indiction, month, and day. Details changed in the course of centuries; but the position of the date and the general pattern persisted. The introduction of the year of grace was a medieval innovation, and the replacement of the imperial year by the pontifical year agreed with the practice which became the rule in the papal Chancery with Leo IX.[3] The next clause of the instrument

[1] P.R.O., C 47/20/4/14, and cf. below, p. 138.

[2] Cf. above, p. 76 n. 2.

[3] In the thirteenth century some German documents and documents drafted by imperial notaries in Italy use the imperial year, but not notarial documents in England. Some English notarial documents omit the pontifical year, using only the year of grace and the indiction.

invariably announces the presence of the notary at the proceedings described. This was in accord with *Novella* 44 'De tabellionibus', cap. 1, which laid down as the normal rule his attendance throughout the transaction. Again, the presence of witnesses which the notary is careful to mention next (usually with the place where they appeared) was prescribed by the civil law. The whole of *Novella* 73 'De instrumentorum cautela et fide' was concerned with the stages in the preparation and authentication of instruments, and its fifth chapter required that the public instrument, to be 'completed', must bear not only the subscription of the notary but also the names of the witnesses who had been present.[1] We have seen what stress the notary public lays upon the idoneity and the summoning of the witnesses (p. 106). This too is following the dictates of the law; *testes idonei, testes adhibiti, testes rogati* are the words of the *Digest*.[2] While it would be wrong to suppose that the notarial instrument was the only channel by which such ideas and phrases could come into English legal parlance (for example, Bracton had already insisted that wills should be made 'coram duobus vel pluribus . . . *ad hoc specialiter convocatis*'),[3] the most consistent reminiscences of Roman terminology are found in notarial instruments. The phrase *redegi rogatus*, which is so widely used in the notary's eschatocol, is in line with the classical law; and *rogatarius* is used in the Middle Ages to designate the notary who at the request of private persons frames their deeds in public form.[4] The terms in which the notary describes his collation of the texts he exemplifies are significantly close to the words of the *Code*. *Code* 6. 33. 3 required that a will certified by a notary should be 'non cancellatum neque abolitum neque ex quacumque suae formae parte vitiatum', and the notary public often uses this phrase with or without elaboration.[5] The notary who says that he has added

---

[1] 'Sed et instrumenta publice confecta licet tabellionum habeant supplementum, adiciatur et eis antequam compleantur, sicut dictum est, testium ex scripto praesentia.'

[2] *Digest*, 22. 5. 11 and 28. 1. 21. Cf. *Code*, 6. 33. 3: 'testamentum . . . depositionibus testium legitimi numeri vallatum sit.'

[3] *De Legibus Angliae*, f. 61 (ed. S. E. Thorne, ii. 181). Cf. above, p. 14.

[4] De Boüard, *Manuel*, i. 40.

[5] Below, Appendix II, nos. 7, 8, 9. Cf. Innocent III, in reference to a notarial instrument: 'cui fides est indubitata adhibenda, cum nec cancellatum, nec

and subtracted nothing 'quod sensum immutet vel vitiet intellectum' could shelter behind Papinian's authority in treating sense as more important than words (*Dig.* 34. 4. 3 § 9), and he echoes Paul (*Dig.* 19. 1. 27) in describing the document he exemplifies as 'sanum et integrum'.[1] These examples do not exhaust the borrowings, direct and indirect, and the reminiscences of classical legal terminology which lurk in notarial instruments. They may suffice to indicate a dependence in actual law which becomes apparent if one studies the civilian and canonist glossators 'de fide instrumentorum' and 'de testibus' and the writers of *artes notarie*.

The quality of scribal composition

The well-equipped notary public was trained in latinity as well as the law. His expertness consisted in great measure in his skill in adapting flexible formulas to standard legal requirements. He must consider closely the formulas and tenor of the act he had to prepare so that, in the words of a fourteenth-century formulary, he could shape them like a wax nose to suit the type of business in hand.[2] Many notaries public did indeed show dexterity in manipulating their terms of art as occasion demanded. But to what extent did their normal procedure offer safeguards against inaccuracy or fraud? So far as one can generalize about a large number of practitioners over a long period of time, English notaries public of the thirteenth and fourteenth centuries seem to have maintained a good standard of accuracy. The law required that they should either write their instruments themselves or verify what was written by their deputy before they subscribed. There is no reason to suppose that the English notaries were better or worse in this respect than their continental *confrères*. Clear evidence of careless errors is scarce. The dating clause offered a traditional trap for the unwary scribe in the indiction; but it was generally

abolitum, nec corruptum sit in aliqua parte sui' (*Extra*, 2. 22. 10). Similar formulas creep into non-notarial exemplifications; e.g. an *inspeximus* by Archbishop Boniface of Canterbury, 12 March 1260 (G. Oliver, *Monasticon Exoniense* (Exeter, 1846), p. 61).

[1] e.g. below, p. 128, and Appendix II, nos. 7, 9, 10.
[2] The Baumgartenberg formulary, in Rockinger, *Briefsteller*, ii. 790.

calculated correctly, although John de Bononia himself was capable of neglecting the rule he cited.[1] A notarial record of profession of obedience made by the bishop of Durham to the archbishop of York, at his consecration in 1311, provides a trivial case of misdating, always supposing it to have been copied exactly into the archbishop's register. It is dated 'die dominico in festo Pentecostes, videlicet vicesimo nono die mensis Maii anno gracie m ccc xi'; but Whitsun fell on 30 May in 1311.[2]

According to an accepted principle of canon law minor erasures and spelling mistakes did not affect the authenticity of an instrument.[3] If corrections on the instrument were obviously made by the hand of the original scribe, it was unlikely that they would be questioned, and special procedure in notarial instruments provided guarantee. For it was normal practice to collate an instrument with its 'original' or protocol before the responsible notary wrote his eschatocol. Examples have already been given of the recording of collation in the eschatocol. That this procedure was taken seriously is shown by erasures and insertions which often occur in instruments and which are almost invariably specified at the end by the notary. As an early instance, take the eschatocol of an appeal by Oliver Sutton, bishop of Lincoln, from the Court of Canterbury in 1290. It reads:

Et ego Willelmus Johannis de Anlauby, Eboracensis diocesis clericus, auctoritate imperiali et alme urbis prefecti publicus notarius, supradictis omnibus interfui, rogatus scripsi et publicavi et meo solito signo signavi. Et sciendum est quod interlineare supra xli lineam descendendo, scilicet *compotum reddituri de eodem et plenarie satisfacturi*, propria manu interserui pro eo quod per collacionem et examinacionem presentis instrumenti ad protocollum ipsius inveni idem interlineare in protocollo esse linealiter contentum.[4]

---

[1] Cf. *Summa*, p. 610, and *Councils and Synods*, ii. 861, where *septima* should be *octava*.

[2] *Reg. Greenfield*, v. 95, cf. 93.

[3] *Extra*, 2. 22. 3 and 11 and 5. 20. 9. For canonists' comments on this matter in relation to papal letters see P. Herde, 'Römisches und kanonisches Recht bei der Verfolgung des Fälschungsdelikts im Mittelalter', *Traditio*, xxi (1965), 291–362, at pp. 340–3.

[4] Lincoln, D. & C. Archives, D ij/62/1/5. Cf. below, Appendix II, nos. 7 13, 16.

Corrections of this sort might be noted either at the end of the text or, as in Anlauby's deed, in the eschatocol. In either case the notary might take the additional precaution of noting that the corrections were made 'ante subscripcionem istam' or 'ante consignacionem istam'.[1] A hybrid document produced by a notary for the official of Chichester in 1341 ends with the note: 'Constat etiam nobis officiali et notario predictis de inter-liniari in verbis *si et quatenus super eisdem duxerit ordinandum* ante sigilli aut signi apposicionem in presencia parcium et testium appositis.'[2] The more scrupulous notary might go further and say that the corrections were in his own hand: 'manu mea feci' or 'illas feci propria manu'; in doing so he covered himself with the protection of the law which justified alterations mani-festly made on an instrument by the hand of the original scribe.[3] In the eschatocol itself a notary might be guilty of a careless slip in writing the familiar form without thereby invalidating the instrument. Even a registrar of the Court of Canterbury, in 1344, the notary Master Henry de Bagworth, might depart from the usual formula by leaving out customary words: 'publicavi et [in] hanc publicam formam [redegi et] signo meo consueto signavi'.[4] A notary public at Bristol in 1386 was so punctilious as to record a correction he had made in his own eschatocol, adding to the usual formula the follow-ing words:

Constat michi notario prescripto de rasura istius dixionis *dioc'* in prima linea presentis subscripcionis mee, quam approbo vicium meum corrigendo.[5]

The best evidence for correction is drawn from collated documents of which the originals exist. Notarial exemplifica-tions usually emphasize, either in the text or in the eschatocol, the careful comparison of original and copy by two or more persons, and usually the persons include a notary public. Thus, the exemplification of a privilege of Pope Alexander III at the

[1] Below, Appendix II, no. 12; cf. no. 7 and 'ex certa scientia mei notarii et ante consignacionem' at the close of the text of a sealed instrument prepared for the abbot of Scone, 17 Aug. 1298, by Robert de Garvalde (above, p. 33).
[2] Above, p. 113.   [3] Below, Appendix II, nos. 7, 13.
[4] Lincoln, D. & C. Archives, D ij/62/1/15. Cf. below, Appendix II, no. 20.
[5] Hereford, D. & C. Archives, no. 570.

New Temple, 15 February 1303, by the notary William le
Dorturer, specifies: 'cum testibus subscriptis diligenter ascultavi et concordare inveni, presentibus in ascultacione predicta
fratribus Henrico Payn et Roberto de Beby monachis, Johanne
de Beverlaco et Alexandro de Mounpelers clericis, testibus ad
hec vocatis specialiter et rogatis'.[1] An instrument drawn up at
royal command on 5 April 1305 has already called for comment.[2]
Included in it was a bull of Benedict XI. The notary, John
Bouhs, declared:

transcriptum, exemplum seu sumptum, per me a suo originali
transumptum, et cum domino Petro le Malore, iusticiario domini
regis Anglie illustris, et magistris Johanne de Cadamo et Gilberto
de Lutegareshale notariis publicis diligenter et fideliter ad suum
originale postmodum ascultatum, nil addens vel minuens quod
sensum mutet vel vitiet intellectum, hic in instrumento presenti
scripsi . . .

The correction of mis-spellings and omissions points to
meticulous care, if not perfect copying. Sometimes an unfamiliar proper name will be mis-spelt by the notary, or he will
have trouble with the squeezed *elongata* in the protocol of
a papal privilege;[3] but his scribal work compares favourably
with that of non-notarial work in royal and episcopal chanceries. When Adam de Swayny collated with two other notaries
public the important bull *Dignis laudibus* of Innocent III, they
only overlooked one mistake in the copy: in the flowery preamble he wrote *caute* for *naute*. But it was a pardonable error.
Adam guarded himself in the eschatocol of his exemplification
by noting that the original was in poor condition: 'quarum
literarum alique sunt delete, alique vero incipiunt iam deleri';
and, sure enough, the original is now illegible at the point
where he went wrong. Apart from this Adam only departed

---

[1] Westminster Abbey, Mun. 12732. John de Beverlaco may be the notary
public John Alani dictus de Beverlaco who appears in 1307 (*Reg. Winchelsey*,
ii. 1164–5). The privilege is printed by W. Holtzmann in *Papsturkunden in
England*, i (Berlin, 1931), 415–17.

[2] Cf. above, pp. 109, 113.

[3] Thus, in copying in 1297 a privilege of 1202, the notary read *eiusdem* for
eiusque, *regulariter* for *regularem*, misinterpreting the abbreviations of the address.
He only made two single-letter mistakes in the following text (P.R.O., E 135/
15/17 m. 1, *BIHR*, xxxviii. 195).

from the original in writing *aliquamdiu* for *aliquandiu* and *imperpetuum* for *in perpetuum*. He scrupulously reproduced the papal Chancery clerk's peculiar spelling of English names: 'Hunteingefeld' and 'Riccardi'.[1]

A notary, after all, did not claim to be utterly faultless in matters of no moment. When he collated documents he guarded himself with the formula which has been quoted from John de Bouhs's instrument of 5 April 1305.[2] In estimating standards of accuracy allowance must be made for the fact that circumstances did not always require that a notary should make a full transcript of the document which he was certifying. He would be justified in copying extracts. But a careful practitioner said what he was doing. When in 1297 the proctor of Tonbridge Priory proved to the bishop of Norwich his church's right to churches in Suffolk, he produced authentic muniments of which certain clauses bore on the business. He then handed over a copy of relevant passages, with the beginnings and ends of the documents, for a notary public to collate with the originals. The notary set out the extracts in a notarial framework, on four membranes, the seams being marked with his sign manual.[3] In making these extracts the proctor and the notary acted in accordance with the law of the Decretals.[4]

It was important that the notary's sign manual should maintain consistent characteristics, and canonists stress that it must not be varied. Dr. Emanuel notes among the English *signa* which he examined lack of symmetry and variation of size between two or more examples of a notary's *signum*, which 'prove that many notaries drew their marks freehand, relying entirely on their own manual *habileté* without having recourse

[1] P.R.O., SC 7/64/22, collated with the original, SC 7/19/17. Gilbert de Seckford, copying a bull of Gregory X in company with two other notaries public, only departed from his original in reading *iminet* for *imminet* and omitting the *gemipunctus* here and there (SC 7/18/22, copied from SC 7/16/9).

[2] It also appears, e.g., as 'nullo addito, subtracto, vel mutato quod sensum mutet vel viciat intellectum'. The clause was in the notary public's oath (below, Appendix II, no. 3), but it went back to the civil law (above, p. 125).

[3] Cheney, *BIHR*, xxxviii. 195. The fact that the notary seems to be copying the proctor's copy may lighten his responsibility for the four errors noted above, p. 128 n. 3).

[4] *Extra*, 2. 22. 5 (Celestine III).

to stamps or stencils. Others, however, definitely made use of mechanical drawing aids. A good example is provided by the *signum* of Robert de Avebury, in which faint traces of a circle, drawn probably by means of a compass of some sort, can be detected underlying the circular upper portion of the design.'[1] An examination of many examples would probably show that over the course of years a notary might introduce slight changes. Dr. Chaplais has kindly called my attention to the case of John Erturi de Cadomo, who disposed the letters of his christian name in one way in the signs on his early instruments written in Spain, but otherwise in later years. John de Cadomo, moreover, provides an example of a negligently drawn sign manual. His negligence was perhaps pardonable; for he was nearing the end of his immense roll of the 'Great Cause' of Scotland, all written in his own hand, and beautifully written. He had penned his large and elaborate sign already twenty-four times across the seams of twenty-five membranes, and when he made it for the twenty-fifth time, across the seam which joins mm. 25–6, he inadvertently substituted a third 'n' for the 'e' which should have followed the 'nn' of 'Johannes'.[2] He must have been a very tired scribe by then.

Fraud and distortion

Granted that the scribal standard was high, what can be said of the accuracy of notarial instruments in matters of substance? Did the public form guarantee the probity of those who were responsible for issuing them? Was fraud common? It would only be possible to answer these questions satisfactorily after examining a large number of records of lawsuits in which notarial instruments were impugned. In the nature of the case, some frauds must have gone undetected; and because the king's court was little disposed to accept notarial instruments as evidence, they do not leave many traces in the records of the civil courts. A London case of 1282, already cited (above, p. 25), shows that *suppressio veri* was practised: that a notarial record of a judgement in the king's court could be used without

---

[1] Emanuel, 'Notaries', p. 5, cf. fig. 17.
[2] P.R.O., E 39/15/1 mm. 25–6. I owe this observation to the eagle eye of my friend, Dr. J. H. Denton.

revealing that an appeal had led to a reversal of sentence. *Suppressio veri* was common enough in ecclesiastical appeals in the old days; but perhaps it had been harder for a litigant's *ex parte* statement to assume the aspect of an authentic record. In twelfth-century Italy the great 'break-through' in the status of the notary public had come about when his acts acquired *publica fides* without the need to be validated by the presence or subscription of a judge.[1] This provided the opportunity for venal notaries. England produced some with dubious credentials in the fourteenth century. In 1312 the bishop of Durham denounced fraudulent men who claimed to be notaries public in his diocese.[2] A papal letter of 1317 spoke of some falsely styled notaries who were at large in the province of Canterbury.[3] Later in the century (1347) the Court of King's Bench reported the activities of a *soi-disant* notary public: 'non constat curie utrum idem Willelmus sit notarius nec ne.'[4] In 1342 the archbishop of Canterbury, making his statutes for the Court of Arches, inveighed against both inexperienced and fraudulent notaries.[5] Finally, a bull of Pope Boniface IX, dated 6 February 1396, was directed to the archbishops of Canterbury and York, in which the pope complained of those who prepared public instruments in defiance of the facts, with false statements or suppression of the truth.[6]

Any profession is bound to produce some rascals. From the point of view of the modern historian, trying to separate the true from the false in documentary evidence, notarial instruments perhaps present greater problems than that of simple fraud. One may legitimately question John Pecham's notary, Robert de Martival, when he introduces his notarialized text of the archbishop's ordinance for the churches and vicarages of Tarring and Patching by telling us that the archbishop himself, on 4 February 1287, at about the third hour, personally read the whole of this lengthy ordinance in public ('legit et

---

[1] Petrucci, *Notarii*, p. 25. Cf. above, p. 4.   [2] Above, p. 68.
[3] *Cal. Papal Letters*, ii. 148–9.   [4] *Sel. Cases King's Bench*, vi. 58.
[5] Wilkins, ii. 681*b*, 687*a*, 692*b*–693*a*. In 1328 the scribe of the chapter acts of Lichfield, Mr. Robert Bernard, notary by imperial authority, had been sacked for financial fraud (*Magnum Registrum Album of Lichfield*, ed. H. E. Savage (Wm. Salt Soc., 1926), p. xx).
[6] Wilkins, iii. 268–9 (cf. above, p. 92).

recitavit in scriptis in presencia mei notarii . . .'). More probably a clerk rattled it off, or else it was 'taken as read'.[1] The problem of veracity was particularly likely to arise when a notary public was not merely called upon to exemplify the copy of a document or prepare an appeal, a proxy, and so forth, in authentic form, but commissioned to give a long narrative account of legal or quasi-legal proceedings in court, council, or convocation. Then the need to abridge produced the temptation to conflate. The wish to lend an air of verisimilitude to a bald narrative encouraged the notary not only to be precise about times and places but to report in direct speech the more significant oral exchanges. Conflation and invention of this sort were not necessarily fraudulent in intent; but they must if possible be recognized for what they are, and they undermine the faith which all this parade of notarial exactitude might otherwise stimulate in the unwary.

It is not often that we can check a notary's thoroughness and fidelity in assembling documents and recording a series of events spread over a long period of time. The records of the 'Great Cause' of the Scottish succession, 1291–6, have already been mentioned as evidence of the civil government's use of notaries public.[2] They form a group which has been subjected to penetrating study by Professor Stones. His findings are of great importance to the critic of notarial instruments. He shows that the public instrument drawn up by John de Cadomo in 1296 was based on a collection of individual memoranda and notarial acts of 1291–3. Two copies of the final instrument exist. Andrew de Tange's even lengthier record, which also included John Balliol's renunciation of fealty to Edward I in 1296, was prepared many years later, and not completed until 1318. Three copies exist. Both records are written on rolls of many membranes. Were John de Cadomo and Andrew de Tange present at all the proceedings, as they declare in their respective

---

[1] Canterbury, D. & C. Archives, Reg. I, ff. 422^v–424^r. Prof. Stones points to the improbability that the chronicle evidences about the Scottish succession were read *in extenso*, as they appear in Tange's Great Roll (*Archives*, ix. 17).

[2] Above, pp. 61–2. John de Cadomo's roll was printed by Rymer, i. ii. 762–84, Andrew de Tange's roll by Prynne, *Records*, iii. 487–543, both imperfectly. These texts must be used in the light of Stones's papers in *SHR*, xxxv and xxxix, and *Archives*, ix, and his *Anglo-Scottish Relations*.

eschatocols? Do they faithfully reproduce minutes of the proceedings made contemporaneously? A few of the documents
used in the composition of these 'Great Rolls', as they have
been called, were themselves public instruments written by
John de Cadomo, and survive in original or transcript. The
fact remains that while John de Cadomo's presence is proved
at many of the proceedings from 1291 to 1293, that of Andrew
de Tange is problematic.[1] If these rolls were actually composed
on the basis of full contemporary notes, the notes were imperfect or imperfectly understood or deliberately abridged when
the time came for them to be edited. Professor Stones insists
that neither of the 'Great Rolls' forms a complete and accurate
record.[2] In fact, Tange's account is not consistent with that of
Caen, and its three versions differ quite considerably in wording, though not in substance. These rolls, then, are far from
reproducing a 'shorthand note' or 'tape-recording' of the whole
proceedings. They are digested accounts of the Great Cause as
the kings of England wished it to be on record, in a form which
was technically authentic; and as such they may have been of
practical use for the next century. But the inventiveness of the
writers is seen in the set speeches, in *oratio recta*, in which the
rhythmical *cursus* produces an unnatural effect. Professor
Stones makes a happy comparison between them and those
parliamentary speeches of the eighteenth century which,
when published, were 'enriched (as Boswell put it) by the
accession of Johnson's genius'. The Great Rolls, says Professor
Stones,[3] are 'selective reports, garnished in a style so elaborate
that its verbal details can never be pressed. But they have other
defects which could not have been so readily anticipated. Their
chronology is in many places demonstrably wrong, especially
when they compress into one day the events of a longer
period. Their omissions, and their extreme compression at

[1] *SHR*, xxxv. 94 and n. 8. While it is not certain that documents of the Great
Cause notarialized by Tange and bearing dates from 1291 onwards (e.g. P.R.O.,
E 39/16/26, duplicated in E 39/16/13) were in fact prepared contemporaneously,
Dr. Constance Fraser has found that Tange was a notary public, employed as
such by the monks of Durham by 1292 (below, Appendix II, no. 22).

[2] *SHR*, xxxv. 97–8. Further evidence was provided in *SHR*, xxxvi. 111–24
by Dr. Grant G. Simpson, when he discussed the inadequate treatment in the
Rolls of the claim of Count Florence of Holland to the Scottish throne.

[3] *SHR*, xxxv. 104 and *Anglo-Scottish Relations*, p. 51 n. 3.

some points, can give a very false idea of what actually happened. The general impression, however, is not one of wilful perversion in the interests of Edward, except at two possible points. . . .' Here we may leave the Great Cause and its Great Rolls, since the only object is to establish a point of diplomatic. In Edwardian England the form of the notarial instrument might be chosen to give an authentic stamp to an official government pronouncement; but it affords no guarantee to the historian that text is contemporaneous with the event or relates the facts fully and correctly.

8. Conclusion

AFTER some years' experience of England, Master John de Bononia remarked the contrast with Italy: 'Italians, like cautious men, want to have a public instrument for practically every contract they enter into; but the English are just the opposite, and an instrument is very rarely asked for unless it is essential.'[1] The difference was not just one of racial temperament. In the first chapter we saw some of the complex historical reasons why the English Common Law eschewed the notary public and why Englishmen in the days of John de Bononia were less prompt than were Italians to put pen to parchment. Yet the fact remains that notaries became established in England in large numbers during the fourteenth century. They were probably far more numerous than has generally been supposed. Forming no professional body, although bound by oath to a code of professional conduct, they had a dubious status. How is their influence on English legal ideas and procedure to be assessed? It is probably true to say that this influence has been underestimated in the past simply because a great many who were notaries public did not always announce themselves as such and because the diplomatic features of their instruments have not been analysed. More needs to be done in this way. If the question cannot be answered at present in any but vague terms, the asking of it may stimulate study; and when more details have been accumulated along the lines indicated above, worthwhile observations may be possible. In the field of ecclesiastical history the importance of the notary public has come to be better recognized of late, and work now in progress should clarify the part he played in secular diplomacy. The present comments are prompted by a cursory and inadequate survey and are of an entirely provisional character.

[1] *Summa*, p. 604. Cf. the comment of Gerald of Wales when at Bologna his creditors called in *tabelliones* to record his debt 'cum solemnitate quam in partibus illis adhibere solent' (*Opp.* (RS), iii. 290–1).

The notary public remained exotic. The Common Law took no notice of him and denied that his signature and sign manual sufficed to authenticate a document. Moreover, ecclesiastical courts and secretariats—established in England before the notary arrived—were only half converted to the use of notarial public instruments.[1] There were hardly any categories of document which were invariably cast in public form, with solely notarial authentication. The process of an ecclesiastical election lent itself to notarial record, but the public form was not always adopted. John de Bononia provided alternative 'public' and 'private' forms for most of the official acts which a bishop's clerk was called upon to draft.[2] Almost every type of document which the clerk could cast in public form and validate, if he were a notary, with his sign manual, could also be drawn up in the form of episcopal letters patent validated by the bishop's seal. The legate Otto in 1237 had specifically required holders of ecclesiastical dignities and offices to furnish themselves with seals which could be treated as authentic. Seals proliferated. So, although the Court of Arches and some other ecclesiastical courts provided many opportunities for notaries to draft public instruments, and although notaries might be used for jobs of exemplification in the king's Wardrobe and elsewhere, notaries public who looked to government departments and ecclesiastical chanceries for employment spent only a small part of their working hours in performing the duties for which they held the title of *persona publica*, that is, producing and authenticating public instruments.

They had time on their hands. Consequently, it is not enough to consider the contribution of notaries public to the use of the public instrument in England. Much of their activity was directed to other types of writing. Their influence spread throughout the world of civil servants and ecclesiastical administrators, and is seen in records of government offices in Church and State alike. One has only to look at John de Bononia's *Summa* to see how much he could teach the clerks in ecclesiastical chanceries about the appropriate forms for all manner of records.

---

[1] Bresslau, *Handbuch*, i. 718 n. 1, on the meaning of *publicum instrumentum*, and cf. above, pp. 3–5.   [2] Above, p. 111.

During the next hundred years English legal documents of all kinds, civil and ecclesiastical, undergo a development common to all Europe: they become at once more exact and more verbose. How much of the change in England was due to the training which notaries public acquired and how much to the infiltration of civilian and canonistic rules through other channels is an open question. It might indeed be argued that the public notariate sprang into being in one country after another in northern Europe between about 1260 and about 1320 precisely because the spread of Roman civilian and canonistic procedure demanded the services of notaries. As for verbosity: the notarial style tended to lengthen documents; but verbosity may be said to have characterized all Latin literary style in the fourteenth century. John de Bononia's remarks on the correct way to return writs of citation are instructive. The English habit of simply replying: 'mandatum vestrum sum reverenter executus' is not good enough for the Italian-trained lawyer. The return must state how, when, where, and on whom the summons was served.[1] This was obviously a sound precaution, whether the return was being made *manu publica* or under seal. In the matter of dating documents, the notary public (it has been shown) believed in being precise.[2] John de Bononia thought that a *scriptura publica* of any kind should be dated by the day, and some of his forms use the hour for dating *acta*.[3] It may well be that the more regular ways of dating introduced into English private deeds in the fourteenth century owed something to notarial practice. Certainly the precise recording of time of day was an innovation with notarial background. The commissioners who received King Richard's abdication in 1399 went to the Tower, according to the official communiqué, 'circiter nonam pulsationem horilogii'.[4] Records of Convocation of Canterbury in this period show the same attention to the hour of the day.[5]

---

[1] *Summa*, pp. 634–9.   [2] Above, pp. 106, 115–18.

[3] 'Ego autem credo diem apponendam esse in omni scriptura publica, sive fiat in iudicio sive extra' (*Summa*, p. 673, cf. 634).   [4] *Rot. Parl.*, iii. 416*b*.

[5] E. F. Jacob (*Reg. Chichele*, vol. i, p. cxv n. 8) gives references from Arundel's and Chichele's times. In 1326 the bishop of Norwich confirmed his appropriation of Ashbocking church to Canterbury in a deed dated 24 July 'hora quasi tercia' (Canterbury, D. & C. Archives, Reg. B, f. 226ʳ).

Precision in dating by the hour of the day was natural in notarial *acta*, where the time of the event mattered more than the time of the drafting of the instrument. Similarly, it appears in *acta* which do not have the marks of public instruments but which seem to derive from the same school as notarial *acta* and which were probably drawn up by notaries. In the style and reckoning of dates, also, it seems that even the royal Chancery could be influenced by notarial custom. A group of royal letters on the French Roll from February and March 1361 are dated 'l'an del Nativite nostre seignur m ccc lxi', one of them adding the further explanation: 'solonc le cours de l'esglise de Rome';[1] this although the Chancery normally dated by the regnal year and, when it used the year of grace, used the Annunciation reckoning.

Resemblances between the notarial and the non-notarial documents extend far beyond mere habits of dating.[2] The structure of notarial instruments influenced other records of both ecclesiastical and civil government. The notarial *acta* of the provincial councils which sat in judgement on the English Templars may have suggested a new way of recording provincial councils. By the end of the fourteenth century the narrative of a council or convocation of Canterbury is elaborated in much the same way as the *acta* of a lengthy ecclesiastical lawsuit. Although these long narratives, preserved in the archiepiscopal registers, are not dressed up with the trimmings of a public instrument, they are entirely modelled on the notarial pattern. It is as well to remember that they were written by registrars and others in the archbishops' service who were probably notaries public. The record was so constructed as to serve easily as the basis of a copy *manu publica*, should one be wanted. The archiepiscopal register thus became the equivalent of a notarial *protocollum* or *cartularium*; but it remained an official record of the archbishop's administration

---

[1] Rymer, III. ii. 598, 608, 612. Cf. ibid., III. ii. 597 for the annunciation style, and see above (pp. 121–2) for use of the nativity style by some English notaries.

[2] Cf. below, Appendix II, no. 7 for the certifying of corrections on the non-notarial *inspeximus* of a notarial instrument. The practice is found in England before notaries public appeared; see the interesting sealed 'littera obligatoria' of 1256 with the footnote: 'Illa rasura facta fuit ante consignationem' (Madox, *Formulare*, pp. 85–7, no. clviii). Cf. Madox, pp. 383–4, no. dcxcvi (1333).

and was not devoted to one notary's acts or to notarial acts alone.[1]

Outside the sphere of English Church government, where notaries public operated freely and where their influence could extend without legal restraint, lay the area of private mercantile transactions. Here there was equal need for the carefully elaborated document, proof against legal cavil, and adopting as a matter of convenience set formulas and clear writing. In an imperfectly literate society much writing of this sort was necessarily left to the professional. Here the habits of the Italian city's notaries public may well have had some effect on English merchants, who formed the class of English society most likely to have encountered them and their acts. The writing of private bonds and deeds must often have fallen to professional scribes, and in the fourteenth century London scriveners formed a guild after the Italian notarial fashion. Professor Postan has suggested that the scrivener, even though the Common Law took no more account of his writings than of a notarial instrument, resembled the Italian notary in keeping a protocol. 'By the beginning of the fifteenth century, and possibly earlier (he writes), they seem to have kept a record of those private documents which passed through their hands, and in transactions of private individuals the entries in the scriveners' books played a part somewhat resembling that of notarial records on the continent.'[2]

Again, the records of a department of State might occasionally reflect the notarial training of its clerks and their 'archive-consciousness'. Thus, in 1392, if not earlier, John Prophet, notary public, began to keep a day-to-day account of the *acta* of the king's Council. His immediate successor does not seem to have maintained the practice, but in 1421 a new clerk of the Council, Richard Caudray—like Prophet a graduate, a notary, and a former servant of the archbishop of Canterbury—began a series of rolls designed as a sophisticated and carefully edited record of selected conciliar proceedings.[3]

[1] Cf. above, p. 100.

[2] Postan, 'Private financial instruments', pp. 34–5.

[3] The series hardly lived up to the intention. John Prophet's 'journal' and the later so-called 'book of the Council' are described and discussed by Dr. A. L. Brown in *The Early History of the Clerkship of the Council*. The journal was printed

When the permeation of government offices and ecclesiastical households by clerks trained in the notarial tradition is taken into account, it must be allowed that their influence on legal terminology and official literary style may have been very great. We have seen that in the fourteenth century John de Bononia had a reputation as a stylist, and that there was a tendency among English notaries public to cultivate 'fine writing'.[1] We should not forget that the great Florentine humanist, Coluccio Salutati, was himself a practising notary by apostolic and imperial authority, whose *protocollum* remains in the archives of the city.[2] Notaries were professionally concerned with calligraphy,[3] literary style, and the law. In England notaries public, who formed no closed corporation, developed no distinctive script, had no monopoly of fine writing, and made no exclusive claim to frame letters and certificates which were not public instruments. But the ablest of them found congenial occupation in the royal Chancery and Privy Seal and Signet offices engaged in diplomacy, and in households of prelates, involved in correspondence with Roman cardinals and in composing sonorous constitutions, mandates, and anathemas.[4] When a letter of more than ordinary importance had to be written, and the task fell to a notary, it was not because the rules of *dictamen* and legal niceties were inaccessible to

by J. F. Baldwin, *The King's Council* (Oxford, 1913), pp. 489–504. Dr. Brown touches on the rarity of archive-consciousness among the clerks of the council (pp. 35–6).

[1] Above, pp. 47–9.

[2] See Armando Petrucci's edition of *Il Protocollo Notarile di Coluccio Salutati, 1372–3.* Coluccio had also practised as notary in his early days (1351–63), but his protocol for those years is missing. A less distinguished rhetorician, Mino da Colle, who practised as a notary, is discussed by Helene Wieruszowski, '*Ars dictaminis* in the time of Dante', *Medievalia et Humanistica*, i (1943), 95–108. Cf. J. K. Hyde, *Padua in the Age of Dante* (Manchester, 1966), p. 122: 'At all levels, from the popular chronicling of Da Nono and Cortusi to the classicising erudition of Mussato, the intellectual life of the commune was dominated by notaries and judges. Paduan literary culture was a spare-time activity of lawyers.'

[3] In England a notarial hand does not develop on lines distinct from other court hands, unlike Italy, where peculiar notarial cursive, derived from the distant past and related to the papal *curialis*, survived in the north and central parts until the twelfth century and in the south much later. See Bresslau, *Handbuch*, ii. 519 n. 3, 546–7, and Brentano, *Two Churches*, pp. 298–300, with bibliographical notes. This is not to deny the Italian features visible in the writing of some English notaries public (cf. above, pp. 103–4).   [4] Above, pp. 62, 48.

others. It was because any stylist or lawyer concerned in such draftsmanship had probably—by the end of the fourteenth century—acquired the professional status of a notary public.

Hubert Hall perhaps had some such considerations in mind and was groping towards a similar conclusion when he wrote: 'Doctors learned in the civil and canon law drafted conventions with foreign princes or repartees to the papal curia, and royal merchants introduced refinements in the bond or recognizance which were turned to good account in official circles. These innovations are of interest if only because they serve to remind us that in spite of the decadence of the ancient diploma the art of diplomatic composition, reinforced by legal subtlety, attains its highest point of development at the close of the thirteenth century.'[1]

For a true estimate of influences it is equally significant that the notarial style and customs spread outside the limits of the profession. Formulary books and works on *dictamen*, it has been shown, were widely read in England in the later Middle Ages.[2] Richard de Bury, bishop of Durham, Keeper of the Privy Seal, Chancellor and diplomat, was no notary himself; but he showed great skill in the *cursus* both in his official correspondence and in his *Philobiblon*. In the tradition of the notaries who practised in courts christian, he compiled an immense formulary of fifteen hundred documents, mainly the more florid products of the papal and royal Chanceries, on affairs of State. If Richard de Bury was not a great scholar himself, at least he struck Petrarch, who met him at Avignon, as 'vir ardentis ingenii nec literarum inscius'. He relished scholarship, collected books on a grand scale, and patronized humanistic studies in England.[3] All this does not make him an example of 'notarial influence'; but it does illustrate the quality and interests of a circle in fourteenth-century English society in

---

[1] *Studies in English Official Historical Documents* (Cambridge, 1908), p. 245; cf. ibid., p. 246: 'Although it is generally assumed that the royal diplomata served as models for all private charters, there are several familiar types of public instruments which are apparently derived from private forms.'

[2] Denholm-Young, 'The cursus'.

[3] N. Denholm-Young, 'Richard de Bury (1287–1345)', *TRHS*, 4th series xx (1937), 135–68. His *Liber epistolaris* has been edited by Mr. Denholm-Young for the Roxburghe Club (1950). For his career in brief, with bibliography, see Emden, *BRUO*, i. 323–6.

which English notaries moved and played their part. Two
generations later, on a much lower level of the civil service
and with greater literary talent, comes the bibulous Thomas
Hoccleve, a clerk in the Privy Seal office and a poet. He too
was a formulary-maker on a grand scale. His bulky collection
(B.M. MS. Add. 24062) was probably compiled towards the
end of his career, *c.* 1420–4; with other formularies it has been
profitably exploited by Professor Perroy in his *Diplomatic
Correspondence of Richard II.*[1] These and others from ecclesiastical and municipal archives open up prospects which deserve
consideration. The detailed study of forms and terms may
show more clearly what England owed in the later Middle
Ages to examples set by continental scribes and lawyers and
to practices originating in alien systems of law.

[1] Camden 3rd series xlviii (Royal Historical Soc., 1933).

John Erturi de Cadomo

(above, p. 21)

THE effort to establish the nationality of 'John son of Arthur of Caen'—one of the first Englishmen to hold the title of notary public by apostolic authority—has involved the examination of many records. It has led to no absolute certainty about his origin, though it is highly probable that he was related to Englishmen 'de Cadomo'. But irrespective of this question, the records reveal a career which throws light on the usual tasks and rewards of notaries employed by the Edwardian government. Their evidence is therefore assembled in this appendix.

John Erturi de Cadomo appears first as a notary in 1268, at Lambeth on 15 October. Just about three months earlier the papal legate Ottobuono had left the country, closing a period of three years during which the English Church had been under his single control; in April he had presided over a council attended by the prelates of both provinces.[1] The Council of London had brought the archbishop of York into the southern province, and may have caused a confrontation with the archbishop of Canterbury which led to the incident at Lambeth recorded by the notary. The perennial dispute over the right of the archbishop to have his cross carried before him in the other province had been revived. Now the archbishop of York sent his proctor to appeal, in writing, to the apostolic see, in the presence of the archbishop of Canterbury, against any obstruction by the latter; and John Erturi was there to record the appeal in a public instrument. Coming so soon after the legate had left England and when other notaries (it has been seen) were active in England on the legate's account, one might suppose that John was a stranger to the country, presumably from Caen in Normandy, whom the events of the last few years might have brought to England in the legate's train. But there are several reasons for rejecting the supposition. First, the family name 'de Cadomo' (Cadamo, Kadomo, Caam, and the like) appears in various parts of England

---

[1] *Councils and Synods*, II. ii. 738–92, cf. 725.

in the twelfth and thirteenth centuries, doubtless all originally deriving from Caen, but naturalized in England. Secondly, John Erturi de Cadomo, although he does not again authenticate any surviving notarial act for twelve years after 1268, does appear again as notary public, under this name, at intervals between 1280 and 1305. Thirdly, since the later notarial documents are all in the royal interest, it is most likely that he is to be identified with a Master John de Cadomo who appears from 1276 to 1310 as an important royal clerk. In this connection it should be remembered that the form 'John Erturi de Cadomo' and the like are hardly ever used in English documents which name notaries in the third person,[1] nor do others normally describe a notary public as such unless the occasion demands. Further, a notary public normally uses the long form of his name only in the eschatocol of a document which he authenticates.

In the following pages these points will be examined in turn.

1. The family name 'de Cadomo' occurs in England long before the time of John Erturi, whose active career (since it only ended in 1310) cannot have begun much earlier than his first recorded appearance in 1268. There were, for example, Robert de Cadomo, a canon of St. Paul's early in the twelfth century,[2] and Ralf, sub-dean of Lincoln *c.* 1161–79[3] and, above all, a namesake of John Erturi, Master John de Cadomo who flourished between 1230 and 1256. This Master John may have belonged to a family with interests in Cambridgeshire and adjoining counties. One Richard de Cadomo appears in Croxton in 1184, and after him Luciana in 1236, Robert in 1279, and Philip in 1299.[4] Master John first appears as witness of Cambridgeshire transactions concerning Barnwell Priory and the bishop of Ely between 1229 and 1232.[5] He attests an act of Bishop Hugh of Ely (probably Hugh of Northwold, 1229–54) as 'officialis noster'.[6] He was rector of Wisbech, Cambs., from at least 1231 until after 1252.[7] Presumably he did not reside, since there was a well-endowed vicarage. He was simultaneously a canon of

---

[1] Above, p. 29, and below, p. 147. P.R.O., E 39/16/13 (4 June 1291) is an exception: Andrew de Tange often gives John Erturi de Cadomo his full name.

[2] Le Neve, *Fasti, 1066–1300*, i. 81.

[3] *Registrum Antiquissimum of Lincoln*, ed. C. W. Foster and K. Major (Lincoln Record Soc.), ix (1968), 105, etc.

[4] W. Farrer, *Feudal Cambridgeshire* (Cambridge, 1920), pp. 180, 181, 203, 204.

[5] Emden, *BRUC*, p. 116b.

[6] Cambridge Univ. Libr., Ely Diocesan Records, Liber R, f. 223vb.

[7] *Patent Rolls 1225–32*, p. 508; Cambridge Univ. Libr., Ely Diocesan Records, Reg. John de Fordham, f. 212r.

St. Paul's, to whom papal mandates were addressed on 5 November 1232 and 4 September 1253.[1] The explanation of these preferments lies in his position as a royal clerk, supposing him to be the Master John de Cadomo who represented the king at a meeting of bishops at Cirencester in 1233, and who went later in the year as the king's proctor to the Roman Curia.[2] Twenty years later Master John received royal gifts of venison in Essex.[3] In 1252 he used his influence as *clericus regis* to obtain exemption from assizes, etc., for his nephew, Philip of Cheshunt (Cestrehunt).[4] Unfortunately, the annals of the Caens in England seem to record no Arthur—a name relatively uncommon in those days. It is tempting, nevertheless, to associate Master John de Cadomo who flourished in the middle of the century with the John Erturi de Cadomo of the next generation. Both were in the king's service, both seem to be interested in the church of Wisbech and associated with the family of Cheshunt. Shortly before John de Cadomo (whom we identify as John Erturi) died in March 1310, he made over land to one Master Stephen of Cheshunt with remainder to John, eldest son of Richard de Cadomo; and, at his death, Stephen was named as one of his executors.[5]

2. A little must be said about the notarial activities of John Erturi de Cadomo. When he first appeared in 1268 he was, Messrs. Richardson and Sayles supposed, 'attached to Archbishop Boniface'.[6] But even if he appeared in the archbishop's chamber at Lambeth on this occasion, the party for whose appeal he drew up the public instrument was the archbishop of York. Walter Giffard had been the king's chancellor until September 1266, and it would not be surprising if his proctor at Lambeth had used a royal clerk who had been known to his master at Westminster. Some colour is given to this conjecture by the fact that in later years John Erturi always appears as a royal clerk, not in the service of the archbishop of Canterbury or of York. The record of 1268, preserved only in a copy in Giffard's register, is not written there in his hand. As to the circumstances in which he had become a notary public we know

---

[1] *Cal. Papal Letters*, i. 130; *Mon. Ang.*, vi. 162*b*. Cf. Le Neve, *Fasti, 1066–1300*, i. 93.

[2] *Cal. Pat. Rolls 1232–47*, pp. 32, 33.

[3] *Close Rolls 1251–3*, p. 319; *1254–6*, p. 320.

[4] *Cal. Pat. Rolls 1247–58*, p. 154.

[5] *Cal. Ancient Deeds*, iii (HMSO, 1900), 179 (E 40/5439) and cf. *Cal. Pat. Rolls 1307–13*, p. 326; *Reg. Reynolds*, p. 17.

[6] *EHR*, xlvi (1931), 544 n. 5. I am obliged to Dr. D. T. Williams, who has studied the household and *acta* of Boniface, for the assurance that John is not otherwise found in connection with the archbishop.

nothing. He may have been one of those thirteenth-century English clerks who had made their way to the Curia on their own business or for the king or a prelate, or who studied at Bologna; in either place they would realize the growing value of the notarial training and title. (Such a one, apparently, was John Alani de Beccles (above, p. 29), the next English-born notary public to be found at work in England, who had been proctor in the Curia for Bishop Thomas de Cantilupe.) But this is pure conjecture. John Erturi's next known public instrument, after that of 15 October 1268, is dated 11 September 1280, and is copied into Archbishop John Pecham's register. By it the archbishop dispensed Master Geoffrey de Eversley from the obligation to proceed to the orders required by his tenure of the church of Harrow. The record has several points of interest. Master Geoffrey was notary of the king of Castile and go-between for that king and Edward I of England (cf. p. 2 n. 3). It was Edward I who had presented him to the church of Harrow, and the archbishop had ordained him subdeacon reluctantly, to judge by the terms of this document. Although it is in form an instrument made *de mandato prefati domini archiepiscopi* (and is sealed with his seal) it includes a guarantee that Geoffrey should not be harmed by any letter issued by the archbishop's authority against him. Clearly it was issued under pressure from the Crown. Since John Erturi never acted for the archbishop again, we may assume that he acted as the king's agent in extracting this concession from the archbishop.[1] Another long interval elapses before he draws up public instruments, this time in 1288, *de mandato domini regis*, in the course of Edward I's visit to Aragon.[2] He was back in England with the court in 1290, and drafted an instrument in the king's presence at Clipstone Regis, 14 October 1290, relating to the king's proposed crusade and the clerical tenth.[3] The next year the 'Great Cause' of Scotland called for the production of various notarial instruments by the English government, and John Erturi was repeatedly engaged upon these.[4] When in June 1300 King Edward I tried to establish harmony between the bishop and the prior and monks of

[1] *Reg. Pecham*, i. 112–13. A notary public of Pecham's household, Mr. John Lewensis, witnessed the document. For Mr. Geoffrey see Denholm-Young, 'The cursus', pp. 77–9.

[2] Rymer, I. ii. 685, 687–92, 695; these are cited as convenient examples in print. Original instruments prepared by John Erturi are in the Aragonese royal archives at Barcelona; and I am obliged to Dr. P. Chaplais for xerox copies of *pergaminos Alfonso II*, nos. 242, 244, both dated 28 Oct. 1288.

[3] Rymer, I. ii. 741.

[4] e.g. Stones, *Anglo-Scottish Relations*, pp. 64, 72, 80.

Durham, John Erturi was present and drew up the abortive agreement at the king's command.[1] The final record of his activity as notary public is dated 5 April 1305, in parliament at Westminster. Here a notarial instrument on the 'processus tangens episcopum Bibliensem' was drawn up by John 'dictus Bouhs' and the work was collated with the help of Peter le Malore, a royal judge, and Masters John de Cadomo and Gilbert de Lutegareshale, notaries public. A second eschatocol follows that of John Bouhs, in which John Erturi de Cadomo 'hoc exemplum una cum prefatis domino P. iusticiario et magistris J. et G. notariis publicis . . . ascultavi . . . me testem subscripsi'.[2]

3. Granted that Master John Erturi de Cadomo was generally described by others as Master John de Cadomo (and so described himself when not engaged on notarial business), are we justified in seeing the notary in every reference to Master John de Cadomo in the reign of Edward I? Messrs. Richardson and Sayles were convinced that they could distinguish two, and taxed such eminent predecessors as Palgrave, Maitland, and Maxwell-Lyte with confusing them. 'By a lucky chance', they wrote, 'both were present at the Lenten parliament of 1305 on an occasion when it was necessary to distinguish them.'[3] They refer to the passage quoted above; but a careful examination of the formulas used by the two notaries who write the eschatocols shows that this is the opposite of the truth. There was one John (Erturi) de Cadomo concerned in this instrument about the bishop of Byblos. John dictus Bouhs referred to his colleague John Erturi de Cadomo as Master John de Cadamo, as was usual in such a context. John Erturi used his full 'notarial' name and referred to J[ohn de Bouhs] and G[ilbert de Lutegareshale], giving them the titles of master and notary public, when he came to add his eschatocol. There were three, not four, notaries present.[4] Messrs. Richardson and Sayles use the two Johns whom they discover in this document to distinguish different functionaries in other references. 'Master John of Caen was employed in the Chancery; master John Arthur of Caen, also simply called John of Caen, was employed in the household. Both were apostolic notaries.'

To prove that Richardson and Sayles have composed two Johns 'de Cadomo' out of one in a single document is not the same as

---

[1] *Records of Antony Bek*, pp. 72–4, from Durham, D. & C. Mun., 1. 9. Pont. 2, being the original notarial transcript by Elias de Cowton of John Erturi's notarial instrument.

[2] See above, pp. 109, 113.   [3] *EHR*, xlvi. 544 n. 5.

[4] I am obliged to Professor Stones for calling this misunderstanding to my notice. Cf. above, p. 29.

proving that there were not two men of the same name working simultaneously for the Crown at the beginning of the fourteenth century, one in the Chancery, another in the household.[1] But is it likely that the name so copiously recorded throughout Edward I's reign in connection with the civil service and church benefices relates to two persons? It is not enough to insist on incompatibility of function. Too little is known about the diversity of function of royal officials and the comings and goings between Chancery and household under Edward I. We need an instance of bi-location or else evidence that one John de Cadomo was dead before the other (which amounts to the same thing). This it has so far been impossible to find. One may, then, provisionally assign all references to one John de Cadomo, versatile in the king's business, based on the Wardrobe, and well endowed with benefices, and assume that all these references relate to the notary public who reveals himself on notarial occasions as the son of Arthur. He is probably styled Master because he is a notary public. This does not preclude the possibility that two men may have to be disentangled if more evidence comes to light; but it is hard to believe that if there were two men of this name, both of them masters (though not necessarily both notaries public), both occupying simultaneously posts of trust in the royal government, those other clerks who record their activities would not have found a way of distinguishing between them.

On this assumption, our notary appears at Westminster on 25 April 1276.[2] His notarial duties account for the next reference on 11 September 1280. In May 1284, described as Master John de Cadomo, king's clerk, he carries orders to La Rochelle, and two years later (February–March 1286) receives safe-conduct and protection for two years, when going to the court of Rome.[3] In 1288 he is found at the king's side in Aragon, engaged in drawing up public instruments.[4] Back in England he acts as notary public in 1290 and the following years until 1296. In January 1292 he sits on a commission of oyer and terminer in London[5] and in December is one of the clerks who record delivery of the Great Seal to the

---

[1] The Mr. John de Cadomo who died in March 1310 was certainly interested in another of the same name, John son of Richard, perhaps a young nephew (above, p. 145). We can leave out of account the John son of Robert de Caam who was killed in self-defence by Andrew de Hengham in Norfolk in or before 1294 (*Cal. Pat. Rolls 1292–1301*, pp. 82, 112) and the John de Cadomo *cementarius*, killed at Bannockburn, according to Richardson and Sayles (loc. cit.).

[2] *Cal. Cl. Rolls 1272–9*, p. 417.

[3] *Cal. Pat. Rolls 1281–92*, pp. 122, 228.

[4] Above, p. 146.   [5] *Cal. Pat. Rolls 1281–92*, p. 513.

new chancellor, John Langton.[1] From 1294 onwards until 1307 he
appears at intervals in the notes on Chancery enrolments, as the
bearer (*nunciante J. de C.*) of royal warrants to Chancery.[2] In the
winter of 1297–8 he is at Ghent with the king, and writes and signs
notes on Chancery warrants.[3] In 1298 and again in 1302 he is one
of a group of three clerks who have custody of the Great Seal for
short periods, first in the absence of John Langton and then during
the vacancy before William Greenfield's appointment.[4] In August
1302 he is made keeper of Hastings castle.[5] From 1300 onwards,
until 1310, he is summoned regularly as king's clerk to parliaments.[6]
He is a receiver of petitioners in parliament in Lent 1304 and
Michaelmas 1305.[7] In the Lent parliament of 1305 he acts (as we
have seen) as notary public. In 1307 he appears in a new role, suing
for the king against the bishop of Chichester in the Court of King's
Bench over the alleged exemption of the prebendal churches of the
castle chapel of Hastings from diocesan control.[8] He is described
as a clerk of Chancery in April and June of this year when passing
letters for the Great Seal.[9] In 1307 he is keeper of the temporalities
of the vacant see of Dublin.[10]

With all these duties went a variety of casual rewards : a legacy from
Queen Eleanor in 1292,[11] robes from the Wardrobe 1296–1301,[12]
venison,[13] oaks from the forests of Essex, Galtres, and Cannock.[14]
But the main recompense lay in church revenues. Here Master
John de Cadomo was particularly well endowed at one time or
another with those benefices without cure of souls which were
the mainstay of the civil service of the time. He was a prebendary
of York as early as 1284,[15] and held a prebend there until he was on

---

[1] *Cal. Pat. Rolls 1292–1301*, pp. 2, 43; *Cal. Cl. Rolls 1288–96*, pp. 276, 308;
Cal. Fine Rolls, i. 317.

[2] *Cal. Pat. Rolls 1292–1301*, pp. 71, 208, 337, 339, 390, 391, 410, 462, 463, 523,
1301–7, pp. 54, 90, 518–19; *Cal. Cl. Rolls 1288–96*, pp. 350, 407, *1296–1302*, p. 224,
1302–7, p. 453 (cf. H. Maxwell-Lyte, *The Great Seal*, p. 360); *Cal. Chancery
Warrants*, pp. 110, 260.

[3] *Cal. Chancery Warrants*, pp. 49, 77, 79, 91, and for the notes, ibid., pp. 85, 89.

[4] Ibid., p. 100; *Cal. Pat. Rolls 1292–1301*, p. 352, *1301–7*, p. 91; *Cal. Ch. Rolls
1300–26*, p. 27; *Cal. Cl. Rolls 1296–1302*, pp. 230, 295, 601, 602, 610; *1302–7*, p. 69.

[5] *Cal. Pat. Rolls 1301–7*, p. 52.   [6] Richardson and Sayles, loc. cit.

[7] *Rot. Parl.*, i. 159; *Cal. Cl. Rolls 1302–7*, p. 345.

[8] *Sel. Cases King's Bench*, iii. 186–90. He had special interests in Hastings (see
below).

[9] *Cal. Pat. Rolls 1301–7*, pp. 518–19; *Cal. Chancery Warrants*, p. 260.

[10] *Cal. Pat. Rolls 1307–13*, p. 6.   [11] Richardson and Sayles, loc. cit.

[12] Ibid.   [13] *Cal. Pat. Rolls 1292–1301*, p. 60; *Cal. Cl. Rolls 1288–96*, p. 301.

[14] *Cal. Cl. Rolls 1288–96*, p. 240, *1296–1302*, pp. 2, 175, *1302–7*, p. 494.

[15] P.R.O., SC 1/14/83. Cf. *CPL*, i. 473 and *Reg. Nicolas IV*, nos. 2871, 7488.

his deathbed in March 1310, if not until the day of his death.[1] For the last three years of his life he was also prebendary of Leighton Manor in the church of Lincoln and he died a prebendary of Wells.[2] Then there were the pickings of royal chapels. In July 1279 he had the king's support, against a providee, for a prebend at St. Martin's-le-Grand.[3] In December 1291 he was granted a prebend in the castle chapel of Hastings.[4] He resigned this early in 1301 in favour of Nicholas de Cadomo, also a king's clerk;[5] but this did not permanently sever his connection with Hastings. In March 1303 the king, describing him as a king's clerk and member of his household, complained that although he held a prebend of Hastings collated to him by the king, the archbishop of Canterbury had cited him as an intruder.[6] On 28 October 1294 John had been granted the deanery of the royal free chapel of Stafford, and still held it in 1300.[7] In the same year 1294 he was canon of Wolverhampton and of Penkridge.[8] On 4 January 1296 he received preferment of another sort: the archdeaconry of Glendalough, which he still held in 1304.[9] This was not all. Master John might also hope to benefit from the dispensation often accorded to king's clerks to be absentee rectors and enjoy livings in plurality. In May 1303—two months after the trouble over Hastings—the king required the archbishop of Canterbury to desist from molesting Master John as parson of Stanford Rivers (Essex) and revoke any process begun against him because he had not been ordained priest within a year of institution. The king's writ to the archbishop asserted the exemption of his clerks from the obligations to proceed to holy orders or to reside. At this date, Master John had been rector of Stanford for at least ten years.[10] Over the years his list of rectories includes Witchampton (Dorset), 1278,[11] Wrabness (Essex), vacated in 1279,[12] Little Laver (Essex),

---

[1] See Le Neve, *Fasti, 1300–1541*, vi. 44. *Reg. Greenfield*, iv. 102 records that on 23 March 1310 he exchanged his prebend with William de Melton for a prebend in Darlington. But John was dead before 28 March (*Reg. Reynolds*, p. 17); so perhaps this was a simulated exchange, written later and antedated to forestall a papal providee to York.

[2] Le Neve, *Fasti, 1300–1541*, i. 83, viii. 81.

[3] Prynne, *Records*, iii. 228 from P.R.O., SC 1/10/34A. Cf. J. H. Denton, *English Royal Free Chapels, 1100–1300* (Manchester, 1970), p. 39 n. 7.

[4] *Cal. Pat. Rolls 1281–92*, p. 463.   [5] Ibid., *1292–1301*, p. 582.

[6] *Cal. Cl. Rolls 1302–7*, pp. 80–1.

[7] *Cal. Pat. Rolls 1292–1301*, p. 106, cf. p. 158 and P.R.O., SC 1/20/183.

[8] *Cal. Pat. Rolls 1292–1301*, p. 119.   [9] Ibid., p. 181, *1301–7*, p. 258.

[10] Prynne, iii. 986 (= *Cal. Cl. Rolls 1302–7*, p. 88); *Sel. Cases King's Bench*, ii. 170–1.

[11] *Cal. Pat. Rolls 1272–81*, p. 278; vacated by 1298: *Reg. Gandavo*, ii. 579.

[12] *Cal. Pat. Rolls 1272–81*, p. 325.

1292,[1] Montgomery, 1293,[2] the chapel of Wykes by Boston (Lincs.), 1298.[3] In this year 1298 he was presented to the rectory of Wisbech (Cambs.), which had been held by his namesake in the mid-thirteenth century; but the bishop of Ely had appropriated the church to his cathedral monastery in 1275; the monks contested the claim of this John de Cadomo *redivivus* and at much expense established their own right.[4] Stratford-upon-Avon is the last rectory on our list, acquired, not without some trouble, in 1300–1, and it is specifically said to have been held in plurality.[5] It is unlikely that these benefices comprehend all the church preferment under Crown patronage which John de Cadomo enjoyed; but they suffice to show that he was a person of consequence in the civil service—always supposing that all references concern one and the same man.

Among the various men called John de Cadomo found in England during the thirteenth and fourteenth centuries one is recorded as a canonist. A fourteenth-century manuscript of Merton College contains an 'Abbreviatio decreti' of which the colophon reads: 'Explicit tractatus decretorum per magistrum Johannem de Cadomo compilatus.'[6] Professor Kuttner notes that it is closely dependent on the *Glossa Palatina*, though compiled after the publication of *Extra*, therefore after 1234. Its old-fashioned form suggests composition soon after that date. So the rector of Wisbech who was the bishop of Ely's official, a canon of St. Paul's, and a royal clerk, whose known career extends from 1229 to 1253, may seem a likely author. If this is the man, his pretensions as a teacher make more plausible Dr. Emden's conjecture that the rector of Wisbech studied at Cambridge. And if so, this commonplace 'Tractatus decretorum' must be among the earliest known literary products of the university. Whether or not these speculations are justified, it is highly improbable that the canonist was John Erturi de Cadomo.

---

[1] Ibid., *1281–92*, p. 488.

[2] P.R.O., SC 1/29/134, cf. *Cal. Pat. Rolls 1292–1301*, p. 119; *Cal. Chancery Warrants*, p. 39. The date of his institution does not appear, but another non-resident rector held it in 1277 (*Reg. Cantilupe*, pp. 137, 168). It is interesting to find Stephen of Cheshunt, subdeacon, presented to this church by the Crown on 18 May 1300, and Nicholas de Caen, acolyte, on 11 May 1315 (*Reg. Swinfield*, pp. 532, 543). For their connection with John de Cadomo see above.

[3] *Cal. Pat. Rolls 1292–1301*, p. 334. [4] Ibid., pp. 347, 365.

[5] *Reg. G. Giffard*, pp. 514, 543, 550; William Thomas, *Survey of the Cathedral-Church of Worcester* (1737), Appendix, p. 70; P.R.O., SC 1/18/24.

[6] Oxford, Merton Coll., MS. 266, ff. 13–129. Kuttner notes another fourteenth-century MS., B.M., MS. Cotton Claud. A. iv, ff. 81–187[v], entitled 'Compilatio decretorum Gratiani', without ascription (S. Kuttner, *Repertorium der Kanonistik (1140–1134)* (Studi e Testi, 71, Città del Vaticano, 1937), pp. 266–7).

Selected Documents

1 (above, p. 74)

Direct papal appointment of Richard 'dictus Ponerel' as a notary public, after examination. Lateran, 7 December 1302[1]

Vatican Archives, Reg. Vat. 50, f. 291ᵛ. Calendared in *Cal. Papal Letters*, i. 608 and *Reg. Boniface VIII*, vol. iv, no. 5081.

Riccardo dicto Ponerel' clerico Exoniensis diocesis. Ne contractuum memoria deperiret, inventum est tabellionatus officium, quo contractus legitimi ad cautelam presentium et memoriam futurorum manu publica notarentur. Hinc est quod nos predictum officium, ad quod examinatus per dilectum filium nostrum Petrum sancte Marie Nove diaconum cardinalem, cui super hec examinationem tuam commisimus, fuisti repertus ydoneus, tibi duximus concedendum, ut illud prudenter et fideliter exequaris et ad te cum necesse fuerit in hiis que ad officium ipsum pertinent recurratur. Nulli ergo etc. nostre concessionis etc.

Dat' Laterani, vii idus Decembris anno octavo.

2 (above, p. 44)

Petition of the prior of Christ Church, Canterbury, to the pope for leave to create two notaries public[2]

Canterbury, D. & C. Archives, Reg. I, f. 245ʳ. Printed by W. Somner, *The Antiquities of Canterbury*, 2nd edn. by N. Battely (1703), part one, appendix, p. 59, no. LI.

Peticio pro tabellionibus faciendis.

Significat sanctitati vestre prior ecclesie Christi Cant' quod per sedem apostolicam frequenter committuntur eidem priori cause

---

[1] The formula closely resembles that in Tangl, p. 329, no. CXXXII, except in omitting reference to the swearing of an oath. For the oath see no. 3 below.

[2] This undated letter was probably addressed by Prior Henry of Eastry to Pope Boniface VIII or his immediate successor. It is copied into Reg. I shortly after a royal writ of 14 Nov. 1302. There is no evidence that the petition was granted or, indeed, that this is anything more than a draft form which was never

et negotia audienda et discucienda ac eciam delegatorum sentencie exequende, propter que necessarium est sibi usus et officium tabellionum, et quia in civitate et dyocesi Cant' rarissime haberi potest copia tabellionum, suplicat sanctitati vestre prior predictus quod placeat vobis graciose concedere sibi potestatem faciendi duos tabelliones.

3 (above, p. 27)

Papal faculty for the archbishop of Canterbury to appoint, within a year, three fit persons as notaries public. Rome, St. Peter's, 25 March 1279

Vatican Archives. Reg. Vat. 39, f. 143^r, no. lxxxij. Calendared in *Cal. Papal Letters*, i. 458 and *Reg. Nicolas III*, no. 488.

Venerabili fratri J. archiepiscopo Cantuariensi, quod possit concedere officium tabellionatus tribus personis.

Ne contractuum memoria deperiret, inventum est tabellionatus officium, quo contractus legitimi ad cautelam presentium et memoriam futurorum manu publica notarentur. Unde interdum sedes apostolica predictum officium personis que ad illud reperiuntur ydonee concedere consuevit ut illud prudenter et fideliter exequantur et ad eas cum necesse fuerit in hiis que ad officium ipsum pertinent[1] recurratur. Cum itaque,[2] sicut in nostra proposuisti presentia constitutus, personarum que contractus legitimos, acta iudiciorum, et alia huiusmodi redigant in publica munimenta defectus in illis partibus habeatur, nos tuis supplicationibus inclinati concedendi infra annum a receptione presentium predictum officium tribus personis quas ad illud post diligentem examinationem ydoneas esse reppereris, prius ab eis iuramento iuxta formam quam tibi mittimus presentibus annotatam recepto, plenam tibi auctoritate presentium concedimus facultatem.

Forma autem iuramenti quod ipsarum personarum quelibet prestabit talis est.[3]

Ego . . ab hac hora inantea fidelis ero beato Petro et sancte Romane ecclesie ac domino pape N. et successoribus eius canonice

used. In later years the prior appointed at least four notaries public by imperial authority (see below, no. 5).

[1] The formula in Tangl, p. 329, no. cxxxiii, here adds 'fiducialiter'.

[2] This sentence, as far as 'tuis supplicationibus', does not occur in Tangl's formula.

[3] The following form of oath agrees closely with Tangl, pp. 50, 33, nos. xvii and i, as far as 'consueto salario'. The next sentence is not in Tangl; nor is it in the form preserved in *Reg. Sutton*, iii. 171.

intrantibus. Non ero in consilio aut consensu vel facto ut vitam perdant aut menbrum vel capiantur mala captione. Consilium quod michi per se vel litteras aut nunctium manifestabunt ad eorum dampnum scienter nemini pandam. Si vero ad meam notitiam aliquid devenire contingat quod in periculum Romani pontificis aut ecclesie Romane vergeret seu grave dampnum, illud pro posse impediam, et si hoc impedire non possem, procurabo bona fide id ad notitiam domini pape perferri. Papatum Romane ecclesie ac regalia sancti Petri et iura ipsius ecclesie, specialiter siqua eadem ecclesia in civitate vel terra de qua sum oriundus habeat, adiutor ero ad defendendum vel retinendum contra omnes homines. Tabellionatus officium fideliter exercebo. Contractus in quibus exigitur consensus partium fideliter faciam, nil addendo vel minuendo sine voluntate partium quod substantiam contractus immutet. Si vero in conficiendo aliquod instrumentum unius solius partis sit requirenda voluntas, hoc ipsum faciam, ut scilicet nil addam vel minuam quod immutet facti substantiam contra voluntatem ipsius. Instrumentum non conficiam de aliquo contractu in quo sciam intervenire seu intercedere vim vel fraudem. Contractus in prothocollum redigam et postquam in prothocollum redigero malitiose non differam contra voluntatem illorum vel illius quorum est contractus super eo conficere publicum instrumentum, salvo meo iusto et consueto salario. Si autem aliquod instrumentum quod falsum esse cognovero ad manus meas contigerit devenire, destruam illud si possim hoc facere absque meo periculo sive dampno. Quod si viderem michi dampnum vel periculum imminere, perferam in notitiam rectoris seu domini iurisdictionem habentis in civitate seu loco in quo ad manus meas devenerit huiusmodi instrumentum. Sic me deus adiuvet et hec sancta evangelia.

Dat' Rome apud Sanctum Petrum, viii kal. Aprilis anno secundo.

4a (above, p. 82)

Faculty granted by Rogerius Mathei de Monte Florum, count palatine, to the prior of Durham cathedral priory, on the petition of W. de C., to create John de B., clerk of the diocese of Durham, a notary public. 1305

Cambridge, Corpus Christi College, MS. 450, p. 178, in an early-fourteenth-century miscellany which includes the works of John de Bononia and Laurence de Aquilegia on the notarial art.

Forma creandi et investiendi aliquos in officium tabellionatus.

Religioso et discreto viro domino priori Dunolmensi ordinis

sancti Benedicti Dunolmensis diocesis Rogerius Mathei de Monte
florum dei gracia comes palatinus salutem et debitam diligenciam
in commissis. Sagax humane nature discrecio, memorie hominum
labilitate pensata, ne diuturnitate temporum que inter contrahentes
aguntur oblivionis defectui subiacerent, tabellionatus[1] adinvenit
officium per quod contrahencium vota scribuntur et scripture
ministerio postmodum[2] longum servantur[3] in evum. Cum itaque
ex parte J. de B. clerici Dunolmensis diocesis nobis extiterit humiliter supplicatum per W. de C. ut discretis aliquibus commit-[p. 179]
tere dignaremur quod possent auctoritate nobis et antecessoribus
nostris super conficiendis notariis vel tabellionibus puplicis a divis
inperatoribus concessa officium tabellionatus concedere Johanni
predicto, nos de discrecione vestra plenam spem fiduciamque
gerentes ac fidedignorum testimonia actendentes que sibi tam super
ydoneitate persone quam aliis probitatis meritis suffragantur,
volentes propterea huiusmodi supplicacionibus favorabiliter annuere
in hac parte, discrecioni vestre tenore presencium duximus com-
mittendum ut si prephatum Johannem sufficientem et idoneum esse
reppereritis ad predictum officium optinendum diligenti examinacione premissa receptoque postmodum ab eodem J. vice nostra sacrosancte Romane ecclesie ac sacri Romani[4] inperii nomine fidelitatis
solite necnon de ipso tabellionatus officio fideliter et legaliter excercendo prout infra annotabitur corporaliter iuramento auctoritate predicta qua vos fungi volumus in hac parte, vos ipsum J. cui exnunc
officium predictum concedimus per pennam calamarium atque cartam que tunc in manibus tenebitis investiatis de officio supradicto,
dantes et concedentes eidem J. dicta auctoritate nobis ut superius
exprimitur in hac parte concessa plenam licenciam tenore presencium
et omnimodam liberam ac plenariam potestatem instrumenta acta
prothocolla conficiendi et litteras exemplandi copiandi et puplicandi
testes recipiendi examinandi et eorum dicta puplicandi testamenta
conficiendi confessiones super quibuscumque contractibus audiendi
et recipiendi, ac insinuandi et scribendi ultimas decedencium voluntates et quelibet alia instrumenta et scripturas sive contractus tam
ultimarum voluntatum quam quorumcumque aliorum negociorum
scribendi puplicandi examinandi, necnon et sentencias iudicum
ordinariorum delegatorum arbitrorum audiendi et formandi, ap-
posiciones excepciones quascumque tam in iudiciis quam extra
conficiendi et ordinandi cum potestate dandi tutores et curatores,
decreta interponendi, alimenta decernendi, necnon emancipare

---

[1] *MS.* tabellionis.   [2] *MS. om.* postmodum.   [3] *MS.* servatur.
[4] *MS.* sacre Romane.

manumittere et adoptare volentibus auctoritatem prestandi, dictumque officium ubilibet et ubique terrarum libere excercendi, ac omnia alia et singula faciendi que ad sepedictum officium quomodolibet spectare noscuntur vel eciam pertinere. Forma autem iuramenti de quo supra fit mencio talis erit. Tu iurabis decetero te esse fidelem sacrosancte Romane ecclesie ac sacro Romano inperio graciam et communionem apostolice sedis habenti michique Ro[p. 180]gerio comiti supradicto, non faciendo aliquid seu facientibus consenciendo quod in contrarium dictorum ecclesie inperii atque mei redundare valeret. Tabellionatus officium perpetuo legaliter et fideliter excercebis non addens non minuens aliquid quod contrahencium alteri prodesse vel obesse valeret. Scripturas vero pro parte in formam puplicam redigendas in carta vero bombacina vel unde alias fuerit abrasa scriptura aut que de facili viciari valeat non scribes et tabellionatus officium semper bona fide et sine fraude aliqua excercebis. In quorum omnium testimonium et certitudinem pleniorem presens instrumentum per H. de H. notarium puplicum infrascriptum scribi et puplicari fecimus mandavimus et nostri sigilli fecimus appensione muniri.

Dat' etc. anno domini m°ccc°quinto.

4b (above, pp. 82–3)

Faculty granted by Bassianus de Alliate of Milan, count palatine, in virtue of his authority from the emperor, to the prior of Christ Church, Canterbury, to create three fit persons as notaries public. Lyon, 5 March 1306

Canterbury, D. &. C. Archives, Reg. I, f. 265^r. Printed by W. Somner, *The Antiquities of Canterbury*, 2nd edn. by N. Battely (1703), part one, appendix, p. 59, no. LIIa.

Venerabili[1] in Christo patri priori ecclesie Christi Cantuariensis Bassianus de Allyate de Mediolano dei gracia comes palatinus salutem et debitam diligenciam in commissis. Sagax humane nature discretio, memorie hominum labilitate pensata, ne[2] diuturnitate temporum que inter contrahentes aguntur oblivionis defectui subiacerent, tabellionatus adinvenit officium, per quod contrahentium vota scribuntur et scripture ministerio[3] postmodum longum

---

[1] *Rubric:* Littera de potestate faciendi unum tabellionem, *the last two words corr. (xviii cent.) to* iij Tabelliones.

[2] *MS.* ve.

[3] *MS.* ministratio.

servantur in evum. Cum itaque ex parte vestra nobis extitit humiliter supplicatum ut vobis potestatem creandi tres tabelliones seu notarios publicos concedere dignaremur, nos huiusmodi supplicacionibus in hac parte favorabiliter annuentes, prefatam potestatem usque ad dictum numerum paternitati vestre, auctoritate nobis et antecessoribus nostris a divis imperatoribus super conficiendis tabellionibus seu notariis publicis concessa, plenarie duximus concedendam, vestram paternitatem ad huiusmodi potestatem optinendam approbantes. Verum quia volumus quod forma solita in creacione notariorum observetur, ne minus ydonei et insufficientes ad huiusmodi officium excercendum deputentur, diligenti examinacione premissa eosdem quos creare volueritis per pennam, calamarium atque cartam que tunc in manibus tenebitis presencialiter investiatis, recepto prius ab eisdem tribus sigillatim, sacri imperii nomine, fidelitatis solite necnon et de ipso tabellionatus officio fideliter et legaliter excercendo, corporaliter iuramento, dantes et concedentes unicuique illorum trium [f. 265ᵛ] auctoritate vobis tenore presencium ut superius exprimitur concessa plenam licenciam et liberam potestatem instrumenta, acta, prothocolla, et litteras exemplandi, faciendi, copiandi, et publicandi, testes recipiendi et examinandi ac publicandi, testamenta conficiendi, aperiendi et approbandi, confessiones super quibuscunque contractibus audiendi et recipiendi, et insinuandi et scribendi ultimas decedencium voluntates, tutores et curatores dandi, alimenta decernendi, decretum interponendi, ac faciendi et scribendi quelibet alia instrumenta et scripturas sive contractus tam ultimarum voluntatum quam quorumcunque aliorum negociorum, et tabellionatus officium libere, prudenter, et fideliter ubilibet excercendi, et omnia alia et singula faciendi et scribendi que ad sepedictum officium spectare noscuntur vel eciam pertinere. Et ad unumquemque eorundem trium cum necesse fuerit in omnibus et singulis supradictis, et que ad predictum officium pertinent, libere recurratur. Forma autem iuramenti per unumquemque eorundem trium talis erit. Dicatur eciam sic cuilibet sigillatim. Tu iurabis ad sancta dei ewangelia quod nunquam eris contrarius Romane ecclesie nec imperio nec nobis. Nunquam falsam facies cartam. Testamentum autenticum et omnia ea que autenticari debent non autenticabis in cartis abrasis, bombacinis vel papiris. Contractus vero, acta causarum, testamenta, donationes, et omnia ea que ad artem et officium notar' pertinent, prout audiveris et rogatus fueris, manu propria cum tuo nomine et signo scribes et autenticabis. Dicta quoque testium bona fide sine fraude scribes et recipies, et generaliter omnia alia et singula que ad ipsam artem et officium notar' spectant iuxta fidelitatem et officii consuetudinem fideliter ac integraliter observare iurabis. In quorum omnium testimonium et certitudinem pleniorem presens privilegium in formam publici instrumenti fieri mandavimus per notarium infrascriptum, et nostri sigilli fecimus appensione muniri. Dat' et act' Lugduni in ecclesia maiori, sub anno domini millesimo ccc^{mo} vi, die v mensis Marcii, indiccione quarta, tempore domini Clementis pape quinti anno primo, presentibus discretis viris Albertino filio dicti comitis layco et Vitale Fargiani clerico Mediolanensis dyocesis testibus ad hoc specialiter vocatis et rogatis.

Et ego Willelmus Thome dicti Coci de Ros, clericus[1] Herefordensis dyocesis publicus sacri Romani imperii auctoritate notarius omnibus predictis interfui, et de dicti comitis mandato presens privilegium scripsi et publicavi meoque signo consueto signavi rogatus.

5 (above, p. 83)

Appointment by the prior of Canterbury of Richard de Norton as notary public by imperial authority in virtue of the faculty received by the prior from Bassianus de Alliate of Milan, count palatine. Christ Church, Canterbury, 10 April [1306]

Canterbury, D. &. C. Archives, Reg. I, f. 266ᵛ. On the preceding page (f. 266ʳ) of Reg. I is another letter of appointment for Richard Norton, of the same date, in the form of letters patent of the prior 'universis sancte matris ecclesie filiis', similarly certified (at the foot of f. 265ᵛ) by the notary Thomas Johannis dicti Barbitonsoris. For the faculty, see above, no. 4b.

Richard Norton was already doing clerical work for Christ Church in February 1298 (*Reg. Winchelsey*, ii. 1319). He prepared an instrument in public form for the prior at London, 15 February 1308, as Ricardus Mayeu filius Roberti Mayeu de Nortone, of the diocese of Lincoln (Canterbury, D. & C. Archives, Chartae antiquae A. 194).

Richard's appointment is referred to by the prior, along with that of John de Berham, in his letter of appointment of John de Watford under this faculty, 27 March 1309 (Reg. I, f. 303ʳ, printed in Somner's *Canterbury*, part I, app. p. 60, no. LIIb). This is in similar but not identical terms. The prior got another faculty from the successor of Count Bassianus, Albertus de Alliate de Mediolano (cf. the witnesses of the faculty, no. 4b above). In virtue of this he created John de Kyngeston, clerk of the diocese of Canterbury, a notary by imperial authority on 30 June ? 1317 (Reg. I, ff. 354ᵛ–355ʳ). John de Kyngeston's appointment was certified by John de Tunstale, clerk of the diocese of Coventry and Lichfield, notary

---

[1] clericus *interlined.*

public by imperial authority. The formula of creation is somewhat different from the earlier ones, and the terms of investiture add to 'per pennam, calemarium [*sic*] atque cartam' the words 'ac pacis osculum'.

Henricus permissione divina prior Ecclesie Christi Cant' dilecto sibi in Christo Ricardo de Norton clerico Lincolniensis diocesis salutem et in agendis viam veritatis tenere. Litteras patentes preclari et nobilis viri domini Bassiani de Alliate de Mediolano comitis palatini, non abolitas, non cancellatas, nec in aliqua sui parte viciatas, in publicam formam redactas recepimus, tenorem qui sequitur continentes : Venerabili in Christo patri, etc., ut supra in primo folio precedenti. Nos igitur probitatis tue merita et sagacitatis industriam considerantes, teque prout convenit in hac parte diligenter examinato, sufficientem et ydoneum ad huiusmodi tabellionatus officium reputantes, receptoque a te ad sancta dei ewangelia corporaliter iuramento super omnibus et singulis articulis superius expressis fideliter et legaliter excercendis et observandis, auctoritate qua fungimur memorata damus tibi et concedimus tenore presencium plenam licenciam et liberam potestatem instrumenta, acta, prothocolla, et litteras exemplandi, faciendi, copiandi, et publicandi, testes recipiendi et examinandi ac publicandi, testamenta conficiendi, aperiendi, et approbandi, confessiones super quibuscunque contractibus audiendi et recipiendi, et insinuandi ac scribendi ultimas decedencium voluntates, tutores et curatores dandi, alimenta decernendi, decretum interponendi, ac faciendi et scribendi quelibet alia instrumenta et scripturas sive contractus tam ultimarum voluntatum quam quorumcumque aliorum negociorum, et tabellionatus officium libere, prudenter, et fideliter ubilibet excercendi, et omnia alia et singula faciendi et scribendi que ad sepedictum officium spectare noscuntur vel eciam pertinere, et quod ad te cum necesse fuerit, in omnibus et singulis supradictis et que ad predictum officium pertinent, libere recurratur. Teque per pennam, calamarium, atque cartam huiusmodi officio tabellionatus seu notarii publici presencialiter investimus. In quorum omnium testimonium presentem paginam in formam publici instrumenti fieri mandavimus per notarium infrascriptum et sigilli nostri appensione fecimus communiri. Dat' et act' Cantuarie in ecclesia nostra predicta, decimo die mensis Aprilis anno et indiccione suprascriptis, presentibus discretis viris fratribus Gwydone de Smerdenne, Ricardo de Clyve, et Alexandro de Sandwyco commonachis ecclesie nostre predicte, dominis Jacobo Sancti Michaelis, Stephano Sancti Georgii, et Thoma Sancti Petri in Cantuaria ecclesiarum rectoribus, testibus ad hoc specialiter vocatis et rogatis.

Et ego Thomas Johannis dicti Barbitonsoris de Cantuaria, clericus Cantuariensis diocesis, sacri imperii auctoritate notarius, omnibus predictis interfui, et litteras comitis vidi, legi et diligenter ascultavi, et de mandato dicti domini prioris omnia suprascripta in hanc publicam formam redegi, scripsi, et publicavi, meoque signo consueto signavi rogatus.

6 (above, p. 83)

Appointment by the prior of Worcester of John de Maddeleya as notary public by imperial authority in virtue of the faculty received by the prior from Bassianus de Alliate of Milan, count palatine. Worcester, 27 May 1315

Worcester, County Record Office, Reg. Worcester sede vacante, f. 79ᵛ (calendared in *Reg. Worcester sede vacante*, p. 134).[1]

Universis sancte matris ecclesie filiis ad quos presentes littere pervenerint frater Johannes prior ecclesie cathedralis Wygornensis salutem in domino sempiternam. Noverit universitas vestra nos litteras venerabilis viri Bassiani de Aliate civis Mediolanensis ac dei gracia Comitis Palestini[2] recepisse, continentes infrascriptum tenorem: Venerabili in Christo patri domino dei gracia priori etcetera. Nos vero dictus Johannes prior auctoritate litterarum predictarum Johannem de Maddeleya per pennam et calamarium atque cartam quam tunc in manu nostra tenuimus, recepto tamen primitus ab eodem iuramento corporali secundum formam et naturam mandati supradicti, eundem Johannem[2] arte et officio supradicto investivimus, et ei postmodum dedimus et concessimus auctoritate supradicta plenam licenciam et liberam facultatem omnia et singula faciendi et perimplendi que ad officium predictum pertinere noscuntur. In cuius rei testimonium huic littere patenti sigillum nostrum apposuimus. Dat' Wygornie, vi kal. Junii anno domini millesimo cccᵐᵒ quinto decimo.

---

[1] *In the margin is added as a rubric*: Forma ad preficiendum notarium.
[2] *Sic.*

7 (above, pp. 34–5)

Exemplification of title-deeds of Norwich Cathedral Priory by John Pecham, archbishop of Canterbury, in the form of a public instrument by John Alani de Beccles. Lambeth, 15 May 1281

B.M., Cotton ch. II. 21, whence portions printed in *Mon. Ang.*, iv. 19–20. Canterbury, D. & C. Archives, Chartae antiquae N. 26 is an *inspeximus* of the same by Prior Henry and the Chapter of Christ Church, dated at Canterbury, 2 April 1302.

The original is on three membranes, *c.* 38·9 × 170 cm. It is all written in the hand of John of Beccles with his mark drawn in the middle across the seams of the membranes and at the foot on the right-hand side. At the end of each document exemplified, the remaining part of the line is filled with decoration. On the dorse, at the foot, is the notarial mark of Hugh de Musele, clerk of Archbishop Robert Winchelsey when he visited Norwich.

In the transcript below, a few words damaged in the original are completed from the *inspeximus* of 1302.

In nomine patris et filii et spiritus sancti amen. Nos frater Johannes permissione divina Cantuariensis archiepiscopus totius Anglie primas religiosis viris . . priori et conventui ecclesie cathedralis Norwicensis salutem et pacem salvatoris in deo patre cum spiritu sancto. Nuper nos in civitate et dyocesi Norwicensi auctoritate metropolitica visitacionis officium exercentes coram nobis et nostris commissariis prout ex officii nostri debito deberemus vos peremptorie fecimus evocari ut super ecclesiis quas in proprios usus detinetis et aliis bonis ecclesiasticis que et quas in civitate et dyocesi supradictis possidetis ius speciale et commune quod habetis compareretis ostensuri. Vos autem coram nobis certo die in prioratu canonicorum sancte Trinitatis Gypewyci eiusdem dyocesis legittime comparentes, privilegia et instrumenta tam super donacione patronatus ecclesiarum quam super collacione episcoporum ac confirmacione pontificum Romanorum coram nobis produxistis; de quorum quibusdam propter nimiam vetustatem timentes periculum in futurum, ipsa ex decreto nostro exemplari humiliter postulastis. Quedam enim quorum sigilla in conflictu inter vos et cives Norwicenses dudum habito qui notorius est toti regno pro magna parte confracta, iusto timore innovari et publicari ex decreto humiliter petivistis. Volentes igitur testimonium veritati perhibere in futurum, vestris iustis peticionibus duximus inclinandum, ne vos inevitabile periculum futuris temporibus pro defectu probacionis invadat, instrumenta vestra que super premissis habetis auctoritate ordinaria coram nobis fecimus presentari et exhiberi, ac ea diligenter inspecta in nulla sui parte viciosa invenimus, vocatis prius omnibus quorum interest seu negocium contingit, vos . . priorem, sacristam, ac procuratorem vestrum, et duos alios monachos vestri conventus iurare fecimus in forma iuris quod ipsam publicacionem calumpnie causa non petistis, quo recepto instrumenta vestri iuris quod super ecclesias quas in proprios usus possidetis, et quod super bonis vestris ecclesiasticis habetis per publicam personam ad cautelam presencium et memoriam futurorum de verbo ad verbum cum suis signis ex decreto fecimus exemplari et publicari, eandem auctoritatem per hoc cum originalibus habitura; quorum instrumentorum tenor in sequentibus annotatur, qui talis est: [*There follow transcripts of ten documents, of which only nos. 1 and 3 are printed in* Mon. Ang. *The others include a bull of Paschal II (J.–L. 6594), a charter attributed to Archbishop Thomas, though probably of Archbishop Theobald (not in Saltman,* Theobald Archbishop of Canterbury *(1956)), and six acts of bishops of Norwich, from Ebrard to William de Ralegh.*]

Nos autem frater Johannes archiepiscopus supradictus literis et instrumentis superius exemplatis, et in hiis tribus rotulis pargameni per manum Johannis de Becles notarii nostri auctoritate et mandato nostro publicatis, sigillum nostrum apponi fecimus in testimonium premissorum. Dat' apud Lamhythe, idus Maii anno domini m⁰ cc octogesimo primo, consecracionis nostre tercio.

Ego Johannes Alani de Beccles Norwicensis[1] dyocesis, [Signum] sacrosancte Romane ecclesie auctoritate notarius publicus, huiusmodi comparicioni, produccioni, peticioni, presentacioni, instrumentorum exhibicioni, iuramenti prestacioni necnon et decreto, cum magistris Alano de Frestona, archidiacono Norfolc', Reynerio de Florencia, canonico Lichefeldensi, et Johanne de Lek' ac aliis ad hoc testibus nominatis et adhibitis presens fui, et predicta sic fieri vidi[2] et audivi, ac easdem literas et instrumenta prout in ipsis originalibus inveni in hiis tribus rotulis pargameni dicti[3] domini archiepiscopi auctoritate et mandato fideliter exemplavi, diligenter ascultavi, rasuras in verbis 'ecclesiam' in lv linea primi rotuli, in xvi linea secundi rotuli 'Aldewinus', et in lvi linea eiusdem rotuli 'ab eo collatis', et in vii linea tercii rotuli 'me', que superius apparent manu mea feci, et quia utrumque concordare inveni, nullo addito vel minuto quod sensum immutet vel intellectum, meipsum testem subscripsi et signum meum apposui.[4]

---

[1] Norwic- *lost by hole in Cotton ch.*   [2] -dicta sic fieri vi- *lost in Cotton ch.*
[3] pargameni dicti *lost in Cotton ch.*
[4] *Two holes at foot for seal-cord, in Cotton ch.*

[*The* inspeximus *of the prior and convent of Canterbury continues and concludes as follows*:]

Interlineare 'ad' supra xxv lineam huius rotuli, item interlineare 'nos' supra liii lineam, item interlineare 'suis' supra lxi lineam, item interlineare 'iusticia' supra lxvii lineam apposita fuerunt ante consignacionem. Nos vero litteras et instrumenta prescripta et omnia in eis contenta ratificantes et approbantes quantum in nobis est tenore presencium concedimus et confirmamus. In cuius rei testimonium presenti scripto sigillum capituli nostri apposuimus. Dat' in capitulo nostro Cantuar', anno domini millesimo trecentesimo secundo, quarto nonas Aprilis.

8 (above, p. 23)

Notarial exemplification by John de Sancto Demetrio of a letter of Pope Gregory X to Robert Kilwardby, archbishop elect of Canterbury, Orvieto, 1 November 1272, and certificate of its delivery to the archbishop elect at Stratford Abbey, 10 January 1273

Canterbury, D. & C. Archives, Chartae antiquae A. 188. The script is conspicuous for regular use of the tittle as abbreviation. The large initial 'I' of the invocation is surmounted by an elaborate cross. *C.* 32 × 26 cm. Cf. *HMCR*, v. 429*b*, *Reg. Grégoire X*, no. 68, and, for the circumstances as related by a monk of Canterbury, *Gervas. Cant.*, ii. 272–4.

+

In dei nomine amen. Anno eiusdem millesimo ducentesimo septuagesimo secundo iiii idus Januarii, indictione prima, in presencia mei Johannis infrascripti notarii ac aliorum testium infrascriptorum ad hoc specialiter vocatorum et rogatorum atque litteratorum, religiosi viri fratres Johannes de Schamelford' et W. monachi ecclesie Christi Cantuariensis ostenderunt quasdam litteras apostolicas non vitiatas, non cancellatas, non abolitas, neque in aliqua ipsius parte corruptas, sub vera et debita bulla et filo integro, et propter casus fortuitos qui frequenter solent accidere et evitari non possunt petiverunt predictas litteras per me supradictum notarium fideliter et de verbo ad verbum transcribi et publicari, quarum litterarum tenor de verbo ad verbum est talis: Gregorius episcopus servus servorum dei dilecto filio . . electo Cantuariensi salutem et apostolicam benedictionem. Est firma in mente nostra fiducia ut ea que nobis sint placida prompto velis affectu et efficaci studio adimplere, maxime que sint equitati congrua et consona rationi. Sane sicut tua novit discretio ecclesia

Cantuariensis olim pastoris solatio destituta dilecti filii conventus eiusdem ecclesie dilectum filium . . priorem ecclesie prefate ad ipsius regimen concorditer elegerunt, cuius electionis occasione tam idem prior quam procuratores eiusdem conventus ad sedem apostolicam accedentes ibidem tum pro eo quod tunc sedes ipsa vacabat tum quia in nostre promotionis primordio multis et arduis negotiis occupati nequivimus expeditioni electionis eiusdem intendere, licet hoc nostris affectibus non modicum immineret, moram diutinam protraxerunt, cumque carissimus in Christo filius noster . . rex Anglie illustris electionem predictam niteretur multipliciter impugnare, idem prior perspiciens ipsius electionis negotium in grave dampnum eiusdem ecclesie prorogari et per hoc eam posse gravibus affici detrimentis, ac volens vitare pericula que poterunt illi ecclesie si vacaret diutius imminere, plus ecclesie predicte commodum quam proprium zelans honorem, iuri quod sibi ex electione competebat eadem in nostris manibus renunciavit libera et spontanea voluntate, ac tam ipse quam procuratores predicti nobis humiliter supplicarunt ut de tali provideremus ecclesie predicte pastore qui curam ipsius ecclesie coram deo et hominibus utiliter gereret et ipsius profectus prudenter auxiliante deo procuraret. Nos itaque huiusmodi renunciacione admissa et supplicationibus huiusmodi paterna benivolentia exauditis, de persona vestra eidem ecclesie de fratrum nostrorum consilio duximus providendum. Cum igitur prior et procuratores prefati in prosecucione negocii electionis predicte gravia subierint onera expensarum, nos dignum arbitrantes et equum ut expense necessarie de archiepiscopalibus redditibus persolvantur, maxime cum dicti prior et conventus nichil de redditibus predictis dum sedes Cantuariensis vacavit usurpasse sive occupasse dicantur, discretioni tue per apostolica scripta mandamus quatenus, et in hac parte nostro coactaris affectui, eisdem priori et conventui de predictis expensis, quas in duobus milibus quadringentis et triginta novem marcis sterlingorum taxavimus, deliberatione habita diligenti, de predictis redditibus archiepiscopalibus sine qualibet difficultate satisfacere non omittas, ita quod devocionem tuam dignis in domino laudibus commendemus et non oporteat nos aliter super hoc suadente iusticia providere. Dat' apud Urbemveterem kal. Novembris pontificatus nostri anno primo. Transcripte fuerunt dicte littere et cum hoc transcripto diligenter absculate Londonie coram hiis testibus, silicet Waltero Lasseburn' et Willelmo Contarell' servientibus dictorum monacorum, et eodem die quasi hora prima fuerunt dicte littere papales presentate et tradite per antedictos monachos domino electo prefato in abbatia monasterii monachorum de Stratfort coram testibus antedictis et coram magistris Constantino archidiacono Subyrie, Hugone de Colibrig' officiale ipsius electi, Bartholomeo de Ferentino et Philippo Sabaldei eiusdem loci, et pluribus aliis.

Et ego Johannes de Sancto Demetrio imperiali auctoritate [Signum] publicus notarius supradictis omnibus interfui et ad preces predictorum religiosorum presens transcriptum ex originalibus litteris sumpsi, et eum cum ipsis litteris presentibus prenominatis testibus diligenter abscultavi, necnon et presentationi dictarum litterarum similiter interfui, et predicta omnia singula scripsi, et in publicam formam redegi rogatus.

9 (above, pp. 57–8, and Pl. 4)

Notarial exemplification by Andrew de Tange of a letter of grace of Pope Honorius IV to King Edward I, 27 May 1286 (Potthast, 22460), prepared in the king's Wardrobe, 26 October 1305

London, P.R.O., SC 7/36/5; *c.* 20·9 × 35·3 cm.

In nomine domini amen. Hoc est exemplum sive transumptum quarumdam litterarum apostolicarum sub nomine felicis recordacionis domini Honorii pape iiii^{ti} conceptarum, cum vera ipsius bulla plumbea ut prima facie videbatur, et filis sericis rubei croceique coloris pendentibus, bullatarum, non abolitarum, non abrasarum, non cancellatarum, nec in aliqua ipsarum parte viciatarum vel corruptarum, set omni sinistra suspicione carencium, nobilissimo principi domino Edwardo "regi Angl' illustri, "dei gracia, directarum, quarum litterarum in omnibus et per omnia tenor est talis. Honorius episcopus servus servorum dei carissimo in Christo filio Edwardo regi Angl' illustri salutem et apostolicam benediccionem. Eximie devocionis affectus quem erga nos et Romanam ecclesiam habere dinosceris promeretur ut personam tuam apostolici favoris plenitudine prosequentes, peticiones tuas ad exaudicionis graciam benignius admittamus. Cum itaque sicut celsitudinis tue peticio nobis exposita continebat, aliqui excellencie tue compares tibi gradu prohibito non coniuncti, quibus filii seu filie tue decenter nubere valeant de facili nequeant inveniri, nos precibus regiis in hac parte favorabiliter annuentes,[1] cum dictis filiis et filiabus auctoritate presencium dispensamus, ut iidem filii et filie personis sibi quarto

---

[1] *In margin at this point, in another hand*: Quod filii regis Angl' et filie possint personis in quarto gradu affinitatis vel consanguinitatis matrimonialiter copulari.

affinitatis vel consanguinitatis gradu coniunctis, impedimento affinitatis seu consanguinitatis huiusmodi non obstante, licite possint matrimonialiter copulari, prolem suscipiendam ex huiusmodi matrimoniis legitimam decernentes. Nulli ergo omnino hominum liceat hanc paginam nostre dispensacionis et constitucionis infringere vel ei ausu temerario contraire. Si quis autem hoc attemptare presumpserit, indignacionem omnipotentis dei et beatorum Petri et Pauli apostolorum eius se noverit incursurum. Dat' Rome apud Sanctam Sabinam, vi kal. Junii, pontificatus nostri anno secundo.

[Signum]¹ Et ego Andreas quondam Guilielmi de Tang', clericus, Eboracensis diocesis, sacrosancte sedis apostolice publicus auctoritate notarius, qui suprascriptas litteras apostolicas sanas vidi et integras, non abolitas, non abrasas, non cancellatas, nec in aliqua ipsarum parte viciatas vel corruptas, set omni sinistra suspicione carentes, cum vera ipsius domini pape bulla plumbea ut prima facie apparebat et filis sericis integris pendentibus bullatas, rogatus eas de verbo ad verbum nichil addens vel minuens quod sensum mutaret vel corrumperet intellectum transcripsi fideliter et exemplavi, London' in garderoba domini regis, sub anno domini a nativitate m° ccc° quinto, et indiccione quarta, mensis Octobris die xxvi, et cum dominis Johanne de Wynton' et Galfrido de Stok', clericis, diligenter ascultavi, et quia presens transumptum post diligentem ipsius cum predictis litteris papalibus originalibus examinacionem inveni in omnibus et per omnia concordare, illud signo meo consueto signavi, in fidem et testimonium premissorum.

10 (above, p. 30, and Pl. 2)

Notarial exemplification by John of Beccles of a letter of the papal penitentiary testifying to the deathbed absolution of Thomas de Cantilupe, bishop of Hereford, produced before the archbishop of Canterbury in Leominster Priory, Thursday, 3 December 1282

Hereford, D. & C. Archives, no. 1414A; *c.* 22·1 × 21 cm. (Cf. *Reg. Cantilupe*, p. lii.) Conjectural readings of damaged and missing portions printed between square brackets.

In dei nomine domini² amen. Per presens instrumentum publicum omnibus [appareat evidenter] quod anno domini m° cc° octogesimo

---

¹ The *signum* is 12 cm tall.   ² *Sic.*

secundo, indiccione decima, die Jo[vis terci]a die mense Decembris
[intrante, co]ram reverendo patre domino J. dei gracia Cantuariensi
archiepiscopo, tocius Anglie primate, in mei notarii et testium subscriptorum presencia constitutus personaliter magister Willelmus
de Monteforti precentor ecclesie Herefordensis, presentavit et
exhibuit dicto domino archiepiscopo quamdam litteram patentem
sanam et integram, sigillo de cera rubea pendenti parvo laqueo de
filo nigro et croceo torto more penitenciarie Romane curie con-
signatam, quam quidem litteram idem pater recipiens gratanter
et inspiciens, mandavit michi notario ut super huiusmodi exhibicione
et recepcione publicum conficerem instrumentum. Tenor autem
dicte littere quem in sequentibus duxi annotandum talis est. Universis presentes litteras inspecturis frater Galfridus domini pape
penitenciarius salutem in domino sempiternam. Noverit universitas
vestra quod nos de speciali mandato venerabilis patris domini B.
episcopi Albanensis curam penitenciarie domini . . pape gerentis,
bone memorie venerabilis Thome de Canterlupo episcopi Herefordensis confessione diligenter audita, ei auctoritate domini pape,
super omnibus peccatis suis que nobis in mortis articulo in sua confessione vere penitens revelavit, auctoritate domini pape beneficium
debite absolucionis impendimus, et consideratis suorum circum-
stanciis peccatorum, super ipsis iniunximus ei penitenciam salutarem.
Postmodum vero sanctissimus pater et dominus, dominus Martinus
papa quartus, quod per nos factum extitit in hac parte ratificavit
liberaliter oraculo vive vocis. In cuius rei testimonium presentes
litteras fieri et sigilli nostri munimine roborari.[1] Dat' apud Urbemveterem, non. Septembris pontificatus domini Martini pape quarti
anno secundo. Act' in camera dicti domini . . archiepiscopi, anno,
indiccione, mense et die primo superius annotatis, presentibus
venerabilibus viris magistris et dominis Ricardo archidiacono
Cantuariensi, Nicholao de Cnovylla canonico Herefordensi, Johanne
de Bekingham rectore ecclesie de Hocton' dyocesis Lincolniensis
dicti domini . . archiepiscopi clericis et sociis testibus nominatis,
in prioratu Leominstr' dyocesis Herefordensis.

Ego Johannes Alani de Beccles Norw[icensis dyocesis], [Signum]
sacrosancte Ro[mane ecclesie auctoritate] notarius publicus,
premissis interfui, ea sic fieri vi[di et audivi et] prefatam
[litteram transcripsi et?] fideliter exemplavi et diligenter
ascultavi, et quia utrumque concordare inveni me te[stem
subscripsi et signum] meum apposui.

---

[1] *Sic.*

11 (above, pp. 20–1)

Notarial instrument by Henry Astensis reciting Master Peter de Radenor's letter of proxy from the chapter of Hereford and his appointment of a substitute as proctor. London, in the bishop of Durham's house, 18 January 1268

Hereford, D. & C. Archives, no. 2930; *c.* 25·5 × 17·3 cm. Noted by Emanuel, p. 6. I am obliged to Miss P. E. Morgan, Cathedral Librarian, for supplying a reproduction of the manuscript.

IN NOMINE DOMINI AMEN. Anno a nativitate Christi millesimo ducentesimo sexagesimo octavo, indictione undecima, die mercurii xviii intrante mense Januarii, pontificatus domini Clementis pape iiii anno tercio. In presencia mei Henrici infrascripti publici notarii et testium subscriptorum ad hec specialiter vocatorum et rogatorum, discretus vir magister Petrus de Radenor canonicus Herefordensis procurator, ut in suo procuratorio prima facie apparebat, capituli Herefordensis habens mandatum ut in dicto procuratorio plenius continetur, cuius tenor de verbo ad verbum inferius annotatur, a dicto capitulo alium procuratorem loco sui substituendi, facit, constituit, ordinat, et substituit suum et dicti capituli procuratorem et substitutum Willelmum dictum Ferbraz quousque ab eodem capitulo vel dicto magistro Petro fuerit revocatus, in omnibus hiis quibus dictum capitulum ipsum P. constituerat procuratorem, dans etiam eidem Willelmo eam et eandem potestatem quam habet in suo procuratorio, et promittit sub ypotheca bonorum suorum se ratum et firmum habiturum quicquid in premissis per eundem substitutum factum fuerit vel quomodolibet procuratorio suo nomine et nomine capituli supradicti. Forma vero procuratorii dicti magistri Petri talis est: Venerabili in Christo patri Ottobono dei gratia sancti Adriani diacono cardinali apostolice sedis legato capitulum Herefordensis ecclesie salutem et cum honore reverenciam, et obedienciam. In causis vobis a domino papa commissis inter religiosos viros . . priorem et fratres ordinis predicatorum in Anglia ex parte una et nos ex altera, dilectos fratres et concanonicos nostros magistros Petrum[1] de Radenor' et Galfridum penitenciarium nostros constituimus procuratores, dantes eis coniunctim et utrique eorum divisim specialiter potestatem alium constituendi sive substituendi procuratorem ad causas ipsas procurandas qualitercunque viderint expedire, ratum habituri et firmum quicquid iidem sive eorum alter qui pro tempore presens fuerit aut constitutus vel substitutus ab

---

[1] *MS.* Petrem.

eisdem vel altero eorum nomine nostro fecerint seu fecerit in premissis, iudicatum solvi pro eisdem si opus fuerit repromittentes.
Idem parti adverse significamus. Dat' anno domini m⁰ cc⁰ lx⁰
septimo viij¹ idus Octobris. Actum est hoc London' in domo . .
episcopi Dunelmensis anno, mense, die, et indictione predictis,
presentibus magistro Ardicione cancellario domini legati canonico
Herefordensi, Philippo de Comite nepote dicti cancellarii, et
Roberto de Altomonasterio testibus vocatis et rogatis.

[Signum] ²Ego Henricus Astensis imperiali auctoritate publicus notarius hiis omnibus interfui, scripsi, publicavi, ac meo signo
consueto signavi rogatus.

12 (above, pp. 24–5)

*Eschatocol of the notarial exemplification by Ildebrandinus Bonadote of
Siena of a letter of proxy, prepared for Bartholomew, merchant of the
company of Bonaventura of Siena, proctor of Master Angelus de Urbe.
London, 15 July 1280*

P.R.O., E 30/14, with notarial sign on left-hand side. The whole document measures *c.* 26·7 × 17·8 cm.

[Signum] Ego Ildebrandinus Bonadote de Senis, sancte Romane
ecclesie auctoritate notarius publicus hoc exemplum ex
autentico fideliter sumpssi³ et postmodum cum Richardo
Aldobrandi de Hocton' et Johanne "clerico de "London'
testibus ad hoc rogatis diligenter cum ipso autentico abscultavi, et quia utrunque concordare inveni de ipsius Bartholomei procuratoris predicti rogatu ad eiusdem exempli
plenam fidem et testimonium me subscripssi. Actum
London' idus Julii indictione octava, anno domini m cc
octogesimo.

---

¹ viij *indistinct in MS.*
² The *signum* appears to be a monogram, ENRIC', formed from the notary's
name. Cf. Redlich: 'Im 12 und 13 Jahrhundert wird auch das *ego* der Unterschrift
oder der Name des Notars in monogrammatischer Figur als Zeichen verwendet'
(*Privaturkunden*, p. 217). ³ *MS.* smpssi.

13

Notarial instrument by Alan de Dersingham recording the renunciation by the rector of Ashby (with Oby), Norfolk, of certain tithes in his parish. Ludham, 11 March 1304

Bodleian Libr., Norfolk rolls 82, no. ff. A copy contained in a roll of title-deeds of the abbey of St. Benet of Hulme, endorsed by Hugh de Musele, clerk of Archbishop Robert Winchelsey, with his notarial sign.

In nomine domini amen. Anno eiusdem ab incarnacione m° ccc tercio, indiccione secunda, pontificatus domini Benedicti pape undecimi anno primo, venerabili patre domino Roberto dei gracia Cantuariensi archiepiscopo tocius Anglie primate suam provinciam visitante, quinto idus Marcii, in ecclesia parochiali de Ludham decanatus de Waxtonesham Norwicensis diocesis, coram reverendo viro magistro Johanne de Ross[1] venerabilis patris predicti commissario seu auditore, et in presencia mei notarii infrascripti et testium subscriptorum, constituti videlicet magister Robertus de Aldeby clericus, procurator religiosorum virorum abbatis et conventus ecclesie sancti Benedicti de Hulmo predicte diocesis pro ut per procuratorium suum predicti patris commissariis traditum patebat expresse, ex parte una, et Willelmus de Haskeby ecclesie rector decanatus de Fleg predicte diocesis, ex altera, super quarumdam decimarum tam maiorum quam minorum percepcione altercantes, quas quidem decimas procurator predictus dicebat dictos religiosos dominos suos infra parochiam de Haskeby predictam percepisse a tempore a quo memoria non existit et ad hoc probandum se artavit, predictus vero rector omni iuri suo super peticione[2] predicta ibidem renunciavit expresse, dicendo se nolle super peticione dictarum decimarum ab illa hora in antea prosequi quovismodo. Acta fuit predicta renunciacio a predicto Willelmo rectore ecclesie predicte coram antedicto commissario predictis anno, indiccione, pontificatu, die, et loco, presentibus magistris Rogero de Snetesham, Rogero de Felthorpe, Willelmo Albon clericis, et aliis[3] in multitudine copiosa testibus.

Et ego Alanus Alani de Dersingham clericus Norwicensis diocesis, publicus sacrosancte Romane ecclesie apostolica et imperiali[4] auctoritate notarius premissis hiis presens interfui, vidi, et audivi,

---

[1] *MS. ? Roes.* [2] *Followed by ? sua erased.* [3] *MS. alliis.*

[4] *MS.* sacrosancta imperiali. 'sacrosancta' *is never used in the imperial title; the conjectural emendation is the form used by Richard de Brenchley in Westminster Abbey, Mun. 9496 m. 9, in 1308.*

et rogatus per predictum procuratorem ea scribere scripsi, in hanc publicam formamque redegi, meoque signo solito et nomine roboravi. Siqua rasura in verbis istis, scilicet 'predicti', 'magister', et 'percepcione' appareat eam approbo ac si nulla ibi fuisset aut appareret, nam illas feci propria manu ante subscripcionem istam et signi apposicionem.

14 (above, p. 104 n. 5)

Notarial instrument by Andrew de Tange, recording quittance by a Spanish knight, Paschasius Valentini Adalyt, of all claims which he might have by reason of his service to King Edward I of England. Carlisle, in the hall of Sir Robert de Cotingham, 20 March 1307

P.R.O., E 30/1676; *c.* 25 × 28·6 cm.

In nomine domini amen. Anno a nativitate eiusdem m° ccc° septimo, indictione quinta, mensis Marcii die vicesimo, constitutus coram venerabili in Christo patre domino W. dei gracia Coventrensi et Lichefeldensi episcopo ac domino Johanne de Drokenesford'[1] excellentissimi principis domini E. dei gracia regis Anglie illustris clerico et ipsius garderobe custode, in presencia mei infrascripti notarii et testium subscriptorum ad hoc vocatorum specialiter et rogatorum, dominus Paschasius Valentini Adalyt de Hyspania miles actionem omnimodam quam unquam tempore vite sue habuit vel habere potuit quocumque iuris titulo, actionis, vel calumpnie qualiscumque, tam eciam peccuniarie quam cuiuscumque alterius usque in diem presentem, erga dominum regem Anglie prelibatum, heredes suos, vel eciam executores, pro se et heredibus suis remisit et quietum clamavit omnino, ita quod a dicto die remissionis, refutancie, sive quieteclamancie ipsius militis verbotenus sic facte, nec ipse nec heredes sui, aut quivis alius eius nomine, vice, vel mandato, a predicto domino rege, heredibus suis, vel eciam executoribus racione alicuius servicii eidem domino regi prestiti per eundem temporibus retroactis, sive amissionis vel dampni cuiuscumque in ipsius domini regis servicio recepti, sive alterius exactionis peccuniarie vel demande qualiscumque, quicquam exigere poterit in futurum, recognoscens palam et expresse organo vocis sue sibi nomine dicti domini regis et pro ipso de omnibus serviciis eidem domino regi qualitercumque prestitis per eundem, arreragiis vadiorum, dampnis et amissionibus quibuscumque equitature vel rerum

---

[1] *MS.* Drok'nesford'.

aliarum et debitis omnimodis competenter fuisse et esse satisfactum et ad plenum. Renunciavit insuper dictus dominus Paschasius palam et expresse, excepcioni satisfactionis predicte sibi non facte, et omni iuris et legum auxilio, quod eidem contra dictum dominum regem, quo ad peticionem vel exactionem alicuius debiti, servicii, dampni, vel amissionis rerum et bonorum quorumcumque aut vadiorum transacti temporis racione prodesse poterit, et dicto domino regi obesse in aliquo vel nocere. Premissa omnia recognovit et fecit dominus Paschasius memoratus ut premittitur organo vocis sue, spontanea et mera sua voluntate, Carleol', in aula domini Roberti de Cotingham, anno, indictione, mense, et die prenotatis, presentibus dominis Johanne de Jageleya, Willelmo de Recteford', Petro de Ware, et Waltero de Langeburgh' cum Johanne de Vyenna, clericis, testibus ad premissa vocatis specialiter et rogatis.

[Signum] Et ego Andreas quondam Guilielmi de Tang' clericus Eboracensis diocesis, sacrosancte sedis apostolice publicus auctoritate notarius, qui premissis una cum dictis testibus interfui, eaque sic fieri vidi et audivi, a prefato domino Paschasio rogatus, super hiis presens confeci publicum instrumentum, et in formam publicam redactum signo meo consueto signavi, in fidem et testimonium premissorum.

15 (above, p. 101)

Draft for a public instrument (?) recording the receipt by the bishop of Salisbury from a proctor of the Hospitallers of 22d (?) for the fruits of the vacancy of the vicarage of Brimpton, Berks., during the last vacancy.[1]
London, 1324

Salisbury, Register of Roger Martival, vol. ii ad fin. (? removed from binding). A separate slip, measuring *c.* 31×4 cm.

. . .[2] anno domini m⁰ ccc^mo xxiiii in capella[3] domini London' comparuit coram eo magister Willelmus de Whiteby clericus, procurator religiosorum virorum prioris et fratrum hospitii sancti Johannis Jerusalem in Anglia litteratorie constitutus, habens ad subscripta sufficientem potestatem, ac eidem domino numeravit et solvit pro omnibus obvencionibus . . .[4] que tempore vacacionis ultime[5] vicarie

[1] 1 Dec. 1323–13 Jan. 1324 (*Reg. Martival,* i. 295).
[2] *Space of 3 cm., perhaps for exact date.*
[3] venerabilis patris *deleted.*　　　　　　[4] *Words missing at beginning of line.*
[5] vacacionis ultime *marked for transposition, followed by* ecclesie *deleted.*

ecclesie de Brympton' Saresbiriensis[1] diocesis[1] provenientibus ad
dictam vicariam pertinentibus quovis modo, et eidem domino
debitis racione vacacionis ...[2] xxii denarios sterlingorum,[3] quos ad[1]
dictos priorem et fratres virtute quorumdam privilegiorum suorum
pertinuisse credidit, sicut dixit, et dominus illos denarios sic per
dictum procuratorem effectualiter[1] restitutos recepit, et nomine[4]
possessionis sue in ipsa vicaria sicut in aliis vicariis sue diocesis
tempore vacacionis earum continuando, illosque liberando tradidit
magistro W. de Selton' officiali suo, liberandos sequestratori suo
qui de eisdem sicut de consimilibus in suo compoto respondebit.
Acta fuerunt hec die et anno predictis presentibus Worth', Selton',
Lobenham, Knossynton', Dorturer, Lughteburgh' notar' et Ayst'.

16 (above, pp. 41–2)

*Notarial instrument by Philip de London recording resignation by
Thomas de Bamburgh, priest, of the chantry of St. Margaret in the
cathedral church of St. Paul's, London. 15 October 1320*[5]

London, St. Paul's Cathedral, D. &. C. Mun., A/75/1987; 20·4×30·4 cm.

In dei nomine amen. Per presens publicum instrumentum omnibus
appareat evidenter quod quintodecimo die mensis Octobris anno
domini millesimo trecentesimo vicesimo, indiccione quarta, pontificatus domini Johannis divina providencia pape vicesimi secundi
anno quinto, dominus Thomas de Banburgh, capellanus, celebrans
ad altare sancte Margarete in ecclesia sancti Pauli London' personaliter constitutus in eadem,[6] cupiensque ex certis et legitimis causis
ab illa canteria totaliter exonerari ut asseruit, predictam canteriam
cum omnibus iuribus et pertinenciis suis universis, videlicet in
libris, calice, vestimentis, et omnibus aliis rebus ad dictam cantariam
quoquo modo spectantibus, in potestatem domini . . decani et
capituli sancti Pauli London' in presencia mei Philippi notarii infrascripti et testium subscriptorum pure, sponte, simpliciter, et absolute resignavit et omni iuri sibi competenti seu competituro in ea

---

[1] *Interlined.*   [2] *Words missing at beginning of line.*

[3] *Interlined, followed by* solvit *deleted.*

[4] *Interlined, followed by* reservans ad (?) *deleted.*

[5] Thomas de Bamburgh had been appointed warden of the old fabric of St.
Paul's by Bishop Ralph in 1308 (*Reg. Baldock*, pp. 74–6). The notary, Mr. Philip de
London, now claimed papal and not imperial authority: cf. above, pp. 86–7.

[6] in eadem *interlined in original hand.*

vel ad eam sub hac forma renunciavit. Pateat universis presentes litteras visuris vel audituris quod ego Thomas de Bamburgh', capellanus, celebrans ad altare sancte Margarete in ecclesia sancti Pauli London', cupiens ex certis et legitimis causis ab illa canteria totaliter exonerari, predictam canteriam cum omnibus iuribus et pertinenciis suis, videlicet in libris, calice, vestimentis, et omnibus aliis rebus ad dictam canteriam quoquo modo spectantibus, in potestatem domini . . decani et capituli sancti Pauli London' coram te Philippo de Lond' auctoritate apostolica notario publico pure, sponte, simpliciter, et absolute resigno, et omni iuri michi competenti seu competituro in ea vel ad eam renuncio. In cuius rei testimonium sigillum meum apposui. Dat' London', id. Octobris anno domini millesimo trecentesimo vicesimo. Acta sunt hec que supradixi anno, indiccione, die, mense, et loco supradictis, presentibus dominis Willelmo de Tillebury rectore ecclesie de Heytford Ebor' diocesis, Johanne rectore ecclesie sancti Gregorii in atrio sancti Pauli London', et aliis testibus ad premissa vocatis specialiter et rogatis. Hoc interliniare supra quintam lineam a capite istius instrumenti descendendo, videlicet 'in eadem', ac si esset in linea recta scriptum approbo ego Philippus notarius infrascriptus.

[Signum] Et ego Philippus de London' clericus, sacrosancte Romane ecclesie auctoritate apostolica notarius, premissis omnibus ut supra leguntur una cum testibus memoratis interfui, ea sic fieri vidi et audivi et ut supra leguntur scripsi, et in publicam formam redegi, meoque signo consueto signavi rogatus.

17

Letters patent of the chapter of St. Paul's, London, arranging the endowment of a chantry and an obit for Master Richard de Neuport, archdeacon of Middlesex, with an incomplete notarial attestation by Henry de Bray.[1] London, St. Paul's chapter-house, 3 July 1309

London, St. Paul's Cathedral, D. & C. Mun., A/70/1772. Fold at foot with slit for sealing *double queue*; *c.* 21·2 × 23·2 cm (folded).

Universis Christi fidelibus presentes litteras visuris vel audituris . . gerens vices domini Arnaldi decani ecclesie sancti Pauli London' et

[1] Cf. *HMCR*, ix. 49*b*, 60*b*. The ordinance for the chantry is copied into St. Paul's Mun., W.D. 2, f. 6ᵛ.

eiusdem loci capitulum salutem in vero salutari. Cum iamdudum magister Ricardus de Neuport archidiaconus Middelsexie, pie consideracionis affectu libros suos deo et ecclesie sancti Pauli optulisset, ad fundacionem unius cantarie perpetue pro anima sua, parentum et benefactorum suorum animabus, et ad obitum suum quadraginta solidatus sterlingorum anniversarium post mortem suam in eadem Londoniensi ecclesia faciendum convertendos, seu ad sex viginti marcas sterlingorum pro eisdem libris, nisi ad tantam quantitatem se extenderent dicti libri, se et bona sua obligasset pro adquirendo et exhibendo cantaria et obitu predictis, nec invenisset, licet solicite ex diu quesito et diligenter, locum vel redditum in quo huiusmodi sex viginti marcas utiliter et secure convertere posset, habita demum per nos provida consideracione quoad domum quam idem magister Ricardus inhabitabat et precipue ad cameram que Rosemunde nuncupatur, quam inquieta fuerit per strepitus et tumultus tam hominum quam equorum calcancium e vicino in strata pupplica sine obiectus cuiusquam interposicione necnon ad serviles prospectus edificiorum alterius partis vici qui ex opposito in ipsam cameram et totum habitacionis illius locum quasi per medium circumquaque dirigebantur, per nos concessum est predicto magistro Ricardo ac eciam per litteras nostras confirmatum quod idem Ricardus libere posset edificare illam aream que super vicum regium abuttat a capella predicte domus in longum continue usque ad murum cimiterii sancti Benedicti, et in latum deversus iamdictam cameram et deorsum in orto illius domus secundum limitacionem quam sibi fecimus et assignavimus usque ad unum pirarium et quasdam vineolas exclusive nec includendas, videlicet pro tollenda huiusmodi turbacione et prospiciendi indecencia, securitate eciam dicte habitacioni providenda pleniori, ita tamen quod huiusmodi edificia post mortem dicti Ricardi remaneant ecclesie sancti Pauli predicte ad huiusmodi cantariam et obitum in forma predicta perpetuo exhibenda sub modo et forma prout dictus Ricardus in vita sua libere ordinabit. In cuius rei testimonium sigillum capituli nostri commune presentibus appendi fecimus. Dat' in capitulo nostro tercio die Julii anno domini millesimo cccᵐᵒ nono,[1] presentibus in capitulo Johanne de Chishulle Colecestr' archidiacono, Roberto de Clothale cancellario, R. de Roos, Johanne de Swynefeld', Bartholomeo de Ferentino, Thoma de Northefleet, Gilberto de Segrave precentore.[2]

[1] The rest in smaller writing by the same hand.

[2] 'Gilberto de Segrave precentore' at the end of the first line of Henry de Bray's subscription, below the names of the last two witnesses which closed the preceding line.

Et[1] ego Henricus dictus de Bray pupplicus sacri Romani [Signum][2] imperii auctoritate notarius concessioni[3] limitacioni et concessioni predictis ac eciam huius scripti consignacioni personaliter interfui et[4] me subscribendo signi mei consueti hanc particulam famosiorem in testimonium rei geste huic apposui.

18 (above, p. 68, and Pl. 3)

Notarial instrument by Henry of Great Sugnall, recording quittance of all indebtedness given by Richard of Gloucester to Thomas de Swanlonde. London, Thomas de Swanlonde's house, in the parish of All Hallows the Less. 8 November 1336.

London, St. Paul's Cathedral, D. & C. Mun., A/77/2067; 20·6 × 19·2 cm.

In dei nomine amen. Per presens publicum instrumentum cunctis appareat evidenter quod anno ab incarnacione domini millesimo ccc^mo tricesimo sexto secundum cursum ecclesie Angl', indiccione quinta, pontificatus sanctissimi in Christo patris ac domini nostri domini Benedicti divina providencia pape xii anno secundo, mensis Novembris die octavo, in hospicio Thome de Swanlonde in parochia Omnium Sanctorum super Celarium London' situato, in mei notarii publici et testium subscriptorum presencia constitutus personaliter Ricardus de Gloucestr' filius et heres ut asseritur Ricardi de Gloucestr' quondam Aldermani London' iuravit ad sancta dei evangelia per ipsum corporaliter tacta coram dicto Thoma de Swanlonde quod ipse Ricardus vel aliquis alius nomine suo a dicto Thoma de Swanlonde vel aliquo alio de suis nunquam infuturum quicquid peteret seu vendicaret virtute alicuius contractus seu convencionis inter ipsos Thomam et Ricardum a principio mundi usque ad diem confeccionis presencium qualitercumque habiti. Acta sunt anno, indiccione, pontificatu, mense, die, et loco predictis, presentibus magistro Waltero de Axe capellano, Stephano de Durham, Ricardo Andreu, Willelmo le Erys, et Ricardo de Gloucestr' fratre Ricardi de Gloucestr' supradicti, testibus ad premissa vocatis specialiter et rogatis.

[Signum] Et ego Henricus de Magna Sogunhull' clericus Lichefeldensis diocesis publicus auctoritate apostolica notarius

---

[1] Preceded in left-hand margin by what appears to be a small letter 'v'.

[2] In the narrow right-hand margin an animal's head (? a lion's) with the name Bray below.

[3] *Sic.*   [4] 'et' *interlined.*

omnibus et singulis suprascriptis una cum dictis testibus presens interfui et ea sic fieri vidi et audivi, scripsi, et in hanc publicam formam redegi, signumque meum apposui consuetum rogatus.

19 (above, p. 70)

Notarial certificate by Henry of Great Sugnall that William de Walton of Lichfield has sworn that his daughter, Maud, was born after he had married her mother, Margery. Margery and two other witnesses have confirmed his statement on oath.[1] Lichfield, in the dwelling-house of William de Walton, 28 March 1344

P.R.O., DL 25/2094; *c.* 34·5 × 16·6 cm.

[I]n dei nomine amen. Per presens publicum instrumentum cunctis appareat evidenter quod anno ab incarnacione eiusdem millesimo cccᵐᵒ quadragesimo quarto secundum cursum ecclesie Angl', indiccione duodecima, pontificatus sanctissimi in Christo patris ac domini nostri domini Clementis divina providencia pape sexti anno secundo, mensis Marcii die vicesima octava, Willelmus de Walton' de Lichefeld' in hospicio suo in civitate Lichefeldensi situato quo tunc inhabitabat, in mei notarii publici et testium subscriptorum presencia personaliter constitutus, volens ut asseruit ex quibusdam causis ipsum moventibus statum et condicionem Matildis filie sue declarare et ad noticiam vicinorum suorum deducere, dixit et ad sancta dei evangelia per ipsum corporaliter tacta iuravit quod contraxit matrimonium solempniter in facie ecclesie cum Margeria uxore sua, matre dicte Matildis, ipsa Margeria per ipsum Willelmum tunc imprengnata existente, quodam die dominico in festo sancte Trinitatis, et dicta Margeria prefatam Matildem filiam dictorum Willelmi et Margerie post matrimonium inter eosdem contractum et ut premittitur solempnizatum peperit; et subsequenter prefata Margeria uxor dicti Willelmi necnon Robertus de Trentham et Robertus de Fulfeu tunc ibidem personaliter existentes iurarunt ad sancta dei evangelia per ipsos singillatim corporaliter tacta quod prefatus Willelmus verum factum recitavit et verum iuramentum

---

[1] The certificate was quoted in evidences produced twenty-four years later, when Maud's second husband was involved in dispute about her inheritance and her legitimacy was in question (cf. P.R.O., DL 25/2095: 'com tesmoigne est par signe de notaire que la dite Maude fille le dit William de Walton' nasquy danz esposailles').

prestitit in hac parte. Acta sunt et fuerunt hec anno, indiccione, pontificatu, mense, die, et loco predictis, presentibus Johanne de Rothewell', Thoma de Pipe, Hugone dicto Rider, Willelmo dicto Taverner, Rogero de Pipe, magistro Ricardo de Bole, Johanne dicto Rider de Lichefeld' et aliis in multitudine copiosa testibus ad premissa vocatis et rogatis.

[Signum] Et ego Henricus de Magna Sogunhull' clericus Coventrensis et Lichefeldensis diocesis publicus auctoritate apostolica notarius omnibus et singulis suprascriptis una cum dictis testibus presens interfui et ea sic fieri vidi et audivi, scripsi, et in hanc publicam formam redegi, signumque meum apposui consuetum rogatus.

20 (above, p. 19, and Pl. 6)

Notarial instrument by Andrew Brito of London, recording the citation by the dean of christianity of Gloucester of the abbot and convent of Gloucester and of Opizo son of Guy of Lavagna and invitation to representatives of the church of Hereford to appear in the court of the legate Ottobuono. Gloucester, 16 December, and Much Cowarne and Hereford Cathedral, 18 December 1266

Worcester, D. & C. Mun., B. 554; *c.* 44·6 × 30·5 cm.

In nomine domini amen . Anno eiusdem millesimo ducentesimo sexagesimo sexto, indictione decima, pontificatus domini Clementis pape iiij^{ti} anno secundo, die Jovis proxima ante festum beati Thome apostoli, per presens publicum instrumentum omnibus appareat evidenter quod in presentia mei Andree notarii infrascripti et testium subscriptorum ad hec specialiter vocatorum atque rogatorum, scilicet Johannis de Wygemor' et Johannis de Keyrwent clericorum, facta fuit quedam citacio peremptoria . . abbati et conventui monasterii sancti Petri de Gloucestria ordinis sancti Benedicti Wygorniensis diocesis in monasterio predicto per . . decanum christianitatis de Gloucestria, in hunc modum, videlicet idem . . decanus personaliter accedens ad supradictum monasterium sancti Petri, citando . . abbatem et conventum eiusdem loci, et litteram venerabilis patris domini O. dei gracia sancti Adriani diaconi cardinalis, apostolice sedis legati, non cancellatam, non abolitam, nec in aliqua sui parte viciatam, eisdem . . abbati et conventui ostendit, legit, et recitavit sub hac forma : Octobonus miseracione divina sancti Adriani diaconus cardinalis apostolice sedis legatus

discreto viro . . decano christianitatis de Gloucestria Wygorniensis
diocesis salutem in salutis auctore. Intellecto dudum quod ecclesia
de Magna Coura Herefordensis diocesis per mortem Johannis dicti
Capel rectoris eiusdem vacabat, ipsam Opizoni clerico, nato nobilis
viri Guidonis de Lavania dicti de Codomo duximus conferendum.
Set quia religiosi viri . . abbas et conventus monasterii sancti Petri
de Gloucestria ordinis sancti Benedicti Wygorniensis diocesis ad
nos propter hoc specialem procuratorem eorum et nuncium desti-
nantes, ecclesiam ipsam in proprios usus canonice obtinere ac eam
aliquamdiu pacifice possedisse firmiter asseverant, nosque per collacionem huiusmodi nulli volentes iniuriam irrogare, discrecioni
tue qua fungimur auctoritate mandamus quatinus tam dictos . .
abbatem et conventum quam eundem Opizonem ex parte nostra
peremptorie citare procures ut infra viginti dies post tue citacionis
edictum per se vel per procuratores ydoneos cum omnibus racioni-
bus et munimentis suis negocium huiusmodi contingentibus compareant coram nobis, suam in hoc iusticiam ostensuri, denunciantes
quoque venerabili patri . . Herefordensi episcopo vel gerenti vices
ipsius, necnon . . decano, . . archidiacono, et capitulo Herefordensibus ut in eodem termino coram nobis compareant si sua in hoc
crediderint interesse. Quicquid autem exinde feceris nobis per tuas
litteras harum seriem continentes studeas fideliter intimare. Dat'
Coventreye, iiii kal. Decembris pontificatus domini Clementis pape
iiii anno secundo. Lecta autem littera dicti domini legati et recitata
prefatis . . abbati et conventui sancti Petri per . . decanum
memoratum, citavit ipsos idem . . decanus peremptorie in forma
que sequitur.[1] Huius igitur auctoritate mandati vos . . abbatem et
conventum monasterii sancti Petri Gloucestrie peremptorie cito ut
infra viginti dies post istius citacionis edictum per vos vel per
procuratores ydoneos cum omnibus munimentis vestris negocium
huiusmodi contingentibus coram predicto domino legato compareatis, vestram in hoc iusticiam ostensuri. Die vero Sabati
sequente proximo in ecclesia de Magna Coura Herefordensis
diocesis per supradictum . . decanum de Gloucestria facta fuit
quedam citacio peremptoria in forma que sequitur. Videlicet idem
. . decanus in presencia mei Andree notarii publici et testium subscriptorum ad hoc specialiter vocatorum ac rogatorum publice legit
et recitavit litteram venerabilis patris domini . . legati supradicti,
et postea citacionem eidem Opizoni directam ex parte . . decani
supradicti in qua continebatur totus tenor littere domini legati
supradicti cum adieccione que sequitur: Huius igitur auctoritate

[1] *MS.* sequetur

mandati te Opizonem predictum cito peremptorie ut infra viginti dies post istius citacionis edictum per te vel per procuratorem ydoneum cum omnibus munimentis tuis negocium huiusmodi contingentibus coram predicto domino legato compareas, tuam in hoc iusticiam ostensurus. Et quia idem Opizo presens non fuerat, idem . . decanus instrumentum citacionis huiusmodi sigillo suo sigillatum super magnum altare eiusdem ecclesie de Coura posuit et dimisit. Eodem vero die Sabati in presencia mei Andree notarii et testium subscriptorum ad hec specialiter vocatorum et rogatorum in ecclesia cathedrali Herefordensi per prefatum . . decanum Gloucestrie facta fuit quedam denunciacio in forma que sequitur. Videlicet idem . . decanus publice legit et recitavit litteram domini . . legati antedictam et postea litteram denunciacionis domino . . episcopo Herefordensi vel vices eius gerenti, . . decano, . . archidiacono, et capitulo Herefordensibus, in qua quidem littera continebatur totus tenor littere domini . . legati, cum hac adieccione: Huius igitur auctoritate mandati vobis, venerande pater Herefordensis episcope, vel vices vestras gerenti, necnon . . decano, . . archidiacono, et capitulo Herefordensibus denuncio ut infra viginti dies a die Jovis proxima ante festum beati Thome apostoli anno predicto connumerandos, ad quem terminum . . abbatem et conventum sancti Petri Gloucestrie quod compareant coram domino . . legato peremptorie citavi pro negocio supradicto, aut infra viginti dies ab hac die Sabati connumerandos ad quem terminum Opizonem memoratum quod compareat coram domino . . legato peremptorie citavi pro negocio antedicto, coram eodem domino legato compareatis si vestra in hoc credideritis interesse. Et quia nec idem dominus . . episcopus nec . . decanus presentes fuerant, huiusmodi instrumentum denunciacionis predicte decanus Gloucestrie sigillo suo sigillatum super quoddam altare ante crucem in medio ecclesie cathedralis Hereford' posuit publice et reliquit. In cuius rei testimonium magister Gregorius de Keyrwent clericus, procurator religiosorum virorum . . abbatis et conventus monasterii sancti Petri de Gloucestria, presens instrumentum per me notarium sepedictum iussit scribi et publicari, presentibus testibus Henrico de Keyrwent, Johanne de Keyrwent supradicto clericis ad hec specialiter vocatis et rogatis.

[Signum] Et ego Andreas dictus Brito de London' sacrosancte Romane ecclesie[1] notarius publicus supradictis citacionibus et denunciacioni interfui et ea que suprascripta sunt scripsi, et in publicam formam redegi rogatus.

---

[1] *N.B., the word* auctoritate *is omitted.*

21 (above, pp. 92–4)

Return of names of notaries public in the diocese of London, sent by the bishop of London to the archbishop of Canterbury with a covering letter dated 14 April 1402

Lambeth Palace Libr., Reg. T. Arundel, vol. i, f. 417ʳ. (The covering letter, which includes Archbishop Thomas's mandate of 18 February 1402 to the bishop in which a mandate of Pope Boniface IX to the archbishops of Canterbury and York of 6 June 1396 is recited, is printed from Reg. T. Arundel, vol. i, ff. 416ʳ–417ʳ in Wilkins, *Concilia*, iii. 268–9.)

Nomina et cognomina notariorum seu eorum qui se officium tabellionatus exercere pretendunt in civitate nostra London' in eadem personaliter apprehensorum per nostros officiales et ministros in hac parte diebus dominicis videlicet diebus nona et sextadecima presentis mensis Aprilis, iuxta vim, formam, et effectum dicti mandati vestri citatorum successive inferius describuntur.

Johannes Perche curia Cantuariensis registrarius
Johannes Penne eiusdem curie actorum scriba
Jacobus Cole
Johannes Tyssebury
Thomas Aude
Willelmus Godman
Thomas Cotyngwith'
Thomas Horstone
Thomas de Lyes
Willelmus Brun de Thornebury[1]

[col. 2]
Petrus Churche
Henricus Brun
Robertus Brun
Thomas Goldyngton'
Johannes Oswaldkirke
Johannes Coumbe junior
Johannes Lovelich'
Johannes Sproxton'
Ricardus Asshewell'
Henricus Ouyng[2]

---

[1] This and the preceding seven names bracketed with the note: 'com*paruerunt* et exhib*uerunt* sufficien*ter*'.

[2] The names in col. 2 bracketed with the note: 'exh*ibuerunt*'.

[col. 3]
Philippus Trody
Johannes Rotsere
Johannes Yonge
Willelmus Wylton'
Willelmus Canoun
Willelmus Daunt
Johannes Santon'
Ricardus Ludlowe
Robertus Wynyngton'
Thomas Fraunceys[1]

[f. 417ᵛ, col. 1]
Thomas Beket
Thomas Bildeston'
Henricus Northlode
Edwardus Husk
Simon Kempston'[2]

Essex.
Nomina et cognomina notariorum seu eorum qui tabellionatus officium se exercere pretendunt in archidiaconatu Essexie nostre diocesis in eodem archidiaconatu personaliter apprehensorum per nostros officiales et ministros in hac parte diebus duodecima et decima septima dicti mensis Aprilis iuxta vim, formam, et effectum dicti mandati vestri citatorum inferius describuntur.

Johannes Litlyngton'
Johannes Wilton de Herewardstoke
Rogerus Puttenham rector ecclesie medietatis[3] de Danbury in Essex'.

Midd'.
Nomina et cognomina notariorum seu eorum qui se officium tabellionatus exercere pretendunt in archidiaconatu Midd' dicte nostre diocesis in eodem archidiaconatu personaliter apprehensorum per dictos nostros officiales et ministros in hac parte diebus duodecima et xviiᵐᵃ dicti mensis Aprilis iuxta vim, formam, et effectum dicti mandati vestri citatorum inferius describuntur.

Johannes Briddeshale
Johannes Hothe

----
[1] The names in col. 3 bracketed with the note: 'exhibuerunt'.
[2] This and the preceding names in col. 1 bracketed with the note: 'comparuerunt et exhibuerunt'.   [3] MS. reads meᵗ'.

Ricardus Gatyn
Johannes Pounde
Petrus Nye

[col. 2]
Colcestr'.
Nomina et cognomina notariorum seu eorum qui se officium tabellionatus exercere pretendunt in archidiaconatu Colcestr' dicte
nostre diocesis in eodem archidiaconatu personaliter apprehensorum
per dictos nostros officiales et ministros in hac parte die nona dicti
mensis Aprilis iuxta vim, formam, et effectum dicti mandati vestri
citatorum inferius describuntur.

Johannes Colcestre alias Pebmerssh'
Johannes Beche
Thomas de Sudbury
Johannes Maunfeld'[1]
Johannes Boloyne non fuit personaliter citatus set per edictum nona
die mensis Aprilis antedicti.

Nomina vero et cognomina eorum qui se in civitate et diocesi
nostris predictis officium tabellionatus exercere pretendunt male
fame et denigrate opinionis, prout informamur, videlicet quorumdam personaliter quorumdam vero publice citacionis edicto in locis
predictis per dictos nostros commissarios, officiales, et ministros
in hac parte, dictis diebus dominicis, videlicet diebus nona et sextadecima dicti mensis Aprilis, iuxta vim, formam, et effectum dicti
mandati vestri proposito prout inferius sequitur citatorum sunt hec.

Johannes Grafton'
Johannes Botheby
Robertus Knygth'[2]
Johannes Corsere
Robertus atte Watier[3]
Rogerus Potenham[4]
Elias Wheteley
Johannes Frenssh'
Ricardus Markwyke
Edmundus Alderforde[5]

[1] This and the preceding three names bracketed and noted: 'exhib*uerunt*
suffic*ienter*'.
[2] This and the preceding two names bracketed and noted: 'personaliter'.
[3] This and the preceding name bracketed and noted: 'per edictum'.
[4] This name noted: 'personaliter'.
[5] This and the preceding three names bracketed and noted: 'per edictum'.

Johannes Tylney[1]
Thomas Styward
Thomas Mountagu[2]

22a (above, p. 66 n. 5)

Receipt given by Andrew de Tange for an instalment of pension from the bursar of Durham, for the period ending at Whitsun 1292[3]

Durham, D. & C. Mun., Misc. ch. 4136g; *c.* 16·2 × 3 cm; sealed simple queue, with separate tie at top of document. The device on the seal is described by Greenwell and Hunter Blair as 'a dog walking in front of a tree'.

Universis presentes litteras inspecturis Andreas de Tang' notarius salutem. Noveritis me recepisse per manus dompni Radulfi de Mordon' bursarii Dunelmensis L solidos de pensione mea, de termino Pentecosten anno domini m° cc° nonagesimo secundo, de quibus quinquaginta solidis, et omnibus aliis pensionibus pro[4] terminis precedentibus, quietum me clamo per presentes. In cuius rei testimonium presentibus sigillum meum est appensum.

22b (above, p. 66 n. 5)

Receipt given by Andrew de Tange for instalments of a pension from the prior and convent of Durham. Durham, 17 December 1303

Durham, D. & C. Mun., Misc. ch. 3456; *c.* 20 × 2·45 cm, with tag for sealing simple queue, bearing fragment of red wax.

Pateat universis per presentes quod ego Andreas de Tang' notarius recepi de religiosis viris dominis meis . . priore et . . conventu Dunolm' per manus fratris Thome de Hessewell' bursarii quinque marcas sterlingorum, pensionem meam videlicet de duobus

---

[1] This name noted: 'personaliter'.

[2] This and the preceding name bracketed and noted: 'per edictum'.

[3] The receipt is not dated but payment must have been made within the next few months; for on 11 Dec. 1292 Tange acknowledged receipt from the bursar of fifty shillings 'de termino sancti Martini', and gave quittance for this and all preceding instalments of his pension (Misc. ch. 4126*e*). Cf. below, no. 22b and *Extracts from the Account Rolls of the Abbey of Durham*, ii (Surtees Soc., vol. 100), 502.

[4] pro *interlined*.

terminis anni domini millesimi trecentesimi primi, de quibus terminis una cum omnibus precedentibus[1] ipsos dominos meos quietos
clamo per presentes. In cuius rei testimonium sigillum meum presentibus est appensum. Dat' Dunolm' die martis proxima ante
festum sancti Thome apostoli anno domini m° ccc° tercio.

23 (above, p. 66)

*Receipt given by William de Maldon for salary paid to him for his
services to the abbot of Westminster during the archbishop of Canterbury's visitation in the city and diocese of Worcester. London, 18
December 1303*

Westminster Abbey, Mun. 29155; *c.* 17·5 × 3·8 cm with tag for sealing
simple queue, bearing remains in red wax of a seal with lozenge and cross
design resembling the notarial *signum* of William de Maldon.

Pateat universis quod ego Willelmus de Maldon', notarius pupplicus, recepi et habui die confeccionis presencium a venerabili
patre domino . . abbate Westmonasterii quindecim solidos sterlingorum per manus fratris Henrici dicti Payn commonachi sui, in
quibus dictus pater michi tenebatur nomine salarii tempore visitacionis domini Cantuariensis archiepiscopi in civitate et diocesi
Wygorn'. In cuius rei testimonium presentibus sigillum meum est
appensum. Dat' London' apud Sanctum Paulum xv kal. Januarii
anno domini millesimo trecentesimo tercio.

[1] *MS. adds and deletes* quietos.

List of Printed Books and Articles, with Abbreviations

Acta Stephani Langton Cantuariensis Archiepiscopi A.D. *1207–1228*, ed. Kathleen Major (CYS). 1950.

Barraclough, Geoffrey, *Public Notaries and the Papal Curia. A Calendar and Study of a Formularium notariorum curie from the early years of the Fourteenth Century* (Proceedings of the British School at Rome). 1934.

—— 'Praxis beneficiorum', *Zeitschrift der Savigny-Stiftung für Rechtsgeschichte*, Bd. lviii, Kan. Abt. xxvii (1938), 94–134.

—— 'The English Royal Chancery and the Papal Chancery in the reign of Henry III', *MIöG*, lxii (1954), 365–78.

Baumgarten, P. M., *Von der apostolischen Kanzlei: Untersuchungen über die päpstlichen Tabellionen und die Vizekanzler der Heiligen Römischen Kirche im xiii, xiv, und xv Jahrhundert* (Görres-Gesellschaft, Sektion für Rechts- und Sozialwissenschaft, 4 Heft, Cologne, 1908).

BIHR: *Bulletin of the Institute of Historical Research*, University of London.

BJRL: *Bulletin of the John Rylands Library*, Manchester.

B.M.: British Museum, London.

Bónis, György, 'Les autorités de "foi publique" et les archives des "loci credibiles" en Hongrie', *Archivum*, xii (1965), 87–104.

Boüard, A. de, *Manuel de Diplomatique française et pontificale*. Tome ii, *L'Acte privé*. 1948.

Brentano, Robert, *York Metropolitan Jurisdiction and Papal Judges Delegate, 1279–96* (Univ. of California Publications in History, vol. 58). Berkeley, 1959.

—— *Two Churches: England and Italy in the Thirteenth Century*. Princeton, 1968.

Bresslau, H., *Handbuch der Urkundenlehre für Deutschland und Italien*. 2nd edn. 2 vols. 1912–31.

Brooke, [Richard], *A Treatise on the Office and Practice of a Notary of England*. 1839. 8th edn. by James Cranstoun, 1925. 9th edn. by J. Charlesworth, 1939.

Brown, Alfred L., *The Early History of the Clerkship of the Council* (Glasgow University Publications, N.S. 131). 1969.

Cal. Ch. Rolls: *Calendar of the Charter Rolls* (1226–1516) (HMSO). 6 vols. 1903–27.

Cal. Cl. Rolls: *Calendar of the Close Rolls* (HMSO). 1892–1913.

Cal. Papal Letters: *Calendar of Entries in the Papal Registers relating to Great Britain and Ireland: Papal Letters*. Vols. i–v (1198–1404) (HMSO). 5 vols. 1894–1904.

Cal. Papal Petitions: *Calendar of Entries in the Papal Registers relating to Great Britain and Ireland. Petitions to the Pope*. Vol. i, A.D. 1342–1419, ed. W. H. Bliss (HMSO). 1896.

Cal. Pat. Rolls: *Calendar of the Patent Rolls* (HMSO). 1891–1916.

Chaplais, Pierre, 'The origin and authenticity of the royal Anglo-Saxon diploma', *Journal of the Soc. of Archivists*, iii, no. 2 (1965), 48–61.

—— 'Who introduced charters into England? The case for Augustine' *Journal of the Soc. of Archivists*, iii, no. 10 (1969), 526–42.

—— (ed.), *Diplomatic Documents, 1101–1272* (HMSO). 1964.

Cheney, C. R., 'Master Philip the notary and the fortieth of 1199', *EHR*, lxiii (1948), 342–50.

—— 'A papal privilege for Tonbridge Priory', *BIHR*, xxxviii (1965), 192–200.

—— *English Bishops' Chanceries, 1100–1250*. Manchester, 1950.

—— 'Letters of William Wickwane, Chancellor of York, 1266–8', *EHR*, xlvii (1932), 626–42.

—— 'Gervase of Prémontré: a medieval letter-writer', *BJRL*, xxxiii (1950–1), 25–56.

Chron. Edw. I and II: *Chronicles of the Reigns of Edward I and Edward II*, ed. W. Stubbs (RS). 2 vols. 1882–3.

Churchill, *CA*: I. J. Churchill, *Canterbury Administration*. 2 vols. 1933.

Clay, C. T., *York Minster Fasti*. Yorks. Archaeol. Soc. Record Series, vols. 123–4. 1958–9.

Councils and Synods: *Councils and Synods with other Documents relating to the English Church*, vol. ii: A.D. 1205–1313, ed. F. M. Powicke and C. R. Cheney. Oxford, 1964.

Curtis, Edmund, *Richard II in Ireland, 1394–1395*. Oxford, 1927.

Cuttino, G. P., *English Diplomatic Administration, 1259–1339*. Oxford, 1940.

CYS: Canterbury and York Society.

D. & C.: Dean and Chapter.

Denholm-Young, N., 'The cursus in England', *Oxford Essays in Medieval History presented to H. E. Salter* (Oxford, 1934), pp. 68–103.

Doehaerd, R., *Les Relations commerciales entre Gênes, la Belgique et l'Outremont, d'après les archives notariales génoises aux xiiiᵉ et xivᵉ siècles*. 3 vols. (Institut Hist. Belge de Rome.) 1941.

Douie, D. L., *Archbishop Pecham*, Oxford, 1952.

Durandus, *Speculum*: *Speculum iudiciale* Guillelmi Durandi. Frankfurt, 1592.

Durham Annals: *Durham Annals and Documents of the Thirteenth Century*, ed. Frank Barlow. Surtees Soc., vol. 155. 1945.

Echt-Forbes Charters: *Echt-Forbes Family Charters, 1345–1727. Records of the Forest of Birse. Notarial Signs, 926–1786*, ed. G. F. Browne. Edinburgh, 1923.

Edwards, Kathleen, *The English Secular Cathedrals in the Middle Ages*. 2nd edn. Manchester, 1967.

EHR: *English Historical Review*.

Emanuel, H. D., 'Notaries public and their marks recorded in the Archives of the Dean and Chapter of Hereford', *National Library of Wales Journal*, viii. 2 (1953), 1–17.

Emden, *BRUC*: Emden, A. B., *Biographical Register of the University of Cambridge*. Cambridge, 1963.

—— *BRUO*: Emden, A. B., *Biographical Register of the University of Oxford to A.D. 1500*. 3 vols. Oxford, 1957–9.

Epistolae et Instrumenta saeculi xiii, ed. B. Katterbach and C. Sylva-Tarouca (Exempla scripturarum, fasc. 2). Vatican, 1930.

Extra: 'Decretalium Gregorii pp. IX compilatio', in *Corpus Iuris Canonici*, ed. E. Friedberg, vol. ii. Leipzig, 1881.

Freshfield, E., 'Some notarial marks in the "Common Paper" of the Scriveners' Company', *Archaeologia*, liv (1895), 239–54.

Galbraith, V. H., *Studies in the Public Records*. 1948.

—— 'Monastic foundation charters of the eleventh and twelfth centuries', *Cambridge Hist. Journal*, iv (1934), 205–22, 296–8.

—— 'The literacy of the medieval English kings', *Proceedings of the British Academy*, xxi (1935).

—— 'An episcopal land-grant of 1085', *EHR*, xliv (1929), 353–72.

Gascon Calendar of 1322, The, ed. G. P. Cuttino (Camden 3rd Series vol. 70). Royal Historical Soc., 1949.

Gervas. Cant.: *The Hist. Works of Gervase of Canterbury*, ed. W. Stubbs (RS). 2 vols. 1879–80.

Giry, Arthur, *Manuel de Diplomatique*. 1894.

Glastonbury Chartulary: *The Great Chartulary of Glastonbury*, ed. A. Watkin. 3 vols. Somerset Record Soc., vols. 59, 63, 64. 1947–56.

Gutteridge, H. C., 'The origin and historical development of the profession of notaries public in England', *Cambridge Legal Essays*, ed. P. H. Winfield and A. D. McNair (Cambridge, 1926), pp. 123–37.

Haines, R. M., *The Administration of the Diocese of Worcester in the First Half of the Fourteenth Century*. 1965.

Hajnal, István, *L'Enseignement de l'écriture aux universités médiévales* (Studia Historica Academiae Scientiarum Hungaricae, vii, Budapest, 1954; second edition, Budapest, 1959).

Herde, Peter, *Beiträge zum päpstlichen Kanzlei- und Urkundenwesen im 13. Jahrhundert* (Münchener hist. Studien. Abteilung geschichtl. Hilfswissenschaften, Bd. 1). 2nd edn. Kallmunz, 1967.

—— 'Papal formularies for letters of justice (13th–16th centuries)' *Proceedings of Second Intern. Congress of Medieval Canon Law* (Città del Vaticano, 1965), pp. 321–45, 355–6.

—— 'Ein Formelbuch Gerhards von Parma mit Urkunden des Auditor litterarum contradictarum aus dem Jahre 1277', *Archiv für Diplomatik*, xiii (1967), 225–312.

Hereford Charters: *Charters and Records of Hereford Cathedral*, ed. W. W. Capes (Cantilupe Soc.), 1908.

HMCR: Reports and Calendars of the Historical Manuscripts Commission 1870– .

Holdsworth, W. S., *History of English Law*. Vol. v, 1924.

Hostiensis, *Summa*: *Summa domini Henrici cardinalis Hostiensis*. Lyon, 1537. Neudruck, Scientia Aalen, Darmstadt, 1962.

Jacob, E. F., *Essays in the Conciliar Epoch*. 2nd edn. Manchester, 1953.

—— 'To and from the court of Rome in the early xv century', *Studies in French Language and Medieval Literature presented to Mildred K. Pope* (Manchester, 1939), pp. 161–81.

JEH: *Journal of Ecclesiastical History*.

Jenkinson, Hilary, *The Later Court Hands in England*. Cambridge, 1927.

J.–L.: *Regesta Pontificum Romanorum . . . ad annum 1198*, ed. Philip Jaffe. 2nd edn. S. Loewenfeld, etc. 2 vols. Leipzig, 1885–8.

Ketner, F., 'Vestiging en eerste Ontwikkeling van het Notariaat in Utrecht (1291–1340)', W. Jappe Alberts and F. Ketner, *Nederrijnse Studien, xiii^e–xv^e Eeuw* (Groningen, 1954), pp. 87–122.

Koechling, L., 'Untersuchungen über die Anfänge des öffentlichen Notariats in Deutschland', *Marburger Studien zur älteren deutschen Geschichte*, II Reihe, no. i. ed. E. Stengel. Marburg, 1925.

Le Neve, *Fasti*: Le Neve, John, *Fasti Ecclesiae Anglicanae*, new edition, *1066–1300*, vol. i, *St. Paul's, London,* ed. Diana E. Greenway, 1968; *1300–1541* 12 vols. by various editors, 1962–7.

Lincoln Cath. Stat.: *Statutes of Lincoln Cathedral*, ed. Henry Bradshaw and Chr. Wordsworth. 3 vols. Cambridge, 1892–7.

Logan, F. D., *Excommunication and the Secular Arm in Medieval England* (Pontifical Institute, Studies and Texts, 15). Toronto, 1968.

Lunt, W. E., *Financial Relations of the Papacy with England to 1327*. Mediaeval Academy of America, 1939.

—— *Papal Revenues in the Middle Ages* (Columbia Univ. Records of Civilization: Sources and Studies no. 19). 2 vols. New York, 1934.

—— 'A papal tenth levied in the British Isles from 1274 to 1280', *EHR*, xxxii (1917), 49–89.

Luschek, Fritz, *Notariatsurkunde und Notariat in Schlesien von den Anfängen (1282) bis zum Ende des 16. Jahrhunderts* (Hist.-Diplomatische Forschungen, ed. Leo Santifaller, Bd. 5). Weimar, 1940.

Lyndwood, W., *Provinciale . . . cui adjiciuntur Constitutiones Legatinae d. Othonis et d. Othoboni . . . cum . . . Annotationibus Johannis de Athona.* Oxford, 1679.

[Madox, Thomas], *Formulare Anglicanum.* 1702.

Major, Kathleen, 'The office of chapter clerk at Lincoln in the Middle Ages', *Medieval Studies pres. to Rose Graham* (Oxford, 1950), pp. 163–88.

Mikucki, S., 'Essai sur les origines du notariat public en Pologne: étude diplomatique', *Revue Historique de Droit Français et Étranger*, xvi (1937), 333–50.

MIöG: Mitteilungen des Instituts für österreichische Geschichtsforschung.

Mon. Ang.: Monasticon Anglicanum, by William Dugdale, ed. J. Caley, H. Ellis, and B. Bandinel. 6 vols. in 8. 1817–30.

Nélis, H., 'Les origines du notariat public en Belgique, 1269–1320', *Revue Belge de Philologie et d'Histoire*, ii (1923), 267–77.

Oseney Cartulary: Cartulary of Oseney Abbey, ed. H. E. Salter. 6 vols. (Oxford Historical Soc., vols. 89–91, 97–8, 101). 1929–36.

Otway-Ruthven, Jocelyn, *The King's Secretary and the Signet Office in the Fifteenth Century.* Cambridge, 1939.

Oxford Formularies: Formularies which bear on the History of Oxford, ed. H. E. Salter, etc. 2 vols. (Oxford Historical Soc., n.s. vols. 4, 5), 1942.

Petrucci, Armando, *Notarii: Documenti per la Storia del Notariato Italiano.* Milan, 1958.

—— (ed.), *Il Protocollo Notarile di Coluccio Salutati, 1372–3.* Florence, 1963.

Pollock, F., and Maitland, F. W., *History of English Law before the Time of Edward I.* 2nd edn. 2 vols. Cambridge, 1898.

Poole, R. L., *Lectures on the History of the Papal Chancery down to the Time of Innocent III.* Cambridge, 1915.

Postan, M., 'Private financial instruments in medieval England', *Vierteljahrsschrift für Sozial- und Wirtschaftsgeschichte*, xxiii (1930), 26–75.

Potthast, August (ed.), *Regesta Pontificum Romanorum A.D. 1198–1304.* 2 vols. Berlin, 1874–5.

P.R.O.: Public Record Office, London.

Prynne, *Records*: Prynne, William, *Antiquae Constitutiones Regni Angliae*, vol. iii. 1672.

Purvis, J. S., *Notarial Signs from the York Archiepiscopal Records* (Borthwick Institute of Historical Research). 1957.

Re, Emilio, 'La compagna dei Riccardi in Inghilterra', *Archivio Soc. Romana Stor. Patria*, xxxvii (1914), 87–138.

Records of Antony Bek, Bishop and Patriarch, 1283–1311, ed. C. M. Fraser (Surtees Soc., vol. 162). 1953.

Redlich, *Privaturkunden*: *Urkundenlehre*, von W. Erben, L. Schmitz-Kallenberg, and O. Redlich. III. Teil: *Die Privaturkunden des Mittelalters*. Munich, 1911.

Reg. Baldock: *Registrum Radulphi Baldock, Gilberti Segrave . . . Episcoporum Londoniensium*, ed. R. C. Fowler (CYS). 1911.

Reg. Boniface VIII: *Les Registres de Boniface VIII* (1294–1303), ed. G. Digard, M. Faucon, A. Thomas, and R. Fawtier (École française de Rome). 4 vols. 1907–39.

Reg. Bransford: *Calendar of the Register of Wolstan de Bransford, Bishop of Worcester, 1339–1349*, ed. R. M. Haines (Worcs. Historical Soc. and HMC). 1966.

Reg. Bronescombe: *The Registers of Walter Bronescombe and Peter Quivil, Bishops of Exeter . . .*, ed. F. C. Hingeston-Randolph. 1889.

Reg. Cantilupe: *Registrum Thome de Cantilupo Episcopi Herefordensis, A.D. 1275–1282*, ed. W. W. Capes (Cantilupe Soc. 1906 and CYS 1907).

Reg. Chichele: *The Register of Henry Chichele, Archbishop of Canterbury, 1414–1443*, ed. E. F. Jacob. 4 vols. (CYS). 1937–47.

Reg. Clem. V: *Regestum Clementis Papae V* (1305–14), ed. monks O.S.B. 8 vols. and index. Rome, 1885–92, 1957.

Reg. Cobham: *The Register of Thomas de Cobham, Bishop of Worcester, 1317–1327*, ed. E. H. Pearce (Worcs. Historical Soc.), 1930.

Reg. Corbridge: *The Register of Thomas of Corbridge, Lord Archbishop of York, 1300–1304*, ed. William Brown and A. Hamilton Thompson (Surtees Soc., vols. 138 and 141). 1925–8.

Reg. Ep. Peckham: *Registrum epistolarum fratris Iohannis Peckham, Archiepiscopi Cantuariensis*, ed. C. T. Martin (RS). 3 vols. 1882–5.

Reg. Gandavo: *Registrum Simonis de Gandavo. Diocesis Saresbiriensis, A.D. 1297–1315*, ed. C. T. Flower and M. C. B. Dawes. 2 vols. (CYS). 1934.

Reg. Geynesborough: *The Register of William de Geynesborough, Bishop of Worcester, 1302–1307*, ed. J. W. Willis Bund and R. A. Wilson (Worcs. Hist. Soc.). 1907–29.

Reg. G. Giffard: *Register of Bishop Godfrey Giffard, Sept. 23rd 1268 to Aug. 15th 1303*, ed. J. W. Willis Bund (Worcs. Hist. Soc.). 2 vols. 1902.

Reg. Grandisson: *The Register of John de Grandisson, Bishop of Exeter, A.D. 1327–1369*, ed. F. C. Hingeston-Randolph. 3 vols. 1894–9.

Reg. Greenfield: *The Register of William Greenfield, Lord Archbishop of York, 1306–1315*, ed. A. Hamilton Thompson (Surtees Soc., vols. 145, 149, 151–3). 1931–40.

Reg. Grégoire X: *Les Registres de Grégoire X* (*1272–6*) *. . .*, ed. J. Guiraud (École française de Rome). 1892–1906.

Reg. Hethe: *Registrum Hamonis Hethe Diocesis Roffensis*, A.D. *1319–52*, ed. Charles Johnson. 2 vols. (CYS). 1948.

Reg. Martival: *The Registers of Roger Martival, Bishop of Salisbury, 1315–1330*, ed. Kathleen Edwards, etc., vols. i–iii (CYS). 1959–65.

Reg. Nicolas III: *Les Registres de Nicolas III (1277–80)*, ed. J. Gay (École française de Rome). 1898–1938.

Reg. Nicolas IV: *Les Registres de Nicolas IV (1288–92)*, ed. Ernest Langlois (École française de Rome). 2 vols. 1905.

Reg. Orleton: *Registrum Ade de Orleton, episcopi Herefordensis*, A.D. *1317–27*, ed. A. T. Bannister (CYS). 1908.

Reg. Pal. Dunelm.: *Registrum Palatinum Dunelmense. The Register of Richard de Kellawe, Lord Palatine and Bishop of Durham, 1314–1316*, ed. T. D. Hardy (RS). 4 vols. 1873–8.

Reg. Pecham: *The Register of John Pecham, Archbishop of Canterbury, 1279–92*, ed. F. N. Davis and D. L. Douie (CYS). 2 vols. 1968–9.

Reg. Pontissara: *Registrum Johannis de Pontissara, Episcopi Wyntoniensis*, A.D. *1282–1304*, ed. C. Deedes (CYS). 2 vols. 1915–24.

Reg. Rede: *The Episcopal Register of Robert Rede, O.P., Lord Bishop of Chichester, 1397–1415*, ed. C. Deedes. 2 vols. (Sussex Record Soc., vols. viii, xi). 1908–10.

Reg. Repingdon: *The Register of Bishop Philip Repingdon 1405–1419*, ed. Margaret Archer. 2 vols. (Lincoln Record Soc., vols. 57, 58). 1963.

Reg. Reynolds: *The Register of Walter Reynolds, Bishop of Worcester, 1308–1313*, ed. R. A. Wilson (Worcs. Hist. Soc. and Dugdale Soc.). 1927.

Reg. Romeyn: *The Registers of John le Romeyn, Lord Archbishop of York, 1286–1296 and of Henry of Newark, Lord Archbishop of York, 1296–1299*, ed. W. Brown. 2 vols. (Surtees Soc., vols. 123, 128). 1913–17.

Reg. Sandale: *The Registers of John de Sandale and Rigaud de Asserio, Bishops of Winchester*, A.D. *1316–1323*, ed. F. J. Baigent (Hants Record Soc.). 1897.

Reg. Shrewsbury: *The Register of Ralph of Shrewsbury, Bishop of Bath and Wells, 1329–1363*, ed. T. S. Holmes. 2 vols. (Somerset Record Soc., vols. 9–10). 1896.

Reg. Stat. S. Pauli: *Registrum Statutorum et Consuetudinum Ecclesiae Cathedralis Sancti Pauli Londinensis*, ed. W. Sparrow Simpson. 1873.

Reg. Stretton: *The First (Second) Register of Bishop Robert de Stretton, 1358–1385 (1360–1385)*, abstr. by Rowland A. Wilson. 2 vols. (Wm. Salt Archaeological Soc.). 1905–7.

Reg. Sutton: *The Rolls and Register of Bishop Oliver Sutton, 1280–1299*, ed. Rosalind M. T. Hill, vols. i–vi (Lincoln Record Soc., vols. 39, 43, 48, 52, 60, 64). 1948–69.

Reg. Swinfield: *Registrum Ricardi de Swinfield Episcopi Herefordensis*, A.D. *1283–1371*, ed. W. W. Capes (Cantilupe Soc. and CYS). 1909.

Reg. Trefnant: Registrum Johannis Trefnant, Episcopi Herefordensis, A.D. 1389–1404, ed. W. W. Capes (CYS). 1916.

Reg. Trillek: Registrum Johannis de Trillek, Episcopi Herefordensis, A.D. 1344–1361, ed. Joseph H. Parry (CYS). 1912.

Reg. Urbain IV: Les Registres d'Urbain IV (1261–64), ed. Jean Guiraud (École française de Rome). 5 vols. 1901–58.

Reg. W. Giffard: The Register of Walter Giffard, Lord Archbishop of York, 1266–1279, ed. William Brown (Surtees Soc., vol. 109). 1904.

Reg. Winchelsey: Registrum Roberti Winchelsey, Cantuariensis Archiepiscopi, A.D. 1294–1313, ed. Rose Graham. 2 vols. (CYS). 1952–6.

Reg. Woodlock: Registrum Henrici Woodlock, Diocesis Wintoniensis, A.D. 1305–1316, ed. A. W. Goodman. 2 vols. (CYS). 1940–1.

Reg. Worcester sede vacante: The Register of the Diocese of Worcester during the Vacancy of the See, usually called Registrum sede vacante, 1301–1435, ed. J. W. Willis Bund (Worcs. Hist. Soc.). 1897.

Richardson, H. G., 'An Oxford teacher of the fifteenth century', *BJRL*, xxiii (1939), 436–57.

—— 'Business training in medieval Oxford', *American Historical Review*, xlvi (1941–2), 259–80.

Rockinger, Ludwig, *Briefsteller und Formelbücher des xi bis xiv Jahrhunderts* (Quellen und Erörterungen zur bayerischen und deutschen Geschichte, ix). Munich, 1863.

Rot. Gravesend: Rotuli Ricardi Gravesend, Diocesis Lincolniensis (1258–79), ed. F. N. Davis, etc. (CYS and Lincoln Rec. Soc., vol. 20). 1925.

Rot. Parl.: Rotuli Parliamentorum; ut et Petitiones et Placita in Parliamento (Rec. Com.). 6 vols. 1783, and index 1832.

Rot. Welles: Rotuli Hugonis de Welles, Episcopi Lincolniensis A.D. 1209–1235, ed. W. P. W. Phillimore, F. N. Davis, etc. (CYS). 3 vols. 1907–9 (and Lincoln Rec. Soc., vols. 3, 6, and 9. 1912–14).

RS: Rolls Series.

Rymer: *Foedera, Conventiones, Litterae* (etc.), ed. Thomas Rymer, re-edited by A. Clarke, etc. (Rec. Com.). 3 vols. in 6. 1816–30.

St. Frideswide's Cartulary: The Cartulary of the monastery of St. Frideswide at Oxford, ed. S. R. Wigram. 2 vols. (Oxford Historical Soc., vols. 28, 31). 1895–6.

Salatiele, *Ars Notarie*, ed. Gianfranco Orlandelli (Istituto per la Storia dell' Università di Bologna: Opere dei Maestri, II). 2 vols. Milan, 1961.

Salisbury Charters: Charters and Documents illustrating the History of the Cathedral, City, and Diocese of Salisbury in the XII and XIII Centuries, ed. W. Rich Jones and W. D. Macray (RS). 1891.

Salutati: *see* Petrucci.

Sel. Cases King's Bench: Select Cases in the Court of King's Bench under Edward I (II and III), ed. G. O. Sayles. Selden Soc., vols. 55, 57, 58, 74, 76. 1936–58.

SHR: *Scottish Historical Review.*

Steer, F. W., (ed.), *The Scriveners' Company Common Paper, 1357–1628* (London Record Soc.). 1968.

Stones, E. L. G. (ed.), *Anglo-Scottish Relations, 1174–1328. Some selected Documents* (Nelson's Medieval Texts). 1965.

—— 'An addition to the "Rotuli Scotiae" ', *SHR*, xxix (1950), 23–51.

—— 'Two points of diplomatic', *SHR*, xxxii (1953), 47–51.

—— 'The records of the Great Cause of 1291–92', *SHR*, xxxv (1956), 89–109.

—— 'An new exemplar of Andrew de Tange's "Great Roll of Scotland" at Exeter Cathedral', *SHR*, xxxix (1960), 86–7.

—— 'The appeal to history in Anglo-Scottish relations', *Archives*, ix (1969), 11–21, 80–3.

Summa: *Summa Johannis de Bononia*, ed. Rockinger, *Briefsteller*, pp. 593–704.

Tangl, M. (ed.), *Die päpstlichen Kanzleiordnungen von 1200–1500*. Innsbruck, 1894.

Tout, T. F., *Chapters in the Administrative History of Medieval England*. 6 vols. Manchester, 1920–33.

TRHS: *Transactions of the Royal Historical Society.*

Wilkins, David (ed.), *Concilia Magnae Britanniae et Hiberniae* A.D. *446–1717*. 4 vols. 1737.

Wilkinson, Bertie, *The Chancery under Edward III*. Manchester, 1929.

Winchester Chartulary: *Chartulary of Winchester Cathedral*, ed. in English by A. W. Goodman. Winchester, 1927.

Woodruff, C. E., 'The will of Peter de Aquablanca, bishop of Hereford (1268)', *Camden Miscellany*, vol. xiv (Royal Historical Soc., 1926).

Index

Note. Only selected proper names are indexed, but all notaries public have been included. The letter (n) after a name indicates a notary public.